No More Can Fit Into the Evening

An Anthology of Diverse Voices

No More Can Fit
Into the Evening

An Anthology of Diverse Voices,
Poetry from the English Speaking World

Edited by

Standing Feather and Thomas Davis

Cover art and design

by Ethel Mortenson Davis

Four
Windows
Press

231 N Hudson Ave., Sturgeon Bay, WI 54235

No More Can Fit Into the Evening

Printed in the United States of America by Ingram Sparks

Cover design by Ethel Mortenson Davis

Book Layout © BookDesignTemplates.com

Library of Congress Cataloging-in-Publication Data available on request

ISBN 978-0-9990077-7-8

Dedication

To Jack Carter North
and the Zuni Mountain Poets
who inspired the journey
toward this Anthology's creation

Acknowledgements

The Editors owe a deep debt of gratitude to **Estella Lauter** who helped with crucial editing tasks to finish this volume. The authors featured in this volume all retain the right to republish the poems that appear in this book that they have written. All others are subject to the copyright of *No More Will Fit Into This Evening*.

Albright, Betty
"Points of Light," *Indra's Net* (UK: Bennison Books, 2017).
"Fog," *Skipping Stones* (Sturgeon Bay, WI: Four Windows Press, 2018).
"To the Sea," *Skipping Stones* (Sturgeon Bay, WI: Four Windows Press, 2018).

Auberle, Sharon
"Angel Fire," *Peninsula Pulse*
"Six Degrees of Separation," *Peninsula Pulse*
"Two Horses," *Verse Wisconsin; Wisconsin Fellowship of Poets Calendar*, 2020
"Waiting for Manuela," *Soundings: Door County in Poetry*, (Sturgeon Bay, WI: Caravaggio Press, 2015).

Blaeser, Kimberly
"Apprenticed to Justice," *Apprenticed to Justice* (Cambridge, UK: Salt Publishing, 2007).
"Refractions," *Apprenticed to Justice* (Cambridge, UK: Salt Publishing, 2007).
"Fantasies of Women," *Apprenticed to Justice* (Cambridge, UK: Salt Publishing, 2007).
"Where I Was That Day," *Trailing You* (Greenfield Center, NY: Greenfield Review Press, 1994).
"Of Fractals and Pink Flowering," *Native Voices: Honoring Indigenous Poetry from North America*. Ed. Dean Rader & CMarie Fuhrman. (North Adamas, MA: Tupelo Press, 2019); *Copper Yearning* (Duluth, MN: Holy Cow! Press, 2019).
"When We Sing Of Might," *Literary Hub* (February 13, 2018); *Copper Yearning* (Duluth, MN: Holy Cow! Press, 2019).

Brenneman, Richard
"Fish Bait," *The Rimrock Poets Magazine*, Vol. 1 No. 3, 1968.
"Gargoyles," *Fifth Poetry Anthology, Friends of the San Jose Public Library*, 1975.
"Heating Bill" *Ibbetson Street #46*, Fall 2019.
"Thin Ice," *Fifth Poetry Anthology, Friends of the San Jose Public Library*, 1975.
"Old Houses," *First Poetry Anthology, Friends of the San Jose Public Library*, 1974.

Chapman, Robin
"Oak Ridge, Tennessee, 1946," *Proximity*, 2014, as "Oak Ridge, Tennessee, 1947", 2014; *Six True Things* (Tebot Bach, 2016).
"Catching Rabbits," *Poetry*, August 1989; *Learning to Talk* (Fireweed Press, 1991).

"The Blue Hat," originally appeared in *The Hudson Review*, 1996; *The Way In*, (Tebot Bach, 1999).

"Holding Open the Doors," *Beloit Poetry Journal*, 1996; *The Way In* (Tebot Bach, 1999).

"Cassandra Looks at Dark Matter Through Hubble's Eye," *Many Mountains Moving*, 2008; *the eelgrass meadow*, (Tebot Bach, 2011).

"Studying Mountains," *The Hudson Review*, 1998; *Smoke and Strong Whiskey* (WordTech Editions, 2008).

"Praying to the God of Sixty-One Orders of Magnitude," *The Spoon River Poetry Review*, 2004; *The Dreamer Who Counted the Dead* (WordTech Editions, 2007).

"The Eelgrass Meadow," *The Fiddlehead* (Canada), 2006; *the eelgrass meadow*, (Tebot Bach, 2011).

"Time," *Alaska Quarterly Review*, 2011.

"Midnight, and people I love are dying," *The Common*, 2015; *Six True Things* (Tebot Bach, 2016).

"Dappled Things," *Dappled Things*, Robin Chapman's poems & Peter Miller's photogravures (Paris: Revue K, 2013).

Davis, Ethel Mortenson

"Swallow," *Here We Breathe In Sky and Out Sky* (Sturgeon Bay, WI: Four Windows Press, 2016).

"Wind," *Poetry Breakfast*, May 1, 2019.

"Presentation," *Under the Tail of the Milky Way Galaxy* (Sturgeon Bay, WI: Four Windows Press, 2018); *A Letter on the Horizon's Poem* (American Forks, UT: Kelsay Books, 2019).

"The Language of the Women," *White Ermine Across Her Shoulders* (iUniverse, 2011); *A Letter on the Horizon's Poem* (American Forks, UT: Kelsay Books, 2019).

"An Evening," *White Ermine Across Her Shoulders*, (iUniverse, 2011); *Under the Tail of the Milky Way Galaxy* (Sturgeon Bay, WI: Four Windows Press, 2018); *Wisconsin Poets* Calendar, 2017; *A Letter on the Horizon's Poem* (American Forks, UT: Kelsay Books, 2019).

"Love Song," *Bramble*, Fall 2017; *Here We Breathe In Sky and Out Sky*, (Sturgeon Bay, WI: Four Windows Press, 2016); *A Letter on the Horizon's Poem*, (American Forks, UT: Kelsay Books, 2019).

"Auschwitz, E. Poland, January 27, 1945," *Gallup Journey, Arts Edition*, Vol. 1, No. 8, January 2011; *White Ermine Across Her Shoulders* (iUniverse, 2011); *A Letter on the Horizon's Poem* (American Forks, UT: Kelsay Books, 2019).

"The Design Teacher," *White Ermine Across Her Shoulders* (iUniverse, 2011); *A Letter on the Horizon's Poem* (American Forks, UT: Kelsay Books, 2019).

"Celestial Bird: The Poem," *White Ermine Across Her Shoulders* (iUniverse, 2011); *A Letter on the Horizon's Poem* (American Forks, UT: Kelsay Books, 2019).

"Death," *Here We Breathe In Sky and Out Sky* (Sturgeon Bay, WI: Four Windows Press, 2016); *A Letter on the Horizon's Poem* (American Forks, UT: Kelsay Books, 2019).

"The Healer," *Poetry Cha Cha* (El Morro, NM: El Morro Poetry Press, 2008); *I Sleep Between the Moons of New Mexico* (iUniverse, 2010); *The Healer* (Sturgeon Bay, WI: Four Windows Press, 2016); *Little Eagle's RE/VERSE,* 2016; *A Letter on the Horizon's Poem* (American Forks, UT: Kelsay Books, 2019).

Davis, Thomas

"A Lover's Song," *The Lyric,* 2016.

"Of Bees and Flowers," Wisconsin Fellowship of Poets, *Museletter,* 2016.

"Break to Manhood," *The Lyric,* 2015.

"The Insight," *Tribal College Journal,* 2002; *Meditations on the Ceremonies of Beginnings* (Mancos, CO: Tribal College Press, 2020).

"Mother Earth's Song," as "Gaia's Song," *Wisconsin People and Ideas,* 2020; *Meditations on the Ceremonies of Beginnings* (Mancos, CO: Tribal College Press, 2020).

"Peach Cobbler, the Beautiful Baker's Song," *Indra's Net* (UK: Bennison Books, 2017).

"The Song of Taliesin," *Wisconsin Academy Review,* 1996.

DancingBare, RedWulf

"Whale Songs," *Waiting on the Monsoons for His Desert Soul*" (Sturgeon Bay, WI: Four Windows Press, 2020).

"A Most Hate Filled Name," *Waiting on the Monsoons for His Desert Soul*" (Sturgeon Bay, WI: Four Windows Press, 2020).

"For the People," *Waiting on the Monsoons for His Desert Soul*" (Sturgeon Bay, WI: Four Windows Press, 2020).

"Waiting on the Monsoons for His Desert Soul," *Waiting on the Monsoons for His Desert Soul*" (Sturgeon Bay, WI: Four Windows Press, 2020.)

"If It Takes a Village," *Waiting on the Monsoons for His Desert Soul*" (Sturgeon Bay, WI: Four Windows Press, 2020).

DeGenova, Albert

"A Good Hammer, " *RHINO,* April 2013, Finalist RHINO Founders Prize; *A Good Hammer* (Timberline Press, 2014).

"Among Friends," *Fifth Wednesday Journal* #15, Fall 2014, Pushcart Prize Nomination.

"Black Pearl," *All Roads Lead You Home,* online journal, Virtual Artists Collective, May 2014; *Black Pearl* (Purple Flag Press, 2016).

Family Album," *The Paterson Literary Review* #31, June 2002; *The Blueing Hours* (Virtual Artists Collective, August 2008).

"Living History," *The Blueing Hours* (Virtual Artists Collective, August 2008).

"One-Sixtieth of a Second," *The Paterson Literary Review* #43, June 2015, Honorable Mention 2014 Allen Ginsberg Poetry Award

"Refuse Pile of Mortal Sins," *Peninsula Pulse,* August 2015, Hal Prize Honorable Mention

"Thanksgiving Poem," *Sphericaltabby.com,* April 2013, words and audio *After Hours #26,* January 2013

"We Thought We Could," Gwendolyn Brooks Open Mic Award Finalist, September 2018, 25th Annual Competition.

Denton, Diane
    "The Lavenders," Collins Poetry Registry, online, 2012.

Grunseth, Langlois Annette
    "Pears," *Bramble*, Summer Issue, 2020; *Dispatches*, October 2020.
    "In the Bloom of the Moment," poetry finalist in *Wisconsin Academy Review*, *Summer 2002* – University of Wisconsin-Madison.
    "Fish for Flowers," *Midwest Prairie Review*, April 2013.
    "At the Back Steps," *Wisconsin Fellowship of Poets Calendar*, 2012.
    "Becoming Trans-Parent," *Becoming Trans-Parent: One Family's Journey of Gender Transition* (Georgetown KY: Finishing Line Press, 2017).
    "When Your Child Comes Out," *Becoming Trans-Parent: One Family's Journey of Gender Transition* (Georgetown KY: Finishing Line Press, 2017).
    "My Mother's Moon," *Portage Magazine*, 2017.

Herron, Elizabeth
    "Winter Solstice," *Poetry for the Ear of God: Healing Trauma Through the Music of Words* (Amazon Create Space Publishing, 2013).
    "Frog Noise," *Poetry for the Ear of God: Healing Trauma Through the Music of Words* (Amazon Create Space Publishing, 2013).
    "Through the Rabbit Hole," *Poetry for the Ear of God: Healing Trauma Through the Music of Words* (Amazon Create Space Publishing, 2013).
    "The Old One," *Poetry for the Ear of God: Healing Trauma Through the Music of Words* (Amazon Create Space Publishing, 2013).
    "Midwife," *Poetry for the Ear of God: Healing Trauma Through the Music of Words* (Amazon Create Space Publishing, 2013).
    "Weathermaker," *Poetry for the Ear of God: Healing Trauma Through the Music of Words* (Amazon Create Space Publishing, 2013).
    "The Wailing Time," *Poetry for the Ear of God: Healing Trauma Through the Music of Words* (Amazon Create Space Publishing, 2013).

Janko, James
    "The Sea," *Zuni Mountain Poets Anthology"* (iUniverse, Inc., 2013).

Jones, Gary
    "At the National Gallery of Art," *Ariel Anthology*, 2014.
    "A British Lit Teacher Tells All," *Pearl*, fall/winter 2009.
    "Snow Falling," *Blue Heron Review*, winter 2016.
    "The Dark Ages," *Möbius Magazine*, online, 2017.
    "Son of Adam," *Ariel Anthology*, 2019.

Kriesel, Michael
    "Grape Jam," *Wisconsin Academy Review*, Honorable Mention, *Wisconsin Academy Review* 2004 Poetry Contest; among a group of poems awarded the Council For Wisconsin Writers 2003 Lorine Niedecker Award.
    "The Washer's Bone Whiteness Laid Bare" won the 2011 John Lehman Poetry Award from Wisconsin People & Ideas Magazine; *Wisconsin People & Ideas*; in different form in *Nerve Cowboy*.
    "Secret Women," Honorable Mention, *North American Review*, 2008 Hearst Competition; *North American Review*.
    "As Crickets Chip Away the Light," *Rattle*.

"Aleister Crowley Lipogram," *North American Review*, winner, North American Review, 2015 Hearst Competition; *New Poetry from the Midwest 2017* (New American Press); *Zen of the Dead* (Popcorn Press, 2015).

"Forgiving the Grass," *Verse Wisconsin* (as Harvesting Light); *Midwestern Gothic.*

"Hidden Snow," *The Writer* and *Verse Wisconsin*; awarded the 2009 Muse Prize from the Wisconsin Fellowship of Poets.

"Zen Amen," *North American Review*, finalist in *North American Review*'s 2007 Hearst Competition; *Free Verse.*

"Early in the Plague," (in different form), *Nimrod.*

"The End," *Shit Creek Review; Saturday Night Desperate* (UK: Ragged Raven Press, 2003).

"Feeding My Heart to the Wind," *Bitter Oleander; Iodine; Tears in the Fence; Wisconsin Trails.*

Lauter, Estella

"How I Met Pable Neruda," "Poetry: John Lehman's Selected Poems," *Wisconsin People and Ideas*, Fall 2012.

"Incubator," first prize for poetry in the Hal Grutzmacher contest, *Peninsula Pulse* (August 2006); *Pressing a Life Together by Hand,* (Georgetown, KY: Finishing Line Press, 2007, #53 in the New Women's Voices Series).

"How To Pray," second place, 2014 Triad: Kay Saunders Memorial Emerging Poet sontest, Wisconsin Fellowship of Poets.

"Peter Piper," second prize for free verse poetry in the Wisconsin Writers Association Jade Ring Contest, 2013; *Bramble, Fall 2017: Everyday Magic.*

Looker, John

"To a Winter's Day Also," *The Wagon Magazine* (India); *Indra's Net* (UK, Bennison Books, 2017); *Poems for My Family* (UK: Bennison Books, 2018).

"On Your 70th Birthday," *Poems for My Family* (UK: Bennison Books, 2018).

"Violin (1778)," *Texas International Poetry Festival Anthology.*

"Made in Mesopotamia," *The Human Hive* (UK: Bennison Books, 2015).

"In the Caves at Nefrja," *The Human Hive* (UK: Bennison Books, 2015).

"The Day They Detected Gravitational Waves," *Collecting Reality, Poems for my Family*, 2018.

Mark, Anna

"Angel in the Snow," *Indra's Net* (UK: Bennison Books, July 2017).

"The Timbre of Frost," *Indra's Net* (UK: Bennison Books, July 2017).

Moran, Chris

"I Myself and Me," *The Pulse of Everything* (UK Otley Writers); *Goodbye Mr. Nash* (UK: Otley Writers}.

"Dancing with Grief," *The Pulse of Everything* (UK Otley Writers); *Goodbye Mr. Nash* (UK: Otley Writers).

"Dad's Hat," *Indra's Net* (UK: Bennison Books, July 2017).

"Past Lives," *Indra's Net* (UK: Bennison Books, July 2017).

Murre, Ralph

"Agrarian, A.M.," *Your Daily Poem*, 2013.

"Cantata for Woodland and Orchestra," *Peninsula Pulse*, 2012.

"Like this morning, crazy with wind," *Verse Wisconsin*, 2010.

"Odds," *Ariel Anthology*, 2014.

"Portrait with Contradictions," *After Hours*, 2011.

"Prayers of Old Men," *Iconoclast*, 2008.

"The Price of Gravity," *Iconolclast*, 2010.

"The Sky is Full of Bluebirds," *Wisconsin Poets Calendar*, 2010.

"Vacancy. Inquire Within," *Wisconsin Poets Calendar*, 2015.

"What is Given," *Your Daily Poem* website, 2010.

North, Jack Carter

"Ions and Prayers," *The Zuni Mountain Poets* (Authorhouse, 2012).

Orlock, Mike

"Origin Stories," *Poetry Apocalypse & Selected Verse* (Lulu Press. 2019).

"On Perdido Beach" received the MUSE award, Wisconsin Fellowship of Poets in 2016; *You Can Get Here from There: Door County Poems & Other Places* (Lulu Press, 2019).

"Poetry Apocalypse" Jade Ring Award; Wisconsin Writers Association, 2014 and appeared in print in their online journal; *Poetry Apocalypse & Selected Verse* (Lulu Press, 2019).

"Dreaming in Italian," Finalist for the Jade Ring Award; 2018 and appeared in their online journal; *You Can Get Here from There: Door County Poems & Other Places* (Lulu Press, 2019).

"Cinderella Spring," *Your Daily Poem* website; 2017 WFOP Calendar; *You Can Get Here from There: Door County Poems & Other Places* (Lulu Press, 2019).

"Buddy and I," *Your Daily Poem* website; *You Can Get Here from There: Door County Poems & Other Places* (Lulu Press, 2019).

"To the Fly Futzing with My Foot" *You Can Get Here from There: Door County Poems & Other Places* (Lulu Press, 2019).

"Finding a God Worth Keeping," *You Can Get Here from There: Door County Poems & Other Places* (Lulu Press, 2019).

Okaji, Robert

"To the Lovely Green Beetles Who Carried My Notes into the Afternoon," *riverSedge*.

"To the Light Entering the Shack One December Evening," *Shantih*.

"What Edges Hold," *Boston Review*.

"Scarecrow Sees," *The High Window*.

"Two Cranes on a Snowy Pine," *Panoply*.

"My Mother's Ghost Sits Next to Me at the Hotel Bar," *The Lake*.

"Diverting Silence," *Taos Journal of International Poetry & Art*.

"September in April," *deLuge*.

Reid, Nathan J.

"We the Firefly," *Great: Poems of Resistance & Fortitude*.

"The Driftless," *Persistence of Perception* (Georgetown, KY: Finishing Line Press, 2020).

"Hindsight," *Persistence of Perception* (Georgetown, KY: Finishing Line Press, 2020).

"Möbius," *Persistence of Perception* (Georgetown, KY: Finishing Line Press, 2020).

"Spring Makes True," *Persistence of Perception* (Georgetown, KY: Finishing Line Press, 2020).

"We the Firefly," *Persistence of Perception* (Georgetown, KY: Finishing Line Press, 2020).

"Bonfire Brown," *Thoughts on Tonight* (Georgetown, KY: Finishing Line Press, 20170.

"Such Sweet Sorrow," *Persistence of Perception* (Georgetown, KY: Finishing Line Press, 2020).

Schroders-Zeeders, Ina

"Chemist," *Moving On*, (Winter Goose Publishing, 2019).

"The Balance," *The Journal*, #46 (UK), 2016; *Indra's Net* (UK: Bennison Books, 2017); *The Balance* (Winter Goose Publishing, 2018).

"The Thought," *Moving On* (Winter Goose Publishing, 2019).

"The Lodger," *Moving On* (Winter Goose Publishing, 2019).

"Making Memories Fly," *The Balance* (Winter Goose Publishing, 2018).

Standing Feather

"Blue Train," *The Glowing Pink* (Sturgeon Bay, WI: Four Windows Press, 2018).

"The Glowing Pink" *The Glowing Pink* (Sturgeon Bay, WI: Four Windows Press, 2018).

Welhouse, Tori Grant

"Bra Burning," *Conclave Journal*

"Endrocrinologist.," *Blue Heron Review*

"Flaming Pajamas," *Passager*

"Spoons," *Midwest Poetry Review*

Winch, Terence

"Psalm," *Innisfree Poetry Journal* #1; *Falling Out of Bed in a Room with No Floor* (Hanging Loose, 2011).

"Social Security," *The Paris Review* 156 (2000); *The Drift of Things* (The Figures, 2001).

"My Work," *In New American Writing 19* (2001); *The Best American Poetry 2003*; *The Drift of Things* (The Figures, 2001).

"Sleep Waltz," *The Paris Review* 156 (2000); *The Drift of Things* (The Figures, 2001).

"Civilized Atmospheres," *The Washington Review* 8, no. 5 (1988); read on *The Writer's Almanac* (March 7, 1996); *The Great Indoors* (Story Line Press, 1999).

"Success Story," *The Writer's Almanac*, March 5, 1996 & April 16, 201); *The Great Indoors* (Story Line Press, 1995).

"Forgiveness," *The Writer's Almanac*, Aug. 24, 2007; *Boy Drinkers* (Hanging Loose, 2007).

"Sex Elegy," *Verse 19* (2003); *The Best American Poetry 2006; Falling Out of Bed in a Room with No Floor* (Hanging Loose, 2011).

"That Little Extra Something," *This Way Out* (Hanging Loose, 2014).

"The Complete Poem," *Pleiades* 36, no. 2 (2016); *The Known Universe* (Hanging Loose, 2018).

Table of Contents

Introduction

How This Anthology Became a Project

No More Will Fit Into the Evening took a while to become a project. For years Thomas (Tom) and Ethel Mortenson Davis traveled from Continental Divide, New Mexico to the Inscription Trading Post and Coffee Company near El Morro National Monument on Sunday mornings to join the Zuni Mountain Poets in their weekly meetings. At the time Tom was the Chief Academic Officer at Navajo Technical College, then University, a writer, and a poet, and Ethel was a poet and artist who had produced exquisite poetry even as a teenager.

What they had discovered at the Zuni Mountain Poets meetings was a magic that engrossed poets into a way of being that lifted them out of themselves and allowed them to improve their craft in a way that escapes most students in college creative writing programs. RedWulf DancingBare, one of the poets, tried to catch the magic's essence in his poem, "Up the Stairs":

> Up the stairs is a procession.
> We each climb one rise at a time.
> We each follow another.
> We are each followed by another,
> not in the locking of our steps,
> but in the stretching of our souls.
>
> Up the stairs
> is a pilgrimage in honoring the poetry of ever-changing mystery:
> as we listen to the heartbeat of the riser,
> as we charge ourselves in the cadence of the pacer,
> as we reflect our own baggage
> against the weight being carried by those who are climbing.

A lot of the magic came from Jack Carter North, the unanointed leader of the group. Tom, in an essay published at www.fourwindowspress.com several years ago, explained the magic like this:

> When Ethel and I became involved in the Zuni Mountain poets, driving from our home in Continental Divide, NM nearly an hour and a half most Sundays, the poetry group was already a strongly going concern. Held at Inscription Rock Trading Post and Coffee Company's outdoor patio in the summer and its loft in winter, the

group was already writing poetry that rivaled anything being written by the Wisconsin Fellowship of Poets, a major arts organization Ethel and I had attended off and on for years. Jack Carter North, the unofficial head of the group, allows almost no negative comments about a poet's work shared during meetings, and the result is astounding. Over the years young and poor poets have joined the group, but over time all of them have improved their work, if they kept coming to the meetings. I would be willing to claim that several of the poets writing, including Ethel, have a poetic genius.

But the real point is that the magic has been going on for decades and is as alive today as when this essay was published in 2011.

For a long time the Davises were satisfied with attending meetings, writing poetry, and getting to know some of the poets whose work is featured in this anthology like Standing Feather, the co-editor, Jack Carter North, Margaret Gross, RedWulf, Donald Sharp, and others. But then Ethel decided she wanted to publish a volume of poetry and the effort to learn how to publish books began. First came *I Sleep Between the Moons of New Mexico* and *White Ermine Across Her Shoulders* by Ethel, then an anthology, *The Zuni Mountain Poets Anthology*, co-edited by Jack Carter North, Margaret Gross, and Tom Davis. Then Tom published a couple of his novels.

When Tom retired from Navajo Tech and he and Ethel moved back to Wisconsin, where they had spent most of their married years and had daughters and grandchildren, they did not lose touch with the poets at Inscription Rock. Then one day Tom, in the area to help with projects at Navajo Tech, came to visit Standing Feather at the Ancient Way Café and started lobbying him to put his poetry together into a book. Standing Feather, always tied up with running the different businesses at Ancient Way, was interested, but wasn't sure he was ready for such a step. Not long after that Tom came to New Mexico again, and *The Glowing Pink* was in the process of becoming.

This was a seminal moment in the development of Four Windows Press and the impetus toward the creation of this anthology. Standing Feather's love of poetry is as obvious as that which can be found in Ethel's work, and when *The Glowing Pink* was brought out by Four Windows after he had started a small gallery, Galleria Carnaval, across from Inscription Rock Trading Post, it was a significant success. Instead of being a self-publishing effort, Four Windows Press was on the way to becoming a small publishing company. As *The Glowing Pink* was being prepared, Tom and Ethel published a book of poetry by Betty Hayes Albright, *Stepping Stones*.

The next book was by RedWulf that came to be titled, *Waiting on the Monsoons for His Desert Soul*, but as that idea started percolating, Standing

Feather suggested, during one of Tom's visits to the gallery, that we do an anthology. The truth was that putting together *The Zuni Mountain Poets Anthology* had been a challenge, and Tom was not sure he was up to dealing with the publishing and relationship dilemmas that accompany any new anthology project. Standing Feather took over two years to talk Tom into this project, but he kept at it, and so here we are on the verge of publishing this volume.

The journey has been as challenging as Tom originally foresaw. The idea was to try to get a diversity of selected poets that would include famous voices, like Terence Winch, the American Book Award Winner and author of the new young adult novel published by Four Windows Press, *Seeing-Eye Boy*, the famous Anishinabe poet Kimberly Blaeser, the wonderful British poet John Looker, and James Janko, a novelist who has won, among other awards, the AWP Award for the Novel for *The Clubhouse Thief*, with a group of outstanding poets from the English-speaking world from diverse backgrounds. They write everything from sonnets to free verse out of world views shaped by race, sexual orientation, nationality, and knowledge of poetry.

The Question About Poetry

The question any anthologist has to face is, how do you decide on of the poets and poems that should be included? In the case of *No More Can Fit Into the Evening*, an early decision was made to invite poets either Tom or Standing Feather knew to submit "the ten best poems they had ever written." There are so many poets writing poetry in the contemporary world that any call for submission results in hundreds of pages of poetry that have to be read before selections can be made. Both Tom and Standing Feather are extremely busy in their work lives, so this was a non-starter as they contemplated putting an anthology together. They also know a lot of poets from around the English-speaking world, so they decided to do an invitational volume.

To a large degree this strategy worked. The poets submitted extraordinarily strong work. After submissions came in, the task was then to winnow through what was submitted and to try to maintain the quality of the poems throughout the volume. One rule was to not exclude poems that have a degree of obscurity. Some poets clamor for clarity, ignoring poets like Wallace Stevens or John Berryman and any number of important movements that have risen and fallen in popularity over the decades. If a poet like Jim Kleinhenz can submit a puzzle to the reader, forcing re-readings before the poem makes sense, part of the joy in reading the poem is to figure it out, to go through the exhilarating work of discovery. Anna Mark demands a different kind of analysis, but also presents an interesting challenge, especially since her work always has an emotional power that cannot be ignored.

Still, a poem can also be crystal clear and absolutely wonderful to read. Usually this happens when theme, image, and emotion fuse together into a statement that delights, startles, frightens, saddens, or exhilarates the reader. Sometimes a simple image put together with memorable language can stick in the mind for months, if not years, after its first reading. Poets like Sharon Auberele or Ethel Mortenson Davis both reach this kind of fused imagery.

Some memorable poets achieve felicity with word music. When Ralph Murre performs his poetry you can catch rhythms and an image of 1960 coffeehouses filled with patrons snapping fingers as a bearded poet peers out into the smoky universe. In Al DeGenova's work the wailing, wild, changing, subtle beat and improvised syncopation of a jazz quartet sweating as they bring a club alive to their soaring rhythms dominates his stage. A performance poet like Nathan J. Reid presents a different rhythm based upon his dramatic structures and the cadence of an actor with an expressive voice.

Others, like Nick Moore or Cynthia Jobin are masters of traditional forms of poetry and achieve a contemporary excellence by going down pathways trod by centuries of poets echoing back into the times of Homer or Beowulf or the great Welsh and Celtic poets.

Still others, and there are several in the volume, like Blaeser. Robin Chapman, or Michael Kreisel, seem destined to achieve a Pulitzer Prize or National or American Book Award. Yet others, like Estella Lauter, Robert Okaji, or Tori Grant Welhouse, write out of a knowledge of world poetry that gifts their work with a true sense of literature.

There are so many poets in this volume that not all of them are mentioned in this essay, but all of them deserve to be mentioned. Mike Orlock, Margaret Gross, Richard Brenneman, and all the others are gifted poets who can challenge, sing, stir up our anger, amaze our senses, or simply leave us dazzled if we spend the time to get to know their work.

The Final Principle

The final principle Tom and Standing Feather wanted to honor is the idea that a healthy sampling of a poet's work is better than a whiff that gives a slight taste of what the poet is all about. Some of the poets contained herein have been published in some of the finest magazines and journals in the world. A few have won major awards for their poetry and their books and have an international audience. Others have never achieved publication outside of their personal blogs, but we wanted to give the reader a deep, rather than a poetaster, sample of their work.

These were not easy decisions to make. Poetry seldom sells to the degree that a publishing company makes any money off any one volume. Small volumes are easier to market than large volumes like this one. We are mainly hoping to come close to breaking even on this effort, but are unsure that even this is possible. However, we are excited that we have included so many poems and wish we could have even gone further down the inclusion road.

Conclusion

What Standing Feather and Tom are really hoping as they bring this project to press is that, perhaps, readers might find themselves on a mesa top where grandmother junipers spread their branches out beneath a full moon, remembering poems that stuck in their spirit after this volume has been read. We are hoping they might have that experience in Door County, Wisconsin where Lake Michigan is tossing wild, white capped waves at the dark dolomite escarpment that runs through Door Peninsula, or maybe in the timeless moment when they are communing with Taliesin, the ancient Celtic bard, in a time before time as he chants the world's beauty into the deep starlight of a Celtic night.

If there are poems in this volume that can achieve any of that, we are glad Standing Feather kept after Thomas Davis until he said, with a sigh in his voice, well, I guess we're going to do a poetry anthology then.

Thomas Davis and Standing Feather

Terence Winch

Terence Winch, originally from the Bronx, New York, but now a resident of Washington DC, is the author of eight poetry collections, the most recent of which is *The Known Universe* (Hanging Loose, 2018). A Columbia Book Award and American Book Award winner, he has also written two story collections, *Contenders* and *That Special Place*, the latter of which draws on his experiences as a founding member of the original Celtic Thunder, the acclaimed Irish band. His work has appeared in many journals and anthologies. He is the recipient of an NEA Fellowship in poetry, a Fund for Poetry grant, and a Gertrude Stein Award for Innovative Writing, among other honors.

Four Windows Press published *Seeing-Eye Boy*, a young adult novel about a boy named Matt Coffey whose world is in turmoil. The novel, Winch's first, presents a dramatic and dynamic portrait of the Irish immigrant world of 20th century urban America.

When Winch won the Columbia Book Award, Barbara Guest, a first generation member of what has become known as the New York School of poetry, said that his poems in his second book, *The Great Indoors*, present an "atmosphere of the bitter-sweet, the expert sense of line, and its many subtle and humorous ways. . ." The literary critic Jack Morgan wrote that "We get this world from no other writer — this last glimpse of the culture of twentieth-century Irish immigrants in America as their first-generation American-born children witnessed it. ...The totality of his work makes for so compelling an Irish mural as to merit George O'Brien's judgment that Winch is 'the voice of Irish America.'" Both of Guest's and Morgan's comments describe the range of Winch's work. His Irish-Catholic roots are clearly stated in a poem like "Forgiveness."

His bittersweet irony and humor, sometimes attached to the Irish American culture alive in the Bronx of his youth, but just as often aimed at himself, is sprinkled through his eight books in what seems like an endless profusion of observations about the world and what it must, should, maybe could, actually mean. Winch's voice is one of the most distinctive and powerful in all of American literature.

Psalm

Leave me alone. Show me no mercy.
Don't heal me. Don't put more joy in my heart.

Your words are abominable. Your actions unspeakable.
I ask you please to take no notice of me.

When it's dark, you make it darker. When we flatter you,
you turn everything clean into a thing of filth.

Please don't eavesdrop on us. Pay no attention to our
adversaries. Do not cleanse me or them of our crimes.

When the earth shakes and the waters flood, I do not think of you.
When I'm on a high place with a song in my heart, you're the last thing
    on my mind.

These are not burnt offerings. They are the hamburgers we eat for
    dinner.
Your power is not in my bones. My cries are not in your ear.

My transgressions give refreshment to my soul. I will cut my clothes up
and throw them off a mountain if you will only abandon us.

Hide your face. Stay away from our dances and funerals.
We write you name in dust then forget all about you.

Social Security

No one is safe. The streets are unsafe.
Even in the safety zones, it's not safe.
Even safe sex is not safe.
Even things you lock in a safe
are not safe. Never deposit anything
in a safety deposit box, because it
won't be safe there. Nobody is safe
at home during baseball games anymore.

At night I go around in the dark
locking everything, returning
a few minutes later
to make sure I locked
everything. It's not safe here.
It's not safe and they know it.
People get hurt using safety pins.

It was not always this way.
Long ago, everyone felt safe. Aristotle
never felt danger. Herodotus felt danger
only when Xerxes was around. Young women
were afraid of wingèd dragons, but felt
relaxed otherwise. Timotheus, however,
was terrified of storms until he played
one on the flute. After that, everyone
was more afraid of him than of the violent
west wind, which was fine with Timotheus.
Euclid, full of music himself, believed only
that there was safety in numbers.

My Work

In my work, at any given point,
the great issues of identity politics
and dialectical absolutism assume
a tight coherence, a profoundly
threatening total awareness

by which I seek to mediate
the conflict between meaning
and the extremes of deconstruction.

I never strike a false note.
I believe in savvy artistic
incandescence as a constitutive
enhancement of racy sexuality,
all as a way to examine the
necessity of self-love.

It's always dangerous to underestimate
my work. I insult the intellectual
dignity of the French. They arrive
in my brightly colored landscape
right after quitting time only to discover
an empty stage set in which all the clueless
actors have wandered off to an installation
of obsolete Marxist sloganeering.

Yeats was deeply immersed in mythology
and so am I. T. S. Eliot preferred Dante
to Shakespeare, but I don't. Charles Bernstein
loves the way my sentences decompose.
John Ashbery will read my work only
while naked. Everything I do is the pure
output of brains, speed, and skill.

A couple of weeks ago, I digested
Aristotle. I found him to be electrifyingly
ahistorical, and he now has been subsumed
into my work. I have open-ended stratagems
when it comes to the Germans, particularly
Goethe and Kant. They live now in my
imagination. I go way beyond alienation
into a new synthesis of desire and content.

My work stands for something invisible,
something inner. I attempt to explain
the risk of appearing. Foucault would know
how well my work succeeds in revealing
the discourse between power and structure.
When you read my work, you may think

"simile" or "metaphor," but what you really
get is the storm, the dark mansion, the servant
girl standing alone in Columbus Circle.
Triumph and loss permeate my work.
People should try to pick up on that.
My technical virtuosity is unrivaled.
Don't talk to me about subject matter.
My work takes "narrative" and turns
it into what never happened. In my work,
"story" becomes language contemplating
its own articulation in a field of gesture.

There is a higher reality at play in my work.
Sacred memories resonate with perceptual
knowledge of the body as primal text. Yet
my work is never subservient to the dominant
ideology. It circulates warmly and freely
through all available channels. My work
is like the furniture you so much want to
sink into, but must wait as it wends its way
from distant points in a giant moving truck
screeching across the country
to your new home.

Sex Elegy

My lovers have vanished. I used to have many.
One moved to Boston and married a Japanese photographer.
Another became a famous actress. Another one, who for a long time
I mistakenly believed to be dead, now lives in Manhattan.

We used to know each other so intimately,
sucking and munching on each other, inserting,
penetrating, exploding. Becoming as one. Funky
smell of sweaty bodies. Clothes strewn on floor
and bed. Candles burning. Smoke of cigarettes and joints
curling up the bedroom atmosphere. Now we never touch,
barely talk. Some I have lost all contact with.

But memories of our pleasure together, my dears,
still play in my mind. My body can still feel your touch.

My tongue still remembers your taste.
Everything else I seem to have forgotten.
The present is the life insurance premium automatically
deducted from your paycheck, while the past burns
out of control in a vacant lot on the outskirts of town.

Sleep Waltz

for mcw

Get old enough so you won't have much to fear.
By then, the music plays inside your head
and everything beautiful must be learned by ear.

In the bathroom mirror I behold my wear and tear.
In our bedroom I try to levitate in bed.
Get old enough so you won't have much to fear.

Meanwhile, my son at six wants to keep me near
and we sing together every night head to head.
So everything beautiful must be learned by ear.

His father's tunes, though, will one day disappear
beyond today's routines and daily bread.
But get old enough so you won't have much to fear.

Remembering my mother was my first career
and the songs surrounding her on which I fed,
knowing everything beautiful must be learned by ear.

We may waltz in the kitchen now, my dear,
or dance out of time in our sleep instead.
Get old enough so you have nothing left to fear.
Everything beautiful must be learned by ear.

Civilized Atmospheres

The bar is filled with a foul odor, something

to do with the sewage system. People don't mind

one bit. They smoke, talk, make time, drink, dance.

We don't mind either. We like to see people having fun.

We think there should be more fun in all our lives.

And more sex and money. We want everyone to have

more power, as much power as they would like,

because we know how important power is to people.

We want everyone we know to be the boss on the job

and at home too. We want them to get what they want

because when they do, they're happy and we're happy.

We want them to have bigger and better houses and apartments.

More beautiful lovers. We want them to have lean, hard

bodies and perfect cardiovascular health.

We want their health clubs to be radiant and spotless.

We'd like to see their children turn out radiant too.

It is threatening to rain. We hate rain. We hate even more

the heavy oppressive atmosphere that precedes rain. We hate

the bad smell in the bar and we don't like the people in the bar

because they seem so pompous. Their breath is horrible

and they have pot bellies and their clothing stinks of cigarettes.

It is getting dark two hours before it should. That really makes

us mad and depresses us too. Darkness. We hate darkness

because it is so scary.

Nobody calls us anymore, so we call them

because we don't want to be left alone up here

in the dark with no one to talk to. But there's no

answer, or we get the answering machine and leave

a message, or they are there but they just can't

talk to us right now because they're too busy, or even worse,

they're expecting a more important call than ours.

It's pouring now. Thunderous skies are opening up.

Everything is wet. We hate to get wet.

We closed the windows just in time, but now

it's airless in here and we can't breathe.

We don't like work. The coming and going,

the politics, the give and take.

We can live without it. The mindless routine

day after day: the bus, the coffee break, the paperwork.

We don't want anyone to have to go to work

with those disgusting bad-smelling people

who think they're so important. Don't they know

that no one is indispensable? What about when you die?

Do they ever think of that?

We don't want to have to come home from work

in the scary wet darkness and then have to leave again

for the smelly bar where those absolutely horrible people

drink their drinks. We don't want anyone

we know to have to do it either.

We'd like everyone to stay home where it's dry and peaceful,

where they can watch movies and eat whatever they want,

sleeping in a chair, listening to the sound of a car horn,

the scary wet darkness enveloping them in its dream.

That Little Extra Something

This is going to be a great piece of writing.
I can just feel it. Can you feel it, too?
I plan to stumble on a profound epiphanic
moment, like one I had tonight while
drinking in a bar downtown. Wish I could
remember that one, but I can't. It's gone,
baby, gone. I could easily address my
feelings about awe, that's always a sure
bet. You know, how awesome everyone

thinks everything is these days? I too
think that everything is awesome.
I have very deep insights into the nature
of art and music, which, if I were to lay
out in this piece of writing, would be
evident to all. Likewise, no one, IMO,
really appreciates sex the way I do.
Man, I could dazzle and entice you with
some very erotic material right here
and now if the situation called for that.
Death, how it's just always hovering
around with its extremely irritating
antipromise, the doom and gloom
scenario that it has mapped out for
all of us. That one is always sure fire.
Along with craziness, love, embarrassment.
Some would add despair, rage, amusement.
Birds and bodies of water could come
into play, as they so often do in these
things. Abandonment, loss, hate, envy.
Pretty much any of the Seven Deadly
Sins can spike up any good piece of writing.
But a truly great piece of writing, like this
one, takes that little extra something,
you know, like a metaphor, simile, image,
sign, symbol, one of those sorts of amazing
tools that can pry open a nuclear payload
of wisdom and understanding and transform
everything and everyone in its wake.

Success Story

My clothes are perfectly contoured
to my body. My shoes & socks
fit just right. My cat is a delightful
intelligent animal. My apartment
is great. The right location,
cheap rent. I eat the best food.
My friends love me. I adore them.
My lover is terrific & beautiful.
The sun is shining. There are trees
even in the slums in Washington.
I have tons of money & a gorgeous
air conditioner. Great art hangs
on my wall. I live a spine tingling life
of delirious sex & intense happiness.

Forgiveness

Father Cahir kept us holy.
He smoked cigars in the confessional
He had a distracted air about him,
as though he wasn't sure what
he was supposed to do next.

I don't remember what he taught.
History, probably. It was his
liberal attitude as a confessor
that made him a legend.

No matter what you confessed to,
he always barked out the same penance:
"Three Hail Marys and a Good Act
of Contrition. Next!" So we tested
this leniency , confessing
to rape, murder, burglary.

Cahir paid no attention.
He knew we were a bunch

of high school punks.
Puffing his cigar,
he'd issue his standard
penance and absolve all sins,
real or imagined.
with godlike aloofness,
his vast indifference to
or total acceptance of the darkness
within the human soul
exactly how I hope the deity
regards us. Take forgiveness
any way you can get it.

The Complete Poem

I bring the car to the mechanic because it stopped
abruptly on 95 on Thursday morning
as you were driving to work.

I go to the nursing home to see my brother.
His fierce defiance never leaves him,
even as he gets weaker and frailer.

I am sitting in the sun room watching two birds
in the tree outside. Something's going on, I say cluelessly.
They're building a nest, you tell me.

On Saturday, my heart spins out of control
for five hours. My doctor explains my electrical system
to me and how something went awry.

It takes the mechanic two days to find the problem
because the car runs perfectly for him.
Finally, for $1000, he installs a new ignition system.

My brother can barely talk. He can't walk, sit up,
or go to the bathroom without help.
Yet he is a commanding presence, and looks beautiful.

When you call me from 95 it scares me. You are in a perilous spot
and have only one bar left of cell phone power.
Keep her safe, O Lord, I pray.

My brother lifts his hand up toward me.
I don't know what to do, so I take his hand in mine.
We've never done anything like this before.

I don't want to give up Sudafed, chocolate, coffee,
or Irish whiskey. I want my heart to keep time correctly,
to thump as always in perfect rhythm, and leave me be.

My sick brother, Kevin, then reaches out his other hand
to our brother Jesse, also at the bedside. Jesse takes Kevin's other hand.
Life runs through us like current.

You are safe and sound upstairs, shredding documents,
drawing pictures of cows. My sister Eileen is in Atlanta
having a glass of red wine and watching Turner Classic Movies.

The mechanic says, Mr. Winch, the engine wasn't getting any spark.
Gotta have the spark to get the thing to work.
But for all I know he's just making that up.

A. Carder

A. Carder lives in the East of England and works as a professional copywriter. She has published one book, *Between Dusk and Darkness*, with Bennison Books. It is a short book, but its prose poems are a model of the genre. Small images of moments skein into an intimacy so filled with longing and memories that they burn into your spirit and make you look at the love in your life and feel just how fragile time makes all of us in our most important relationships. In one poem, "A Lot to Talk About," Carder says

> That I sat among dry bones in this room, my arms a straight-jacket, the paralysis of loss stopping everything, the day leaving without speaking.

The language is original and beautiful, of course, but what is important is the deep emotion conveyed, the sense of loss and how that loss has stopped everything in life, even the day that leaves without speaking.

There are endless examples of this deep emotion and analyses of the few moments left as the moments between dusk and darkness, after what is obviously a tragedy in the poet's life, create a tension that keeps you feeling the power of the images of moments.

Prose poetry can be traced to 17th-century Japan, and France and Germany in the early 19th century. Many prominent writers have used the form including Oscar Wilde, Gertrude Stein, Amy Lowell, Walt Whitman, Rainer Maria Rilke, John Ashbery, Charles Bukowski and the Beat Generation. Carder's work is subtle and evocative rather than robust in the style of Whitman or Bukowski, but is nevertheless powerful in its understated way.

Nefertiti in Jeans

Then, on the bus, you turned and kissed my left temple. And the old men half-puckered and the women shining above their shopping, and me Nefertiti in jeans.

The woman in the bakery folded our French stick in half as if subduing a wrestler. And so began our stockpile of private treasures. In such moments lives are arranged, more final than a marriage. And every bakery since, every inhalation of fresh-baked bread, a reminder of that consecration.

You made curry, its exotic aroma narcotic, and everything changed for all time.

Dark Furniture
and Tall Sash Windows

I remember that room. Its vastness and draughts, the high ceiling and ancient beds. Dark furniture and tall sash windows.

You, barely 20, watched my sleeping face. And the moonlight really did move across it. And you wept. Because, you said, your heart had broken open, quietly. The perfect match of pitch and resonant frequency shattering a glass.

I had a name then. You tasted it in your mouth.

Now, if I run a moist finger around the rim of a glass, I can hear the ghostly hum of that resonance. And hear again my name in your mouth. It is sweet.

Accretions

I don't know, I say.

We waited so long in the café. The waitress had her apron on inside-out. You took pristine paper napkins and folded them into your pocket. The croissant wasn't warm, your toast came without jam. We had the conversation with our eyes and fell a little in love with her, our inside-out waitress. A tip for all the tenderness she aroused and the white napkins fluttering to the floor as you stand to dig out your change.

I smooth and fold them like pages, like sheets, like all the days and tuck them back into your pocket.

I don't know how not to do this, I say.

Do you see me? I don't say.

'Accretions' has a number of meanings. In biology it refers to a growing together of parts that are usually separate.

Kintsugi

And often now, my mouth on your half-mouth, a blunt knife, the quick of you uncut.

You can't explain, you write on water. But you have a genius for repair, the fissures filled with polished gold. This is a broken thing, we are joined here.

Is this then stronger and more precious? The scars gleam like a nightlight. It is a way of seeing.

Kintsugi is Japanese for 'golden joinery': the Japanese art of repairing broken pottery with lacquer dusted or mixed with powdered gold, silver or platinum. The philosophy behind this is suggestive of treating breakage and repair as part of the history of an object, rather than something to disguise. The Japanese philosophy of wabi-sabi embraces the flawed and imperfect.

Shards

Fragile as ancient glass unbroke, too exquisite to recall, they rise. In this no-place between sleep and waking there is no choosing. I press my fingertips to the bone of my breast, bone to bone, to feel time pass.

These times, long time, are built on fleeting moments that pierce me. Before the brushing of teeth and making of tea I am with you on the threshold still, called back, shored against, your eyes intense and blue.

Jack Carter North

Jack Carter-North grew up in the Midwest, earning a degree in secondary education from Miami University in Oxford, Ohio. His career brought him to the Southwest, where he was both an English teacher and teacher-trainer. He created a curriculum for teachers called *The Project-Oriented Classroom*. North has been the unofficial "leader" of the Zuni Mountain Poetry Group for over 20 years, providing dozens of people an opportunity to share their work, improve their public poetry reading skills, and receive weekly inspiration from several good regional writers.

One of North's strongest attributes is his teaching methodology used in the Zuni Mountain Poets Meetings. Rather than use the methods popularized by the University of Iowa School of Writing, better known as the Iowa Writers' Workshop, with its emphasis upon critical feedback given by both professors and students to works produced by students, North believes that creativity is a positive attribute that has to be emphasized, avoiding all critical comment while concentrating on each individual poem. The result of this methodology has been an explosion of poetry in the area surrounding the El Morro National Monument in New Mexico.

As Thomas Davis, an educator in his own right, has said, "Jack North taught me more about how to nurture creativity than any other individual, and the proof of the success of his teaching methods can be found in how poets improve so dramatically once they join the Zuni Mountain Poets group. It's almost like magic. New poets come in, writing, at best, awkward or poor poetry, and within six months their work has grown so much you would swear they are on their way to becoming professional poets."

North's work has appeared in *The Zuni Mountain Poets* (Authorhouse, 2012), *Poetry Cha Cha* (El Morro Poetry Press, 2008), and the literary journal, *Querencia*, (Jack Carter-North, ed., 2013).

In North's poetry we are quickly seduced by the emotional content of his physical landscapes, and the transference of the physical place into physical movement. His characters can often showcase a gritty unraveling of their circumstance while gracefully keeping love in the center of the choreography, as highlighted in his short poem, "The Fall."

The Fall

the firebox was empty,
his axe under
summer rubble.
man's intolerance
and fickle love —
their caroms haunted him
like november sleet.
his gods ignored him.
he took a pull
on his wine,
kissed the cheek
of the last gladiola,
and shut the gate behind him.

Dreamsicle Splash

a misplaced dream slipped inside the sunset,
a dreamsicle splash, and I awaken to its light:
    in the dream i am carrying books and folders,
    a lit professor on his way home
    from classes on a clear friday night.
    the family greets me, but nobody moves
    from the TV room.
    i go to the basement,
    mix a gimlet and lean on the fireplace.
    i shut the basement door.
the gerbils stir and scratch the newspaper.
i hear a line from donne in my head
about pastoral awakening and see ravens on lake michigan.
the family calls me to blueberry muffins.
i smile and chug the gimlet.

Gypsy Woman

she took him by the hand to a black lit room,
pointing him to a stuffed green lame ottoman.
she sat on the stool and faced him, taking his hand,
opening her other hand which revealed finger cymbals.
she took a modest fold of dollars from her bra,
and he pressed two hundreds just above her breast.
she smiled, and with one hand wrapped the hundreds into the fold,
returning it to her bra with a come-on smile.
she played the cymbals, got up, and returned
with plate-sized round cards.
she lowered herself slowly on the ottoman with him.
her hair, braided indigo laces, fell in front of her
as she dealt him one card, an orange and black bird
flying into sunset clouds with deep red sunrays.

     you will always be writing in your head
she said as she reached for a crystal,
which she placed on top of the bird.

      and then you will be quiet enough
        to write the treatises and make the pictures
        which tell the stories.
        this is the bord of good fortune.
she placed the crystal into his hand,
folding his fingers around it as she picked
another card, a group of flamingos in a shallow pond.

     your friendships will last for many years,
and you will follow them and love them
when you are not working the earth.
these flamingos bring harmony and soft rains.
she hummed a lullaby and tapped her cymbals.
she spread the cards out on the ottoman,
extending her hand in a sweeping invitation
to pick his own card, and he turned over
a kingfisher diving into a stream.

     three birds mean you will be blessed
       with three miracles.
       these will be windows
       into what you may suspect is divine.

Crescendo

I want my crescendo to last forever.
I want to stomp on the big-boy pedal,
Ride my Harley into a thousand sunsets,
And explore mankind from the inside out.
There are no bucket lists.
I want the sun on my neck.
I yearn to dance the cha-cha in Tijuana
And the jitterbug in Manhattan.
I want to strum flamenco riffs that stun the world.
I must relearn the French horn and take up
With the Boston Pops.
I will grow sweet corn that draws crowds.
I will accept all people as brothers,
Remembering that the complex thing is to simplify,
Inch by humble inch.

Rudders

Sometimes we are at sea,
trying different rudders
to avoid the snapping sound
of a broken boat
adrift,
pieces of us to be found
by vagrant, disinterested
gulls.

Brotherhood

his meeting with himself began alone in the garden
by a golden bale of three-strand straw.
he felt them churning in him, and they came too:
the father, the romantic, the builder,
and the gladhander, the teacher, and the dancer.
all breathed together at this moment, so softly, and walked

among the gladiolas, quiet greetings on their lips.
their darling, river boy poet, the sweetest,
the soft one everybody wanted to be near, was close,
his presence coming from them.

the romantic nudged the edge of the bale and said,
we should have listened to river boy poet. . .
our man was happiest
when he sold flowers in the rain in cincinnati.
he needs to sell flowers or truck farm his corn or something.

the teacher put his arm around the father, set his hat back and said,
long ago we voted — he taught, joined sher, raised the boys.
wanderlust gave way to the truest love.
look where we are —
he waved his arms at the mesa and the sky and the house.
i have been happy with him.

let him build one more thing in his life and then let him go
said the builder,
have him set his hands in the mud one more time.

the father:
        get at him ... wake him up ...
        he needs to chase thoreau and let random
        take him and sher for its own pair ...
he wiped a tear from his cheek.

the dancer, in fine turquoise, spoke:
        we raise boys, we teach, we build, we grow corn,
and we grow gladiolas.
        always with love in his heart.
        remember, once he wanted a professor's life in a city,
and he had a meeting at the bar,
 and we talked him away from that.

a memory, and he laughed and pulled wheat straw from the bale:
free in hawaii, before he came back,
before the degree, the jobs, and the family.
he sat down next to the romantic, braiding the teacher's hair.

a chuckle came, river boy poet's soft chuckle, and it was silent
except for the chortles of gladness going up

into the twilight from his huddled brotherhood.
there he was, pulling his cap off and setting his bundle on the bale.
he pulled a pencil from behind his ear and reached for a leather-bound
    diary.
they all hugged him, patted his curls, and sat in a tight circle around him.
river boy poet always spoke softly.
his brothers nuzzled around his face.
he stuck a piece of straw into the side of his mouth and smiled,
then cuddled each brother's chin or cheek — he was the youngest —
a blessing upon them — teardrops spilled onto the earth.

pulling a piece of turquoise from his pocket, he whispered:
    we're happy with him and us ...
he shook his scarf out and chuckled,
      as long as the family, gladiolas, poems, and sweet corn make him
      who he is, we're lucky we're with him.
to this the seven of them hummed an assent, a soft chant, for several
seconds.
they put their arms around each other, a tribe of seven.

everyone rose when river boy did.
hands stroked his tender cheeks, and they pulled
him into their arms, whispering to him the hopes they had.
he caressed and kissed their hands, and a murmur came from river boy.
he spoke for them as he always did at the end:
    we are good with him, and we love this man,
    but he must not see the end, though he senses it.
    let him spend his years like pearls,
    and we will be a silver string for them.
he buried the turquoise beneath the bale, and the meeting was finished.
noise from the straw, their boots stirring the golden dust,
and they were gone.

he cut a strand on the bale across from him and pulled out a fistful of
wheat straw and threw it into the wind ...
and then hugged a clump to his chest,
chuckling like river boy poet.

ions and prayers

the zuni farmer explained
that ancestors send the rain,
praying to ancestors and feeding them
bring blessings from them.
their rain is magic.

the grower-teacher across the creek from us depends
on monsoons to bring his crops
from the scorch of summer
to harvest in September.
with a bottle of wine last night
he explained the molecular construction
of soil when rain is added to begin
the ionization and electrolysis processes,
making particles charged with nucleoids
for developing the sucrose needed
for plant proliferation from shlorophyll.

I told him its magic.
he said if we can explain it, it's not.
I said if we can explain it, *we're* magic.
he shook his head and chuckled,
a chardonnay disbeliever.
in dreams that night, he was visited
by rain gods who tickled his chin and cheeks.
next day he said
he couldn't explain growing really,
and that it was probably magic
in the ions and electrolytes.

Kimberly Blaeser

Kimberly Blaeser, writer, photographer, and scholar, served as Wisconsin Poet Laureate for 2015-16. She was awarded the Edna Muedt Poetry Book Award from the Council for Wisconsin Writers in 2019. The author of five poetry collections — most recently *Résister en dansant/Ikwe-niimi: Dancing Resistance, Copper Yearning,* and *Apprenticed to Justice,* and editor of *Traces in Blood, Bone, and Stone: Contemporary Ojibwe Poetry,* Blaeser is a Professor of English and Indigenous Studies at UW—Milwaukee and a Master of Fine Arts (MFA) faculty member for the Institute of American Indian Arts in Santa Fe, New Mexico. Her work is widely anthologized with selections translated into Spanish, French, Norwegian, Indonesian, Chinese, and Hungarian, and her photographs, picto-poems, and ekphrastic poetry have been featured in various venues including the exhibits "Ancient Light" and "Visualizing Sovereignty."

Anishinaabe, an enrolled member of the Minnesota Chippewa Tribe, Blaeser grew up on the White Earth Reservation. She lives in the woods and wetlands of Lyons Township, Wisconsin and spends part of each year at a water-access cabin adjacent to the Boundary Waters Canoe Area Wilderness in Minnesota.

Blaeser is a significant voice within the American Indian Renaissance that started with the publication of *House Made of Dawn* by Scott Momaday in 1968. Her poetry explores what it means to have the past history of Native America, with all that means in historical trauma, as part of her background in the contemporary world. At the same time, like the Turtle Mountain Anishinabe writer Louise Erdrich, she explores the German side of her ancestry, often juxtaposing what that means to her life. Sometimes beautiful, sometimes haunting, often unforgettable, usually crying out for justice, she is writing some of the most interesting poetry being published.

In her poem "After Words" she writes,

Because the gesture of after words
means the same thing no matter
who speaks them.
Because faith belief forever
are only words, no matter.
Because matter disappears
always and eventually.
Because action is not matter

but energy
that spent, changes being.

Blaeser is always trying to define all of our places, as well as her own, in
an uncertain world.

Apprenticed to Justice

The weight of ashes
from burned-out camps.
Lodges smoulder in fire,
animal hides wither
their mythic images shrinking
pulling in on themselves,
all incinerated
fragments
of breath bone and basket
rest heavy
sink deep
like wintering frogs.
And no dustbowl wind
can lift
this history
of loss.

Now fertilized by generations —
ashes upon ashes,
this old earth erupts.
Medicine voices rise like mists
white buffalo memories
teeth marks on birch bark
forgotten forms
tremble into wholeness.

And the grey weathered stumps,
trees and treaties
cut down
trampled for wealth.
Flat Potlatch plateaus
of ghost forests
raked by bears

soften rot inward
until tiny arrows of green
sprout
rise erect
rootfed
from each crumbling center.

Some will never laugh
as easily.
Will hide knives
silver as fish in their boots,
hoard names
as if they could be stolen
as easily as land,
will paper their walls
with maps and broken promises,
scar their flesh
with this badge
heavy as ashes.

And this is a poem
for those
apprenticed
from birth.
In the womb
of your mother nation
heartbeats
sound like drums
drums like thunder
thunder like twelve thousand
walking
then ten thousand
then eight
walking away
from stolen homes
from burned out camps
from relatives fallen
as they walked
then crawled
then fell.

This is the woodpecker sound
of an old retreat.

It becomes an echo,
an accounting
to be reconciled.
This is the sound
of trees falling in the woods
when they are heard,
of red nations falling
when they are remembered.
This is the sound
we hear
when fist meets flesh
when bullets pop against chests
when memories rattle hollow in stomachs.

And we turn this sound
over and over again
until it becomes
fertile ground
from which we will build
new nations
upon the ashes of our ancestors.
Until it becomes
the rattle of a new revolution
these fingers
drumming on keys.

Refractions

for Bill Harrold

Why should it happen
that the smallest
zig-zagging black cricket
one stick leg raised —
a musician's baton,
holds and then releases
the same song
as my canoe paddle
slicing into glass?

Boundary Water's evening lake
still, mirroring
like memory doubles
you here and gone
now leaning akimbo
a cricket musician
message encoded in meter
in the rhythm of my own arms
paddling side to side
as if I could find you
in the funnel of each stroke
in the blue sluice of time.

And light grabs my breath again:
peering into that one space
where ledge rock dissolves into color
cascades grey and rust and moss green
effortlessly transforming at water's edge
tumbling headlong into repetition
unfolding mirror image
into the depthless eternity of reflection
until, in that moment, I forget
which side of vision
is mere reality.

And that this bent black line of insect
can sing
and more — that every chirp should count
in precise degrees
just how cold is loss.

Fantasies of Women

for Carol Marefka

They say:
there was an old woman
who lived in a shoe —
children, spanking, bed, no food
it's an old story,

one to rival the Peter tale
who kept his wife in a pumpkin shell,
or Jack Sprat who coveted
all the 90% lean cuts of meat,
while his ever-expanding
squat round wife
tumbles over the sides
of a tiny kitchen chair
over-filling the page
on which she is drawn.
We keep turning that page
but one caricature follows another.

Some claim:
women were always the delicate sex —
fainting, timid, helpless souls
you know that line
the length and breadth of those
whose names have scrambled
the letters of femininity
into unrecognizable derivations
Annie Oakley, Gloria Steinem
Wilma Mankiller
Rigoberta Menchu
Mother Teresa of Calcutta.
In pants or full veil
in every state of dress or undress
Cher's navel
the jewel on Cleopatra's forehead
burn like all beacons of dissent.

I heard:

A nation is never defeated
until the hearts of its women
are trampled upon the earth —
this one I believe
for I grew up among women
who could swallow a raw heart
whole or in infinitesimal pieces
deer heart, rabbit heart, turtle heart
and did swallow and chew
chew and swallow their own red hearts

beating *for survival*
       for survival
       for survival
       for survival.

And this is the single story
we write with our lives
women of travois, ox, or minivan,
of African brown barefoot toes
bound Chinese feet
or seventy-five dollars a pop Birkenstocks.
Together we walk on our houses of history
track true
the paths of indentured servants,
girl babies slain and buried,
this black dirt of bias exposed
overcome in
story cycles of scarlet fecundity
told through the fires of many tongues
and translated again
in the labor of women.

Now we sing:
There was a young woman
who lived in a shoe-obsessed
commercialized overstocked world
she had many children
and knew just what to do —
raise them to share the burdens
of all the people
to unearth the fantastic lies
they were taught to walk upon
to devour fear
chew and swallow
and to cast their hearts
for survival.

Where I Was That Day

It wasn't just the pill bugs
gray, many-legged
pulling that stunt like they always did —
closing in on themselves
contracting into the tiny round mass
like an image of the origin circle.
And it wasn't the turtle alone either
who became so neatly one half of the earth's sphere.

It was partly that day
when I stopped at the little creek,
noticed the funny bumps on that floating log
and how they seemed to be looking at me,
how they were really little heads with beady bulging eyes,
how when I came back a half an hour later
the bumps had been rearranged on that log.

It was partly the butterflies
who materialized out of the flower blossoms,
the deer that appeared and disappeared into the forest
whose shape would be invisible one minute
and would stand out clearly the next
like an image in one of those connect-the-dot puzzles.

It was the stick bugs, the chameleon
the snakes that became branches
the opossum who was dead — then suddenly alive.
And it was me
who fit and saw one minute so clearly
and then stumbled blind the next,
that made me think we are all always finding our place
in the great sphere of creation,
made me know I could learn a way
to pull the world around me, too —
color myself with earth and air and water
and so become indistinguishable,
match my breath to the one
pulse in and out with the mystery,
be both still and wildly alive in the same moment,
be strangely absent from myself

yet large as all creation —
to know
to know
to know and to belong
while the spell holds
learning to hold it a little longer each time.

That's where I was that day
I watched you from the arbor
never blinking
while you looked all about for me
then turned back home
thinking to find me in another place
while I was there everywhere you looked.
I knew then the stories about Geronimo
were true
that he did turn to stone
while cavalries passed him by
mistook him
for just a part of the mountain
when he had really become the whole mountain
and all the air they breathed
and even the dust beneath their horse's hooves.

I walk about
trying to find the place I was that day,
but getting there seems harder now
I feel heavier, my spirit weighted down.
I'm thinking I must shed something
like animals shed their hair or skin
loose even their antlers annually
while I hold on to everything;
I'm thinking I must change my colors
like the rabbit, the ptarmigan, the weasel.
I'm thinking I must spin a cocoon
grow wings and learn to fly.
I'm thinking I must hibernate and fast
feed off my own excess for a season,
then perhaps emerge
in the place I was that day
and stay there longer this time.

I watch the creatures

tree toads becoming and unbecoming a part of the tree
rocks in my path that crack open into grasshoppers and fly away
the spider who hangs suspended before me
then disappears into mist or air
and I feel comforted
knowing we are all
in this puzzle together
knowing we are all just learning
to hold the spell
a little longer
each time.

Of Fractals and Pink Flowering

after Eric and Heather ChanSchatz "The Next Generation"

Imagine the geometry of flower
is hunger for balance,
is my child's hand on the gears of beauty
layering and interlocking color.
Picture me prone, a small center point —
one copper dot in the white Minnesota winter.
Picture my mother drying her hands
placing the compass and spinning
arcs and intersecting curves,
woodland flowers growing
into many-petaled mandalas
into limitlessness: a universe
of circles, of symmetry — sun,
stars, blooms and orange-hued fruits,
the berry, squash, ripe tomato wonder
of belonging.

        My own spirograph bursts
rush forth ornate like paisley, like fireworks
against dark summer sky. Spokes and wheels
and gears meshing — each pencil thrust
a tentative mark, a hopeful threading
of the cogs of longing. Imagine my fingers
holding tight to the friction,
watch the intricate flourishes appear

on white paper — the tabula rasa
transformed by oval,
just another language
another voice saying hello
to the spiraling bodies of self.

Imagine my psychedelic crayola
yearning, my January pining
after the purple florals
the cosmos, the daisy mix
(he loves me, he loves me not)
on Gurney's seed packs.
Now watch as we carve splendor:
my world is medicine wheel and hand drum,
is pow-wow bustle and beadwork in woodland design.
The sweep of nature tallied by curve,
by eye, assembled now as scarlet fractals,
as collage of vines, tassels, seed pods,
and a child's simple pink infinity.

When We Sing Of Might

i.

In this part I switch clothes with a woman I just met
shed my phone, my metal — pray to the scanner gods.
I walk freely through each lock, each clanging door;
here the prison air, the elastic waist of her patterned skirt
settle like a new identity around my body.

ii.

This is the part where it used to be game — a child
moving like a worm through the blades of cool,
through soft evening grass. Firecrackers our only sin.

From here I watch the patrol car, count to ten to twenty,
count the pointed edges of a star driving by,
remember the chorus about *sin and error pining* —
hold my breath, spend an old longing born of beer,
born of bible talk and men.

iii.

This is the year when no one followed the tin star
or the wonder star of Christmas hymns,
when the trail between the courthouse and my grandma's
grew shorter and everybody's hands got tired
picking the rice clean enough for baby Jesus,
clean enough to sell at the Model Meat Market
on Main Street where all the cars parked on an angle,
and I used to think the sign said "angel parking"
and I wondered who would park an angel
if they could find one.

iv.

Right here *weary world* I park the flashbacks
about all the arrestable moments — a past of illegal
brown bodies eating out of season, boys the wrong color
for love, a past of too many: fish, fists, and bottles
broken, the brown drip of spilled brandy — arrestable
edges of lives made jagged and dangerous
(*His law is love and His gospel is peace*)
star-jagged and dangerous as the moments where I see
and maybe you do too the faces sharpened
into angles of rage, of disgust sharpened
on all the low-wage jobs and lying songs
their children learned in grade school
and sang at concerts with fingerplay
and warm kool-aid, when we all still drank
the kool-aid and believed the liberty lyrics —
(*and in His name all oppression shall cease*).

This is the part where arrestable moments
could go either way — and do
depending upon the time of night
the county and the star-wearing body.
So that quiet grass and breath-holding
was training. That counting, one to ten,
ten to twenty — this is where
seconds can become years for some
when it goes the wrong way
when they are the wrong color
when their pockets are empty
when liberty and justice for all — is all used up.

v.

But when we sing of might, this is the part
the part where my jailed brown uncles
my shackled cousins angel their way in
where children fostered and lost reappear.
I dress in their stories patterned and purple
as night. I dress in old songs of prison trains
and men covering their eyes to sleep,
songs of women on one side of a sliding panel
of lives shattered but mosaiced by might—
the angles of survival a many-cornered wholeness.

Ward O'cean

Ward O'cean is an El Morro, New Mexico poet who appreciates how poetic muses wander inside of desert southwest dwellers. He is a devoted metatician, sound awareness practitioner, salvage-assembler, and future-pop scavenger. He has self-published poems for many years (*Reikitazer, Instagram*) and is a founding member of *The Secular Stretching Society* and journeyman member of the *Wave Riders of the Ancient Way Healing Center*. A student of movement technologies, both verbal and vibrational, Ward entered the Zuni Mountain Poets group *(El-Morro, New Mexico)* in 2016 with delicate, sparse poems that made big waves in the group discussions. He likes to think of himself as riding between empty boundaries of waiting words. In his words he developed his trade by leaving various friends in wild, unknown places:

Touching heavens, that wave into twilight hours
often speak such separation;
such wandering paths we may have crossed
out of sheer exaltation in our shaky successes.

O'cean's work often presents readers with an alternative view of the universe, while planting hidden proposals that unravel the abstractions of the ethereal. He blows off cobwebs, then kindly places the concepts back into fundamentals of elemental awareness. The poems suggest that we are never far from the things and ideas we see as distant:

Burnt to dust
By desert sun
By water creatures
Chewed like gum
Faded streamers
Birthday fun
Plastic always suffers

Needed more
With every year
Yet banished to
a blue bin near
enough to keep
a conscience clear
Plastic always suffers

You came to me in a day-dream/ 2

Dripping the vibration
Of growing things

Audio slips through
Waking hours
For seconds seeming
Pressed between

Your voice
And humming now

You came to me in a day-dream/3

The Moon holds
My gaze out the
Back-seat window

On landscapes
Over-turned
By the

Phantom weight
Of your head
In my lap

And the driver asks
"Is Everyone still
With Us?"

You came to me in a day-dream/4

A matador
A bull

Curving horns
Believing dance
To be a spectacle
Of reaction
And victory

At the end accolades ...
Bravos ...

You came to me in a day-dream/5

On all four horses

I am frozen
In the known

Cacophony
Of many hooves

Over-ridden
And riding
to me

Chimpanzees

Some like it
Being put in dresses

Learning how to talk

Some smear their dismay
On the walls

Jane Goodall
Locked away bananas
For timed dispersal

We are so alike
When near ripe fruit
Is Unreachable

Plastic always suffers

Never loved
beyond the day
Your usefulness
Begins to fray
You're torn apart
Then thrown away
Plastic always suffers

Burnt to dust
By desert sun
By water creatures
Chewed like gum
Faded streamers
Birthday fun
Plastic always suffers

Needed more
With every year
Yet banished to
A blue bin near
Enough to keep
A conscience clear
Plastic always suffers

Compassion Addict

In the deep program
There is often Addiction

Hugging
Cuddling
Coddling

If the environment
No longer holds,
What structure
Do we reach with?

In the spirit
Of love
We pray to be
Filled
With the listening
Of others

10 of Spaces (Ace of Dishes)

The last thing the trees said
was in a language like our own
but reflected back on itself
Like whispers in the wind
or ripples as we fall
Laughing
Into the water.

The Courage of Water

Ready to carry heavy elements
Satisfaction Is somewhere inside

Hidden as dew before The sun rises
I ask it for saving like stability

To Freeze at the first striking light
In the valley of the poets

I cannot doubt dry days
Where other flowers flourish

I cannot doubt the clouds
With the desire to fall

Or run through me along
The pull of the Planets love

Hare 2 Turtle

to slow down limbs
that could not rest
in casual paces

what brings the sleep
of satisfaction
If the catching up
is done?

If winning wont
Be waiting
Without dreaming

Don't wake me
Don't wake me

How Do You Like It?

Do you like it from a box
CNN or maybe FOX
Chairman Mao and chicken pox
How do you like your fascism?

Do you like it on the air
Waves that dance like Fred Astaire
With entertainment self aware
How do you like your fascism?

Guess we like it good enough
Rolling credit off a bluff
Until the world runs out of stuff
How do you like your fascism?

Mike Orlock

Mike Orlock, a retired high school teacher and coach, says he enjoys travel, reading, writing, films, and spending time with his two children and five grandchildren. His short fiction has appeared in *Tri-Quarterly*, the literary journal of Northwestern University, and *Another Chicago Magazine*. His poetry has appeared online in "Your Daily Poem" website, in the WFOP yearly calendars, *Verse Wisconsin*, the *Los Angeles Times*, *Blue Heron Review*, the *Peninsula Pulse*, and various other venues. He has published three books of poetry: *You Can Get Here from There: Poems of Door County & Other Places; Poetry Apocalypse & Selected Verse;* and *Mr. President! Poetry, Polemics & Fan Mail from Inside the Divide*. His work has received awards from the Illinois Arts Council, the Wisconsin Writers Association, and the Wisconsin Fellowship of Poets.

Four ideas describe most of Orlock's poetry: idiosyncratically funny, sarcastic or ironic, romantic, and original. He often takes his cue from contemporary culture, as in his poem, "Poetry Apocalypse," in this case the current fascination with zombies, and then leaves the reader to puzzle out the big meaning he is conveying, all the time making sure there is at least the snort of a laugh in there somewhere. "On Perdido Beach" is a poem that brings out his romantic side as he takes a walk, with someone he clearly cares about addressed in the poem as "you," on the beach:

> We are engulfed by the detritus of living things
> long dead, dormant yet yearning.
> We listen for angels, pray for ghosts
> in cathedrals and cemeteries, but what we seek is here
> in oceans,
> in earth,
> underfoot.

The one thing true of almost everything Orlock has published, even in his politically enraged, funny, sarcastic *Mr. President! Poetry, Polemics & Fan Mail from Inside the Divide*, where he attacks all things Trumpian, is that he is always entertaining, barbing meaning into the originality of his lines. There are few poets that can enliven a page the way Orlock can.

Cinderella Spring

for Rori Michele, my princess of every season

April wears the sun like silk,
a girl in swirls of yellow folds
that drape her days
    in lingering light —
        as she steals minutes from the night.

Like Cinderella dreaming dresses
cleaning her step-sisters' messes,
April too has work to do —
    washing winter from the world
        so dreams of daffodils come true.

Her sisters May and June deride
April for her moody swings,
impatient of meanderings —
    they want summer! want it now!
        want the sun to scrape and bow!

But April takes her time with things.
In fields muddy with melting snow,
steps uncertain, progress slow,
she pauses, clouds of skirt lifting —
and gives to all a peek of spring.

Poetry Apocalypse

In the end the dead will live again. They will rise
from graves and crypts in putrid clothes,
in moldering shrouds, to walk (or run: scientists
disagree on this detail) in great hordes, driven
by an insatiable need, buried deep within
their rotting cerebral cortexes, to feed.

In the accounts I have seen on TV and in IMAX 3D,
the dead always seek living flesh to rip apart with hands

and teeth, gouging out chunks of bloody meat and oozing entrails;
but this part is wrong. This part is just Hollywood
hokum, because the reality would be too hard to swallow,
let alone imagine. The truth is this:
What the walking dead hunger to devour is poetry.
They have an atavistic need to read!

They are inexorably drawn to cities and villages, to schools
and public libraries — any place that once held the promise of poetry.
There they scrounge through rubble and refuse searching
for Poe, Whitman, Pound, Frost, Eliot, Yeats, Merwyn.
They fight like dogs over anthologies and textbooks,
drool over collected works, gnash their teeth on chapbooks.
Their filthy fingers rip through rhyme and meter with a savagery
no civilized audience could comfortably countenance.
The squeamish want their poetry refined, elegant, and polite — not a
bloody feast of steaming syntax and regurgitated refrain.

Scientists aren't sure what caused this poetry apocalypse.
Some speculate cutbacks in social programs
the last half of the last century,
when politicians wrangled over funds for new weapons,
created an imbalance in the cosmos.
Others point the finger at TV, video games, social media,
teacher unions, healthcare reform, and even climate change
as likely causes for this "zombie flu."

But the truth is much less cataclysmic,
as it usually is in an apocalyptic event.

What happened was this:
An American man visited Japan
and concocted a toxic haiku.
Seventeen syllables later, the world we once knew ended

Origin Stories

A Love Tome

There was no beginning in the Beginning.
There was only Blank — immense as Sky in the imagination of Child,
limitless as Horizon sheaved white as snow.

What came after was Word, hollowed out,
thumbed into Sound and knuckled into Idea.
Word left tracks whichever direction it vaulted, wild with impulse
bloodying its courses, feral with the stink of messy inspiration.

Word begat Poem, long before Form and Order,
before the yoke of Trope and the dogma of Devotion,
broke its spirit on the wheel of Prayer.

Poem became cantation, lyrical exhalation,
aesthetic refinement too fine for the masses
to feast upon. Let them get their fill of swill —
vulgar verse, silly shanties.
Poem had gone to University, and what it learned there
was how to hide in Book, Classroom, Library —
what rhyme to wear with a sonnet, what meter goes best with a triolet.

Its fingers white with chalk dust, its eyes glassy through
a be-ribboned pince-nez, Poem forgot what once it was
and became that thing it once forswore:
Civilized. Analyzed. Annotated.

Then Poem met Man-child, hawk-eyed and wild-whiskered,
shaggy as a buffalo still roaming range;
a man profane in the manner of men common and crude;
a child direct in ways offensive to those prim and prude.
He spoke of Body. He sang of Sex.
He reveled in Smell, used nose to Taste, fingers to See.
He gulped huge mouthfuls of World until his belly swelled
with Word bursting forth in ways wonderful and free.

Man-child was new to Poem, yet familiar,
a memory buried somewhere deep in cerebral Syntax:
Barbaric. Unbridled. Beautiful

as the Blank there was in the Beginning before Word,
before Poem ever ventured onto white.

Poem knew him by Whitman, lionized him as Walt.
And Walt — he knew Word as Song, Poem by heart.
He sang until Silence was drained and Blank filled,
beginning the Beginning again.

On Perdido Beach

Walking with you this beach bleached white by sun,
smoothed by waves flat and straight
as any county highway we've driven in Door,
you stoop to study a cluster of shells
glittering along the waterline
like pieces of pottery from some lost civilization
waiting for someone to tell its stories.

Just think, you say in that unique way you use
to caress a thought into something more than just chitchat,
*each of these shells was once a home
for something that lived,
looking for a place safe and snug
from which to see the world.
Reminds me of those houses we see
along the highways back home.*

Eyesores, abandoned, abused by time,
folding into themselves,
brought to their knees,
the bones of their frames just shells, really,
suggesting stories of lives we intersect
every time we happen by, usually
too consumed to notice.

We are engulfed by the detritus of living things
long dead, dormant yet yearning.
We listen for angels, pray for ghosts
in cathedrals and cemeteries, but what we seek is here
in oceans,
in earth,

underfoot.
It speaks in tongues that lick smooth shell and bone,
wood and stone, and wraps itself like roots
around us, wanting.

Press your ear to the open door of an empty house —
that could be ocean you hear,
murmuring secrets in the shadows.
Look closer into the chaos of the waterline —
that's a history you see written in shards of shell,
of a world so choked with life
it's bursting.

Dreaming in Italian

per il buon amico e campagno di viaggio, S. K.

Io sono Americano
from the tip of my ball cap pledging allegiance to a mediocre team
of multimillionaires back home, to the heels of my expensive cross train-
ers
cushioning every step around the *Duomo* and up and down the stone
bridges
in the *calles* of Venice — yes, I am that American.

I stick out like a fully dressed Chicago-style hot dog at a Tuscan *trattoria*,
so you can imagine my surprise when I returned home from my travels
to find myself dreaming in Italian.

Mio Dio, le cose che ho potuto dire ora!
Words rolled from my tongue like fresh *gnocche* off the fork!
Phrases flew through my mind like swallows in the *Piazza da Santa Maria
Novella!*
I could punctuate, parse, and postulate entire subsets of verse
con studiosi discuti i canti della Divina Commedia di Dante!

I was a different person in these dreamscapes:
no longer the brash *Americano* who regarded anything foreign as sus-
pect,
but a bold *Mediterraneo* who embraced life *con la passione e il desiderio
di piena festa sulla bellezza del mondo.*

I wanted everything under the Latin sun, from the lemons that hang heavy
in the trees of Sorrento, which render themselves upon ripening to that most Italian
of elixirs, *limoncello*; to the wild boar of the Arno valley, that feast on grapes
and olives until their flesh is sweet enough for a *primo piatto of tagliatelle al cinghiale*.
Tale munificenza! Tali splendor!

My days have settled back into comfortable routine, as familiar as the NFL logo shirt
I wore on the tour through the Doge's palace in Piazza San Marco;
but my nights are strong as espresso, my dreams drunk on *grappa*.
I dive into sleep, *sperando di risvegliare nell'immagine del David di Michelangelo,*
a man emerging from the marble of himself, perfectly content with the enormity
of what faces him, captured in a moment so pure it is divine.

Buddy and I

The streets around my house are aflame with fall
as Buddy and I make our daily rounds.
There's a briskness to these days of late October,
a crispness to the sound leaves make
skittering in the curb,
and a smoky tang lingers in the air.

If Buddy notices he doesn't care.

He keeps his nose pressed to the ground
(no telling what new smells are there)
and pulls me by the lead from tree to shrub,
as if he's the one taking me for a walk
and is impatient that I grasp all he wants to share.

We have a sort of understanding, he and I,
if a dog can think along those lines:
I'll pause long enough for him to sniff out things
at every post and pole or sign
if he'll pretend to listen when I talk
and answer with a lick from time to time.

I still call Buddy "Pup"
although he's anything but a puppy anymore,
having turned twelve of my years this past summer.
People tell me that's old for a dog his size,
and I realize that's true;
his muzzle, once brindled brown, is now white
and cataracts nibble at his sight.
Where once he'd charge across the yard
after any critter brazen enough to test him,
he now labors to his feet to sniff the air and look.

But I've slowed down a step or two myself.

Like alternating chapters in a book,
Buddy's time and mine seem juxtaposed.
It's in the quiet of these autumn afternoons,
with Buddy a black shadow at my feet,
that the grief I can't help but presuppose
dissipates in a blizzard of falling leaves.

Neither of us look with much enthusiasm to winter:
Buddy struggles to climb the piled snow
in search of those remembered places that
still carry a scent of himself;
and I dread the chill that seeps like wet
through my shoes and socks,
and the lengthening nights that close like the lid of a box.

To the Fly Futzing with My Foot

Is "Danger" your middle name
or were you born with reckless disregard
for existential realities?
Is teasing my ankle, buzzing me
while I page through *The New Yorker,*
worth the risk of no longer having
anything left to risk?

On your own terms I admire, I suppose,
the bravado with which you greet
each minute of life, each second

you accept everything the world
has to offer, be it the rim
of a coffee cup, the core
of an apple, or the skin
of my foot, exposed between the bottom
of my pants leg and the top
of my sandal; but is life
of such arbitrary significance
you compulsively court its absence
over and over, despite the signs
of my increasing aggravation?

If we exchanged places, if *I* were
suddenly free of all expectations
for what is to come, fully alive
in the moment, and *you* were prisoner
of what you did yesterday
and what it will mean tomorrow
tethered, therefore, to an impatient
today, would you do as I have
done, fold the magazine in half
and wait—and would I do as you,
foolishly linger on the summit
of an ankle bone to admire the view
one moment too long?

The world is rife with conflict
and resolution, my little friend,
and as one famous writer
famously observed, *Everything ends
in death, everything*—sometimes sadly
sometimes badly, and sometimes even
oddly in the pages of *The New Yorker.*

Finding a God Worth Keeping

It takes some looking.
He's not in words, She's not in hymns.
Neither are boxed in bricks
or behind fancy painted glass.
I didn't find Him hiding
in a Sunday mass,
didn't spot Her standing at a pulpit.
They weren't where you'd think.

I saw Him
in the eyes of my dog,
soft brown globes without a glimmer
of guile. There was no Hallelujah
in that look, just acceptance
of a kind so subtle
like a dog's smile,
there for a moment
just long enough to believe in
then gone,
so its memory becomes
a matter of faith.

I met Her
while filling the gas tank
of my power mower,
a mindless step in a procession
of mindless steps completing
a mindless chore.
She descended as a Monarch,
in vivid orange and black, and lighted
on the handle near the pull cord,
flexing Her wings open and shut
open and shut open and shut
waiting for me to re-cap the tank
before commencing Her benediction.
Then She fluttered off among
the hydrangeas, Her work with me
done, leaving me to think
about something more
than the dimensions of my lawn.

If that's not a God worth keeping,
what is?

Standing Feather

Standing Feather is a poet, painter, sculptor, performance artist, and cross-dressing trickster healer. He is the author of *The Glowing Pink* (Four Windows Press, 2018) and a long-time member of the fabled Zuni Mountain Poets. He has also published in the poetry anthology, *The Zuni Mountain Poets*, (Authorhouse, 2012) and the literary journal *Querencia* (ed. Jack Carter-North, 2013). Founder and ring mistress of Galleria Carnaval, an art gallery in El Morro, New Mexico, Feather is from Salt Lake City and studied at the University of Utah. He co-founded the Wilderness Trout Expeditions guide service in 1998, guiding and teaching fly-fishing for many years before retreating to the Zuni Sandstone mesas and Ponderosa forests of western New Mexico.

The award-winning novelist and poet James Janko, in reviewing *The Glowing Pink*, said that "...Feather reminds us of the almost unspeakable intimacy shared by all beings. I view the poems of this collection as passageways to the sacred, to the sheer beauty and wonder of life. Reality is luminous." Janko's perception is borne out in a work like the long poem, "Cross Dresser," where the poet both struggles with who he is as a human being, but also realizes the glory that rises out of that struggle:

> With the cats trailing
> underneath him
> and the crows
> observing from above,
> the man swayed
> and tilted
> over the steamy streets
> like the empress
> of celestial passion.

His language in this poem can have an original twist that matches images that can be both poetic and intense, exploring a state of being that is reaching for substance and stability. This in a world that can be uncertain and in need of acceptance and a deep spirit that gives meaning to moments and daily life.

He is, as Thomas Davis said, "a searing edge part flame and part cool, silver moonlight, mixed with the fragrance of deep emotion. . ."

In the end his poetry cries out for the acceptance of all human beings in humanity's community and for the glory of the earth community in which humanity exists as part of the whole. It looks both inward and outward with a mystical intensity.

Cross-Dressers

I.

The yellow moon
rises over the dingy city
and shines in slivers
upon the storefronts.
The smokestacks
that bellowed fiery steam
across the glossy skyline
have cooled and quieted,
leaving the cold steel
headframes
to loom as sentinels
that witness and protect
a row of cheap hotels
near the edge of town.

Inside Room 12
the man dressing
in women's clothes
does not feel shame
because he knows
it is not shameful
to be a woman.
Tonight, there would be
no indignity.
The lust of the salty sea
floating hidden
in the summer breeze
was toning with the sighs
of lonely jazz
trickling away
from the smoky clubs.

One cannot predict
an evening's outcome
when the intention itself
is rowing upstream.
The privileged people
had escaped
from the sultry streets,
fanning their painted faces
as they entered
plush velvet parlors
or stepped into
wooden riverside boats
that would carry them across
the romance of the dark water.

II.

Outside the room
the crows hopped
and squabbled
in the parking lot
and cawed to the elegance
of the fabrics
caressing the man.
He emerged majestically
from the red room
to dance through the birds
in gallant ceremony.
He had been shunned
by transgendered kings and queens
for not taking hormones
and was implicated as being
just a cross-dresser.

The voice is the action
of the heart,
and plants can feel ambiguous
until they flower.
The song had grown
from deep in his bosom,
a swirling cauldron
of suspicious disgrace
and immaculate ecstasy.

The crow's gathered
in the stifled trees
along the dated boardwalk.
The sparkle of the man below
met the dimness from the moon above.

III.

As a young boy
he had waited patiently to be a girl.
Like an unloved dog,
time began to choke
the light from the thought,
and the anticipation
of becoming
soft and beautiful
had subtly vanished
under the cloak
of pedestrian reality.
The pounding waves
of cultural expectations
kept the flower away,
like a fugitive boat
escaping slowly from the shore.

There is nothing on earth
that resists obstacles
more stubbornly
than the
courage of water.
Super Bowl Sunday
and cold November
duck hunts
with Labradors and decoys
veiled the man's
emerging requirements
to notice
the pulsing lips
inside the stirring blossom.

The conception crawled
from deep inside
the trombone

and pushed itself
into the perplexed world.
The man flung himself
at the planets and stars
and toppled
to the mud and dirt.
The wind punched
low bellows
from his bleeding heart
into the fear of his throat.
He wanted to rope the moon
until he ascended
from the smothered city.

The birth itself
was like turning a sock
inside out.
It was timed to release
with the detachment
of the falling summer.
This left only the insistence
of his breath
to warm his anxious heart.
The divine feminine
was a medicine
he had ingested,
and with tonight's rising moon
he could feel it take.

IV.

Won't somebody shake
their body tonight?
The wild cats
that make love
under the plummeting
yellow streetlight
have gathered atop
the ashen brick wall
to examine the man
clicking down the crumbling
sidewalk. They stretch
and raise their tails

and prance seductively
along the dark edges
of the deceptive
limelight.

V.

The broken down
can easily dance
on shabby stages
and can feel
the rawness of the wood
and can shimmy
long into the deep
of the crazed night.
They close their eyes
and dream
of fiery stars
that burn rapture
into their damp
cold guts.

The unlucky
build their dreams
from the suffocation
of their rhapsody.
The trenches
dug by the people
can swallow
the sacred child
inside of us, leaving only
our raging innocence
to strangle the hymn
before it escapes
the throat.
The unlucky
bury their determination
into the trenches.

VI.

With the cats trailing
underneath him

and the crows
observing from above,
the man swayed
and tilted
over the steamy streets
like the empress
of celestial passion.
The hot yellow moon
gazed impatiently
between the rushing clouds
and begged the man to
release his soul to the sky.

Now the tender
of his own
furious flame,
he gracefully
shuffled and shifted his long limbs
over the fractured sidewalk,
arms outstretched
in supple cohabitation
with his waving torso.
The once strangled parts
of his body
heaved in gasps
of indebted devotion.
The moon was soft
and yellow.

The trance became thicker
as the man
approached the crossroads.
Leaving the old behind
he began to ascend
into the pearly
sophistication
of the gleaming avenues.
He was black creeping lava
hiding fire deep below
his glistening skin,
a parading altar
dedicated to the fidelity
of awakened dreams.

He had received himself
fully now.
The man, the ravens
and the street cats
used the shadows
to convert their fears
into sophisticated prowess.
The stars winking
in the midnight sky
bent with the nodding
moon, and the vested
procession
descended from the hilltop
and moved towards
the lights
of the city.

Blue Train

The earth
at the bottom
of dark hollows
is perpetually wet.
It must contain
a stillness
that the trees
blowing bent
on the rimrock
cannot relate to.

The stiffness
of the grasses
and the dampness
of the dirt
in the stillness
of these bottoms
have manifested
slowly through
the chaos from
above.

My troubled
mind is full
of intellect.
Coltrane must have
lost his trouble
and listened to
the stillness,
like jagged rocks
listening to the roundness
of the river stones.

Roots

The lichens are slowly crawling up the throat
of the mesa. They are blue and red
from eating the giant rocks
and usually outlive the pinon trees
that root themselves into cracks
on the surface of the stone tongue.

I want to bury the strength of the rocks
into the fears of my gut.
I want to sink the elegance of the trees
into the sorrows of my mind.
If I could do these things
time would spread itself inside me
and my roots would drink
from the origins
of their assurance.

I would then be a tree woman
harnessed to the clay,
standing with a silent mind
in the place of placid refuge.
I would take long, deep breaths
and my nourished blood
would quench the enduring crusade
of my dreams.
I would petrify like ancient trees
and gently lay my mind
into the stillness of my heart.

Saints

As boys we would defy our mothers
and sneak down to the sprinting river
to lay under the stars
and listen for boulders
rolling slowly along the riverbed.
The rocks were being pushed along
from the influence
of the spring runoff.
Under the stars the low rumbles
sounded like elephants
summoning songs
from the throbbing pulse
of their lineage.

Later in the summer
the nights would be hot
and the river was lower
and we would lay on the grass
and listen for the stillness
beneath the water.
The sound was like swans
gliding through the backwaters.
Cherishing the scent
of the honeysuckle
growing along the banks
prepared us for the upcoming
losses of autumn.

Love is wild
like thorns and petals.
The river runs through me now.
It dilutes the pains of losing love
and carries with it
the desire for more.
From the porch rocking chair
I can hear
the drumming nighthawk.
The soft glow of the desert sunset
is being chased
by the ferocity
of the dark night.

La Fleur

Ants pollinate flowers
by walking
on their velveteen floors.
Their tiny tracks
move from the entrance
to the glowing center
and back again.
The light shining through
the soft pedals
illuminates the temple -
and the sweet nectar
drips into the chalice
of the flower.
A concerto pulses from the opening
to draw the ants.
They sing its refrain
along the return path home.

The Glowing Pink

A frumpy man in a brown suit
beckoned me to the water's edge.
Ducks and geese floated away from him
as I approached, and he told me with his hands
to slow down. He was centered
on his stage. With a gesture, he proposed
that he could put me in a trance
with his flute, so I sat on the grass
to join him.
The afternoon sun and the cool breeze
met the surface of the pond
in shiny crystals, and the ducks and geese
paddled towards him again. He smiled
and pointed to a pink carnation
standing dignified among the summer grasses.
Then he summoned his flute
and told me with his face
to relax and close my eyes.

The herons on the opposite shore
spread their wings in homage
to the song of the flute,
and the sun rays slivered through their feathers
and onto the shimmer of the pond's façade.
The trance approached like a slow carriage,
and the golden leaves twirled down
from above. The mask of the pond
was awake.

The voices of the man's soul choired a psalm
that met the tempo of his tune, and the waves
spread up through the trees
and into the vastness of the sapphire sky.
He watched the geese as a boy,
and had learned to breathe more fully
waiting for their descent. When they circled low,
he could see himself
in the blackness of their eyes.

The voices of the song honored creatures
that may spend their entire lives inside a flower —
birthing and decaying away
without our ever having known of them,
and that universes are met and reconciled
inside spirals that stretch into time
we have not yet understood, and that all of this
can fit inside the carnation
glowing pink on the water's edge.

The honking of the geese had taught him
that music was the silence
between their notes. He was a magician
transmuting limitations. He could wrap himself
around a ripple and hold it still,
or let it go like angelic echoes
floating down through the rocky walls
of a lonely desert canyon.

Robin Chapman

Robin Chapman's award-winning books of poetry include:

Six True Things, poems of growing up in the Manhattan Project town of Oak Ridge, Tennessee, and recipient of the Wisconsin Library Association's Outstanding Achievement in Poetry Award

The Way In and *Images of a Complex World: The Art and Poetry of Chaos* (with J.C. Sprott's fractals and explanations), recipients of the Posner Poetry Award

The Dreamer Who Counted the Dead, selected as for a WLA Outstanding Achievement in Poetry Award

Abundance, winner of Cider Press Editors' Book Award. Recipient of Appalachia's 2010 Poetry Prize

She is Professor Emerita of Communication Sciences and Disorders at the University of Wisconsin-Madison and a member of the steering committee of the UW Chaos and Complex Systems Seminar, a weekly, campus-wide seminar on the new sciences of chaos and complexity.

The poet Ilya Kaminsky, in a review of Chapman's most recent book, *The Only Home We Know*, says that in Chapman's poetry, "memory functions as a spirit guide through the various details, wonders and terrors of our world." Her poetry ranges from memories of her childhood in Oak Ridge, Tennessee through contemplations drawn from the suicide of students to examinations of the large phenomena of the world: mountains, black holes, and the meaning of life itself as it teeters on the brink of environmental collapse.

In a significant body of her poetry, science plays as much a role as language. Chapman's science is not only drawn from a careful piling up of observation and results from scientific experiment, but also attempts to bring alive what the evolution of scientific knowledge means to individual lives and the memory of those we know, have known, and loved. She seems to always be trying to wake up the universe of human beings so that they know what they are doing to themselves and the world, and she says, over and over again, you had better pay attention and consider what all of this means.

Ending her poem, "Studying Mountains," she demonstrates just how powerful her unique approach to poetry can be:

> Studying mountains, I too, feel
> The body begin to loosen
> Deep in its roots, flowing with what rises
> Through the small dark body of the mule deer
> From the immense dark body of the earth.

There is obviously deep empathy here as she conveys a mystical sense that the mountain is tied to herself and that the immense body of the earth is alive. This is simply powerful poetry.

Oak Ridge, Tennessee, 1946

It's the morning of the world
I want to tell you about,
my world of east Tennessee red clay
and crabgrass in its spiky rosette patches,
a child's morning after Cream of Wheat
or cinnamon toast, the years before
the school bus loomed for us, late again,
racing down the road — the mornings
when the fathers had bicycled or carpooled
off to work, the mothers had turned
to making beds, and we burst out
of our Cemesto six-basic-floorplan houses
to the backyards and greenbelt woods
left by the Army Engineers for camouflage
in our gated town, place we already knew,
dimly, proudly, to be the home
of the Atom Bomb.

It is the everyday mornings I mean,
when we rushed out eager to find
what new rabbit trails could be seen
in the wet grass, what ripe blackberries
could be found in the briar patch,
whether the plums and apples
were still green, whether Honeybunch's
kittens had opened their eyes yet.
The mockingbird sang us the songs
of every bird in our kingdom
in one long stream from a corner tree.
It was paradise, seeing the world

through morning eyes,
and the mockingbird's knowledge
what we took from the tree.

Catching Rabbits

Child in the southern summer
Stalking prey, I propped up the flap
Of the army knapsack with a crooked stick,
Tucked inside the carrot that Bugs Bunny waved
Under Doc's nose every Saturday, hid
Myself in the briar-patch brush, ready to jerk
The string that would topple the trap shut;
Waited all that day, and the next,
For cartoon rabbits to come to the bait,
While, under the porch, the cat stashed
His half-eaten carcasses and, each night,
Rabbits cropped the blackberry shoots; why

Is this still important, that vision
Of the soft creature I would catch, befriend,
Stroking away the fright? And the damp heat,
The loud scold of the mockingbird,
The scratching thorns? I wanted
The knowledge I don't have yet,
Of how our two real lives might intersect,

As the long week, later, I tried to care
For the fierce marsh bird, wings full of lead,
That I found in the storm sewer and brought home
To the tub, feeding him the only food
I could imagine, night crawlers wriggling
Through my fingers and down his craw. He lay
In my arms, twisting his head, the day he was
Dying, and I walked him out to see the trees
And the sky. I don't know yet what marsh birds
Eat, or how to repair their thin-boned wings,
Or if I could have saved him with such tutelage;
Now it's the child who teaches me.

The Blue Hat

Now, while so many of our daughters are dying
Because they are not thin or young
Or beautiful enough, it is the blue hat
I want to explain, a royal blue fedora
That I bought because I knew Betty,
Fashion coordinator of the town's largest department store
Who dressed in Vogue magazine styles and feather boas
In the middle of Tennessee hills
And denim-dressed Unitarian wives.
Betty wept at the beauty of her husband Arthur's sermons
And decorated her Christmas tree with red velvet ribbons
And came to Mom's funeral in a black Homburg
With Chantilly lace drape and silk pajamas
And a choker of crystals —

Betty, who was the first to have watermelon placemats
And real candles in a wrought-iron chandelier,
Who looked me over as I swung my legs
On the turquoise loveseat and said to Mother,
What are we going to do with her?
Betty told me I would be beautiful
With the right clothes and a little older
And gave me a cashmere sweater for college
And false eyelashes for graduate school
And said sex was wonderful

And when a stroke shut Arthur down
Except for a little roar he could make
Sometimes when he heard her voice on the phone,
Betty believed that behind his immobile face
And arms and legs his mind raced on,
Got 24-hour-a-day care and a hospital bed,
Played MacNeil-Lehrer news and his favorite videos
Every evening, wearing her best red negligee
To climb in bed with him for an hour or two,
Tell him about her day, the way she'd chat
With her friends at work about what Arthur had thought
Of the last foreign film or the latest political news,
For seven years before he died;
This blue hat honors Betty.

Holding Open the Doors

for P.K., P.S.

How could it be
　　you cut short your own life, my
　　　　student of life, in a cold afternoon

of drizzle; or you, old colleague
　　of words, ending yours in a late night rain?
　　　　Even as the black-and-white-warblers

circled the tree trunks,
　　even as the barred owl who-whooed
　　　　through the dark? How could it be,

as we paddled down the cold Wisconsin
　　past the maples downed at the river's edge
　　　　whose roots sucked air and whose

beautiful drowning heads made music of water,
　　one of you opened the bathwater tap, laid
　　　　your head in that backwater?

And the other shut the garage against night?
　　When the sun came out today and we entered
　　　　our elevators saying *yes,*

too nice to be inside, but all
　　　that work to catch up, we could only
　　　　　hold the doors open minutes to learn

you had both gone from us, in spring,
　　even as lilacs opened in wind
　　　　and the scent trailed toward us;

oh, those among us who know
　　how this could be, stand up,
　　　　that we may know to hold onto you.

Studying Mountains

Under the whispering trees he limps,
Brown-furred, white-rumped, black cap and antlers,
Four points on one side, three on the other,
Stumbling a bit in the snow.

Kneels on a little promontory
As though he is too tired or hungry or cold
To go farther, trees already browsed well over his head,
The hoof-raked snow yielding only last year's needles,
A month of thirty and forty below behind him;
Or perhaps it is simply noon, and time for his usual rest.

Now he beds down,
His head raised for long minutes looking out
At the mountain.
                    And now he lowers his head,
Stretching his neck, a sort of bow, laying it
On the snow, where he lies long minutes
As though he were dying, or giving up, or sleeping.

And now again he raises his head to that still, high face
Of the mountain that, dying or living, he chooses to see.
The sun picks out the fuzz of his antlers,
Down of his muzzle, black of his nose, brown of his eyes.

His ears flick to the sound of my chair shifting;
He looks at me, a shadow behind glass, then turns his head back;
Slowly, his jaws begin to chew,
And I turn back to my work.
                    And now the sun has moved on;
There's only the mark on the ground where this long balance
Was struck.
                    Studying mountains, I too, feel
The body begin to loosen
Deep in its roots, flowing with what rises
Through the small dark body of the mule deer
From the immense dark body of the earth.

The Eelgrass Meadow

And what if we are no more than ribbons of grass,
    waving in the tide?
We could be an eelgrass meadow, subtidal zone.
    Our roots would clutch sand. Our leaves
would soften the waves, transmute sunlight to food,
    decay to a rich and rotting broth.
The larvae of ghost shrimp
    would browse among us, beginnings
of story; and in the dark abyss our bodies
    would nourish the rattail fish.
If we were an eelgrass meadow,
    brooding anemone would grow to flower
their stinging barbs among us, the moonshell
    seastars would creep out into tidal pools.
The young salmon we sheltered would venture
    at last into the ocean's openness, travel
thousands of miles with the taste of our estuaries
    in their mouths to guide them home.

Cassandra Looks at Dark Matter Through Hubble's Eye

Winter again, and all that futile calling out
against the specters of lost childhoods, famines,
greed and drought, wars and terror
quiets, as, putting her eye to Hubble's past light,
thoughts of hurling herself over a cliff subside,
replaced by the faint shape of what's been missed:
the unseen mass of the universe that aligns
our fears, brought into focus by gravity's lens.
Beneath each fear its antidote: the pull
of the lovely lumpiness of life.
The beautiful archaic blues of the night sky
lit by stars and moon, the glitter and shine of snow,
the long patience of trees, and on each face
on our path the joy of watching
the fawn sleep, the pine marten play.

Praying to the God of Sixty-One Orders of Magnitude

Dear God, out of the whole wide beach
the children have chosen the driftwood ark,
salt enclosure, for play; with glad cries
they throw over their buckets and trowels,
the castles and moats at ocean's edge,
to climb into the lean-to of logs. What box
have I built for you? The play father,
coming home from work, the play mother
making tea and bread? Who can you be
in this world that unfolds within worlds?
Maker of flood and rainbows?

Six billion of us chant or pray or cry
our needs, hosts ourselves to congregations
of eyelid mites, dissident colonies of e-coli,
riverine dwellers in lymph and blood,
and those strangers we carry in every cell,
Eve's mitochondrial energy wheels,
with the hijacked machinery of limb buds
and bilateral symmetry, of memory's buzz.
Are you god of a trillion billion stars?

And of smaller worlds yet, curled into spaces
of vibrating string, god of the quantum
universe? Are you the god of the child
who invents her absent father?
Are you god of the mother giving birth,
and the lovers who wish only to touch?
Of the prairie vole retrieving her pups
from fire? Oh god of every magnitude
and attraction, bend and warp, of beginning
and end, are you small enough for planet Earth?

Time

My neighbor, 87, rings the doorbell to ask
if I might have seen her clipping shears
that went missing a decade ago,
with a little red paint on their shaft,
or the iron turkey bank and the porcelain
coffee cup that disappeared a while back
when her friend, now dead, called the police
to break in to see if she were ill, and have we
had trouble with our phone line, hers
is dead and her car and driver's license
are missing though she can drive perfectly
well, just memory problems, and her son
is coming this morning to take her up
to Sheboygan, where she was born
and where the family has its burial lots,
to wait on assisted living space, and she
just wanted to say we'd been good neighbors
all these how many? years, and how lucky
I am to have found such a nice man
and could she borrow a screwdriver,
the door lock to her house is jammed.

Midnight, and people I love are dying,

and I can't sleep so I'm up thinking
too hard scribbling these words in the dark
because the physics science news I read
before bed is making me crazy now
with incomprehension — it makes
no sense to me that gravity should exist;
what I know about is love:
that flaring up of caring connection
that lasts life-long and does not depend
on distance, and it makes no sense to me
that the speed of light in a vacuum

should be a constant in this universe
transforming at every instant along the way,
speeding and slowing, and it makes no sense
to me that there should have been an origin
of the universe and before that nothing —
surely it was everything, waiting there?
When our lives are spun out of star furnaces
and our histories of DNA mutable, shifting,
remaking themselves in us — all that stuff
of the universe spun out of nothing?
It makes no sense, and it makes no sense
that time should have a beginning and no end,
for what was the constant face of love
before time began and before matter
assembled and before that small dense crush
exploded into what, so very briefly,
would, some small fraction, run through
our bodies, changing daily, the days
of our lives — and where do they go?
Those we love? It makes no sense to me
that the light of their countenances
or the love we carry should wink out
and light, that constant of the universe,
speed on in nothingness, undeterred by loss.

Dappled Things

Always the world-spun light casts patterns
raveled through the wind-thrown clouds, the forest's
branch-broken loom, across the hoof-scraped moss
and snow-banks, the backs of browsing mule deer
whose swiveling ears listen for the whispered sound
of the tawny cougar's padding walk. Dark and light,
sleep and wake and dream course through our lives
to make us what we are — sun and shadow-clothed,
bedrock and layers of fertile soil, green climb
and blight of history, wind-taken, time-wound
and wounded, heart-bound to world's warp and weft.

Nathan J. Reid

Nathan J. Reid is a spoken word poet and actor whose work has appeared in *Bramble Literary Magazine*, *Wisconsin People and Ideas*, *Poetry Hall*, *GREAT: Poems of Resistance & Fortitude* poetry anthology, and other publications. He serves on the boards of the Council for Wisconsin Writers and the Wisconsin Poet Laureate Commission, is the former senior editor for the *Wisconsin Review*, once one of Wisconsin's most important literary and science journals, a member of the Wisconsin Fellowship of Poets, and host of *The Reid Poetry Hour*, an annual show on WORT 89.9 FM in Madison, Wisconsin. His chapbook, *Thoughts on Tonight*, was published in 2017, and his first full-length collection, *Persistence of Perception*, was released in 2020.

Central to Reid's poetry is its dramatic structure. Gifted as a powerful performer, his poetry pulses with rhythms tailored to oral presentation that purposely seems like it comes from a storyteller telling an unwritten tale out of his trove of stories. In some poems you can almost see Reid sitting before a great fireplace in a castle performing his stories and rhythmic free verse in the same way old Irish bards did before the Christian era in Ireland.

A poem like "The Driftless," portraying a man becoming a landscape, exemplifies both the creativity and narrative drive of this approach.

> I sat leaning against the old well, my back relaxing into the rock
>   slab
> with surprising ease, and before I knew it the grass was
>   sprouting through
> my legs, wrapping around them in a thick coat, warming my
>   bones

This passage demonstrates how Reid can mix poetry and prose into a poem that is innovative while, at the same time, achieving both the narrative and oral presentation he works to create. This is not the storytelling of Homer or the author of *Beowulf* with meters and mnemic devices drawn from an ancient practice of reciting poetry, but it is still from that tradition updated to a contemporary search for what presentation poetry can be.

The Driftless

I had been walking along a gravel path for several hours
without meeting any crossroads, cars, or people

eventually there came a break between the trees and tall grass, where
    a field
opened up, guiding my eyes toward an old well dotted in the distance

having grown ever so thirsty I dragged my feet across the field
and found a tin cup of icy clear beverage waiting for me

I downed the drink and felt refreshed enough
but my body was still a heavy bundle of exhaustion

so the evening sun convinced me to stay and rest
while it forged on ahead to scout out tomorrow's terrain

I sat leaning against the old well, my back relaxing into the rock slab
with surprising ease, and before I knew it the grass was sprouting
    through
my legs, wrapping around them in a thick coat, warming my bones

and as night fell more and more into its deep dive
my head turned more solidly into a wooden bucket rotted
and stamped with the jagged grin of a brown jack-o'-lantern

a frozen expression fixed atop the neck of a slouching scarecrow
all my candles reignited, all my dreams cast in stone

We the Firefly

Today: We are all unraveled, our lives pulled, exposing the accordion that blooms from the fragile bonds of our paper doll folds. We realize we are time travelers, lovers and killers, telepaths and dumb-luck dreamers. I am my father and my unborn son. I am the woman on the bus, the child in her arms, the driver cussing to himself as his pancreas flinches against each pothole. And the universe reveals to us how we are the most unlikely of every fat truth, and the walls we climb daily are laden with false bricks that can be pushed in like a button, unlocking doors that lead to new space, but even there we get the feeling *We have been here before* over and over and over.

Somewhere in a run-down apartment there is an ancient prince. He's on his seventeenth life. He doesn't understand where he is, the noise in the street, or why these colosseums are dripping from his eyes.

There is a sparrow resting her wings. She's the embodiment of short and sweet and every day she's pretty sure that you and I and this whole damn world are something she dreamt up last night in her sleep.

We are loopers, rabbit hole divers, matrix upon matrix. There is the illusion we are each an individual essence, when in truth we share one soul. It is a firefly caught between the canvas and the paint and it floats across this portrait of existence, filling each life as it does so. Meaning someday, somehow, you will be the person sitting next to you. Someway, some life, you will see yourself from across the room.

Trust me, for I have been you. I have smiled all your smiles. Your hearts pump my blood. Our pulses are the waves, humanity the moon, I have been you. You are loners and regretters. Heavily you sit without a dream to hold your hand. I have seen you trying to crawl back through the rooms you have already walked through. As if you could rewind, cut, copy, paste, and create anew. As if that were some kind of miracle. But tall and glowing and tall and alive you have already walked through, I have seen you, you starlight, you midnight wanderers.

Don't worry about the phone calls from family you ignored, they have already forgiven you with hugs and pot roasts. Don't worry about the dead friends who visit your dreams again and again, they are not tormented or lost, it just means you love them so much more than the time they were given, for you are them and they are you. I have been you.

Do not fester in a heap of sour love gone wrong but rise above it so opportunity may find you. If you have hurts at the bottom of your heart, do not go looking at them through the bottoms of your drinks. Reach down, take them in your hands, crumble them to pieces and toss them up to the heavens that swallow everything yet say nothing. Because this life is a moving cliff and the day we were born was the day we let go, so unclench your fists, learn to make music with the air around your fingertips. The only moment is right-here/right-now and, right-here/right-now, you'll find every other moment. Be a moment. Be the wind that blows through the cemetery where children play. Be the relief in somebody's smile at the end of the day. Be these words, for they are no longer mine. Be soft lips for the springtime. Be boogie-woogie, jazz, and soul; be boogie-woogie, jazz, and soul. When something wrong is going down be the voice that yells, **NO!** *Be the Sun! Be the Moon! Be a cry for a cry and a truth for a truth!*

Today: Unravel with me. You are free. Me, I have been you. I have seen you without a dream to hold your hand — so hold my hand, and we the firefly will flow out a new path, resting now and then on the canvas, absorbing rich paint. For I have been you. And when I walk around this world, stare into your faces,

I know

you have been me too.

Möbius

I will be am who was before
the am who is, who was no more
who will be then when then is now
till now is not quite here somehow

Give me a half-twist — this band, this width
this single boundary reaching forward for that asymptote.

My eyes are pillars of books that out-stack those alpine heavens
stories flapping open-faced along this strip of verity
of dreams alive and giant, the way your dreams use to be.
But now you fade from our *mise-en-scène*, afraid
of being sliced out from that colossal film reel
and left behind on the cutting room floor.

When I was a boy I once asked if you believed in a god.
You said gods perhaps only exist when you are thinking about them
and probably not even then. I asked if you believed the world as myth.
You said faith is a moment and this moment is missing.

This moment is missing.

Or maybe faith, as a concept, has been turned inside-out,
worn on the wrong hand…Do I believe in a god?
   I believe in light, I believe in darkness.
   I believe in all the love found in-between.
I believe the calmness that keeps old age from fearing death's
      apparent horizon
is in knowing how this line, if continued, will meet its starting point
      again — a persistence of perception.

One day you announce to us: *Family and friends,*
   I have cancer, I am not dying.
   I have cancer, I am not dying.
And that day you aren't. Neither are you the day after.

But as each new terror is detected the calendar grows heavy with
emptiness our home three times its gravity where I must sit
witnessing this anti-miracle of breath to bones. I read books
describing how we one day translate back to our projection point
not understanding the moral to this story. My burdens get the best of me
like the anxious shepherd with his out of control flock, sheep pulling
woes over our eyes as we behold you, your future history slipping away,
struggles cementing into permanence, bankrupting unfinished business,
slowly ripping you from us with no regard to quality, until one day
I lose faith in the middle of a cold shower, drowning in
every innocent tear I hear suffer, and wish a silent wish
for you to die, betraying the bonds of brotherhood, of friendship,
the spirit of survival — forgive me, please, my friend,
      forgive me, please!

You woke from your soon-to-be-eternal sleep to tell us two things:
1. Be sure to spread happiness, move time forward.
2. I love each and every one of you.

The reel uncoils itself from the projector, lies flat,
then is raised from the floor in ceremony.
It's given a half-twist and joined start to finish.

Is this not what now is?
Is this not what faith is?
Is this what I am?

I will be am who was before
the am who was, who is no more
who will be then when then is now
yet now is not quite here somehow

Spring Makes True

Spring makes true the wild trails
we dreamt ambling all winter
where the weather smiles so brightly
we must step off the road to meet it
without soaked laces or muddy soles
where gravel is friendly, inspiring folk songs

Spring makes true the unlocked sun
where rainbows escape through prism bars
coating our skin with a simmering sense
we possessed formerly in hibernation
where not the bird, nor the song, nor the nest, nor the tree
but *the egg* is eyed as most beautiful

Spring makes true forgotten rain
rebirthing our spirits, thawing thoughts
over sunflowers, converting us from
adult to embryo to child to adult again
where warm nights keep windows yawning
as loose cloth giggles on toward summer

Hindsight

Hindsight is not a time machine. She can't pendulate
back and forth, just BACK, RESET, and BACK again.

    I built her bones inside my garage.
Forking through scrap-metal salads, I clicked and cranked together
triangle after triangle until they formed a skeletal globe, extended
struts and joints from its crust to the junkyard car seat at its core,
installed a central nervous system of magnets, lights, electricity.
By the time I finished it looked like a particle collider had been
    swallowed up by a Hoberman sphere.

Back then I kept in my breast pocket a folded-up piece of paper
with different months and cities written on it, months like

    November 2008 – Mumbai, India
    April 1995 – Oklahoma City, Oklahoma
    May 1974 – Ma'alot, Israel
    November 2015 – Paris, France
    September 2001 – New York City, New York

    …To name a few.

Sitting in that junkyard car seat, I balanced the dials on my arm rest,
    tugged my seat belt, flicked the switch.

The lights darted inward. Positive magnets chased them
in hot pursuit, toward Hindsight's negative core. The frame
collapsed upon itself. When the light reached the center
with nowhere else to run, the magnets caught up, bumping
light off continuum's cliff. The framing followed.
    My ship and I winked away.

The little silver ball fell back with yester-daze
down ruffled trails of cosmic fabric
rolling to a rest on an empire shiny and new
where a dozen shadows once crashed into the daylight
toppled people over, left rubbles of stolen dreams.

    I arrived as the shadows were shaping
raced to warn the kings, philosophers, children, to tell them about the

bomb but they looked at me a fool, squeezed their egocentric blankies
    said, *Goddamn and kingdom come!*

    I hastened to their parents — who knew!
Who saw this falling nightmare, this oncoming curse!
I begged and I begged but they looked at me with pity
    while stating, *Nothing can be done.*

So I infiltrated the darkness to curb the shadows alone,
stomping on combat boots and a rebel gun...Except
trying to fend off darkness is like trying to capture light:
hands struggle for a grip yet hold nothing in the end.
Where I thought I brought newfangled variables, I found myself
within the equation, hidden behind unknowns. For every shot
I meant to block was another innocent couple dead on their loveseat,
stray bullet hole staring at them through their living room wall.

As gloom pushed heavy on the quivering city, I dragged myself back
into my spheroid ship, RESET Hindsight's bearings, switched away.

Restored inside my garage, I slumped over the seat belt, waiting
for heart and stomach to join the team. A neighborhood breeze
escaped from the street, through a window, caressing freshness
on my wet and furrowed brow. My ship said,

    The universe can't take back what it has already spoken.

Nodding, I jettisoned my list of dates where history seemed too cruel
and vowed to only fuss with the ever here and now.

Now I ride, a tourist, through that scope of god-like memories.
And she graciously takes me. Not a time machine.

    Just Hindsight.

Bonfire Brown

You're on the left side of the bed. I am on the right.
A vanilla candle roasts across the room, illuminating with an olive glow
your bare shoulder peeking out from under the blanket.

Two nude spoons roll in a heavy napkin. I curl my arm
around your waist, caress the bottom of your left breast.
Your purring hand arrives at my face like five golden leaves
gliding onto a gentle pond. You turn my way, rose petal lips,
        a kiss.

We nestle into a pillow gaze, strung together
by the one light reflected in both our eyes. As stars
live and give a motley existence, so your irises
breathe fiery truth, in an earthly hue, where I find myself
exposed and elated in the view of bonfire brown.

Embedded with frequent leaps of fire, rippling
with the smoke of toasting timber, your eyes
wear a rare brown born of abstract and magic
that ever burns and ever calms with endless heat — like a cryptic color
from some other-dimensional rainbow, unique as soul.
No crayon will ever bear the label, no painter will ever replicate
        bonfire brown.

Assuming a sacrosanct pose, we even up our eyebrows,
pet nose with nose. A kiss. Eyes closed we bathe ourselves
in secret prayers only two can share. A silent washing away of
        wishes now come true.

Deep in meditation, my mind gasps. I can feel
that sense-of-something-higher connecting our carnal coil
to every ancient curved corner of the universe. I find how
the answer to each little cosmic question is bonfire brown.

        Another kiss.
Nibbling my bottom lip, smirking like a frisky kitten,
you say, *What do you call a spectacular spasm?*
With a voluntary neck-twitch, I reply, *A fantas*-tic!
A better kiss. I continue with, *What do you call a glorious grossness?*
Feigning a disgusted frown you return, *A fantast*-ick!
        Giggle fits, a longer kiss.

Then your honey crisp cheeks fall just slightly,
sobering thoughts struggle with tipsy words,
and with a bold healthy bit of fear you ask me,
        What is love?

Like those miraculous moments
when two raindrops are two yet two raindrops are one,
I lean in again with not just a kiss but all of me to all of you.

Vanilla's glow, middle of the bed, you have
sunrise in your smile and a sunset in each brown eye.
With my naked hand cradling your naked face, I confess,
Dearest dreamy darling: Love is bonfire brown.

We mold the blanket up around us.
Two nude spoons rolling in a cozy calm.
Before the olive light is gone: good night lips,
         a kiss.

Such Sweet Sorrow

when are you leaving, soulmate?
        kiss the tear-stained cheek
        cradle the neck like holy grail
when will you go?
        late light, the frightening feeling
        as two minds savor the last memory meal
soulmate?
        new egg crackling loud as the lightning-struck mountain
        recalls country drives through handheld days of silent love
are you?
        yester-laughing calm sheet rising chest—kiss me
        stay until all this richness
                gone?

Ethel Mortenson Davis

Ethel Mortenson Davis was born in Wisconsin where her parents were dairy farmers in Marathon County. Influenced by the imagist poets, she has had several books of poetry published: *I Sleep Between the Moons of New Mexico, White Ermine Across Her Shoulders, Here We Breathe In Sky and Out Sky, The Healer,* and *Under the Tail of the Milky Way Galaxy* (a 2019 Wisconsin Library Association outstanding book of poetry).

Davis studied art at the University of Wisconsin-Madison. Her pastels have been featured in galleries in New Mexico, Minnesota, and Wisconsin and appeared in publications and as book covers.

Central to Davis' poems are tight, sparse lines with concepts that are surprisingly spacious. Repeatedly, the temperament of her poetry leads into the most poignant layers of human experience, a direct line into the 'blood of the heart'. Once there, we are able to witness the rawness of universal truth while gently overhearing declarations of arcane wisdom:

I wanted to gather you
up in my arms,
like a mother
gathers up her young,
and bring you back to New Mexico —
a place you once loved.

I wanted to take you away
from the suffocating
people in that room
so I could listen,
alone,
to your ragged
breathing.

Davis presents the natural world as the most trusted healing element in our lives. Encased in the poems are examples of how earth's flora and fauna provide behavioral roadmaps to achieving resiliency through struggle, forming compassion through loss, and expanding awareness through nature:

Because the night is filled
with black-winged pelicans
coming in to land,
a sail being taken down,
a sliver of moon
climbing above
the white birch trees,

and laughter from young girls
rising above the lapping waves,

no more can fit
into the evening.

Davis's most recent book, *A Letter on the Horizon's Poem*, *(Kelsay Books, 2019)*, features poems that traverse the numerous panoramas of her writing career.

Swallow

All the holy books
of the world
could fit on the tip
of a swallow's wing
as she dips and sways,
diving for flying
insects.

All the wisdom of mankind
could balance on her
unpretentious head
as she cares for
her young
under the eves
of our house,
eyes showing no deception,
fighting off the blackness
that sits all around her.

Wind

She is the freest
of all women,
the wind.

The sound she plays
through the pinion trees
is a loud, sweeping sound,
like a great, spiny broom
cleaning away from the earth
things unnecessary.

Invisible,
yet she stirs the winter skies
to bring deep canyon snows today—
and then tomorrow
life-giving thunderstorms.

She makes us ask,
what is necessary?
What do we need
on our temporary trek
across the earth?
Our suitcase in hand?
What is it we really want?

Only life from the wind.

Presentation

The young father
bound
his newborn daughter
across his chest
and then slipped on his skis.

This was a cold February
in the land of lakes and trees
with dancing green lights.

Here he connected
just as his ancestors
before him connected,
to the starry night,

just as his daughter
will someday bind
her infant
across her heart,
presenting a new life
under the milky-green
foam of stars,

under the great tail
of the Milky Way Galaxy
above her shoulders.

The Language of the Women

The women of the village
started to weave
a new language
into their fabric —
shapes and forms
into their dress,
so they could communicate
with each other.

The men of the village
had treated them cruelly,
along with the children
and the animals
(whose spirits are interwoven).
Girls that tried to escape
had their ears and noses
cut off or worse.

Now, when the women
are in the market,
watched and separated,
they are able to send

messages to each other.
They are getting stronger
every day —

*Mighty like the great river
that one day will flow out of that country.*

An Evening

For Sophia and Phoebe

Because this night is filled
with black-winged pelicans
coming in to land,
a sail being taken down,
a sliver of a moon
climbing above
the white birch trees,

and laughter from young girls
rising above the lapping waves,

no more can fit
into the evening.

Love Song

When scientists discovered
the wings of a cricket
preserved in stone
from the Jurassic period,

they played its wings
and heard
an ancient love song
never heard
in our world before,
a new song.

This morning,
while driving home:
A colt had been flung
to the side of the road,
killed in the night
by a passing car,

its little body
nearly missed
because it was
so small —

small enough
to still be brought
to its mother's belly,

its mother gone,
too,

a love song
unfinished.

Auschwitz, E. Poland
January 27, 1945

Deep January
never felt so warm —

when the strong arms
of the Red Army
picked up
the skeleton-like people
and set them
on blankets in the snow.

The evil snake
had reached down
deep into their bodies
and tried to snatch
their very souls,

but the soldiers
gathered them
like sick dogs
in their arms
and set them
into the sunshine.

Libertacja was like
the swinging
of a thousand swings
up into the air — a day when poetry
began to be written.

The Design Teacher

She taught him
to look at the dragonfly,
its color, design,
and to look at why it
moved the way it did.

They searched near
the small pond
and found the black and whites,
the emerald greens,
the slim turquoise,
and the orange and blues.
All had whirling lace wings
above their heads.

One day they saw
a golden dragonfly,
or so they thought —

so they came to find
the new dragonfly
in the late afternoon light
near the small pond
in a universe

that slipped through

a hole in the basket
never to be found
or picked up again.

Celestial Bird: The Poem

One
became caught
last night
in my net.

This morning
I untangled him —
eyes true and bright,
magnificent iridescent feathers,
and a warm beating heart
that stayed in my hand
as I threw him up into the air
so he could
continue his flight
across the universe.

Death

I'll tell you
what it's like.

It's like a train
coming
and rolling
over you.

You can't get
out of the way
or
stop the train
because
it's too late.

All you can do
is take it —
let it run over you,
let the train
finish its job.

The Healer

"…you have been yourself at the edge of the Deep Canyon and
have come back unharmed" An Elder of the San Juan Pueblo.
1959. V. Laski. *Seeking Life*.

"I was invisible" An Asiatic Eskimo. 1980. D. Cloutier. *Spirit Spirit,
Shaman Songs*.

In the snowy canyons
you came to me
as an eagle
and whispered
(in almost audible sounds)
"the key to the secret
of healing. . ."

For my wounds
had gone beyond wounds
and had festered
into deep holes
in my sides,
and gangrene had set in,

but, in a whisper,
you came and said,
"you have the keys within you.
You are the stars
in the starry night.
You are the source
at the mouth of rivers.
You have the medicine
to heal
already in your bones."

And my wounds became

as faint as the sound
of feathers,
as pale as the ringed moon.

And the healer
came to me
in the face of the wolf.
She came
and nodded to me
with her deep intelligence,
and her eyes told me,
"your spirit is strength.
Your force is as great
as volcanoes,
for your goodness prevails
over the dark;
your goodness
has brought you out
of the deep canyon."

And again the healer
came to me.
This time as a bear,
a joyous white bear
with great white paws,
and she told me,
"you were invisible,
but now I see you.
You have gone
to the edge of the great canyon
but have come back
unharmed.

"And now your laughter
will become
as mountainous as thunder,
and your tears
will be the tears of glory!"

I tell you.
I have put my ear
to the great Earth
and have felt your presence.

Cynthia Jobin

The late Cynthia Jobin was a New England poet with a large following through the Internet. She held a master's degree from the Massachusetts College of Art and Design and a doctorate from the American Institute of Holistic Theology; she worked as a secondary school teacher, a professor of graduate students, and managed her own calligraphy studio. In retirement she wrote poetry and translated poems from the French, including medieval French. She published one poetry collection in her lifetime and a second compiled by the English poet John Looker after her death. Her work has appeared in literary journals, magazines, and at least one anthology, *Indra's Net*. Jobin was a master of both traditional poetic forms and free verse. Her poetry can contain a wide range of literary, mythological, and symbolic elements that demand the reader spend some time appreciating what she is exploring. Often, however, as in Looker's poetry, there is an elegance of language wedded to meaning that is accessible to the average reader. The emotional content of the poetry can be complex, but also can delight, veer off into humor, or delve into the meaning of loss, joy, fear, or even the imminence of her own death, which is at the heart of "Night Draws Near, Brother Ass."

> Night draws near, brother ass
> pale sister moon ascends the dark
> brother wind makes a chill pass
> from long ago and far away
> where Francis dogs still bark —
> they echo sorry old beliefs
> that make you lesser than
> a thing that's called a soul.

As with so many accomplished poets, Jobin's best work is memorable, sometimes a puzzle, and often worth the effort to plumb its depths.

Disciple

Come to a place each morning
before the world begins,
while sleeping dogs still lie
and the cats are somewhere, breathing.
Outside the sound of rubber on tar
ebbs and flows, comes and goes
in waves, far from any ocean.
Off and on, unidentified birds
tweet into the absence of language.
No human voice yet, except those
faintly recalled from dreams
now silencing into thought.
There is nothing to do or be.
There is only the here, the now.
Do not fail to come,
and it will be revealed:
the what, the how.

The Sun Also Sets

Without a bedtime story or a lullabye
the evening's blush sinks to a deeper red
then slips into a slit between the earth and sky
leaving our goodbyes lingering, unsaid.

I do not want to go, or let you go.
I want to dare this ending, call its bluff,
delay our parting with a sudden overflow
of words — too many and yet not enough —

while you, my dearest one, would choose
blunt disappearance, the mute way
to stanch an agony — those deeper blues
along the skyline fire — as if to say

the sun rises, the sun also sets.
So let it set. Let us let it. Let's.

The Palpable Obscure

All souls own this evening, love,
blurring borders between quick and dead.
And even if the fearsome moans of man
did not appoint this time as hallowed,
our backyard trees announce it, as they
lose their glory and become their bones.
The veil is at its thinnest now, that
suddenly obscured you and left me
bereft, dumbfounded in the desolately clear.
Once a day, at least, I stop to wonder
where you are. I do not think of
you as being here. Except, tonight
a heightening of powers in the darkness
wants to break november from october
with a cold slap and a small wail in the wind.
Something more than me, something much
more sure that you abide, this night, brings
you, in ways that I can almost touch.

North, Early December

Let me down easy
the way hints of winter
fall exquisitely today
scattering icy lacy flowers
from a cloud bouquet
flutter, waver just a bit
unhurried and unworried
to get on with it.
A deeper cold will come
but stay its harder hand
let play a little longer
the november grey indefinites
let me down easy.
The longest night is still ahead
weighs heavy in the apprehension
threatening dismay

let me go haltingly into its
frozen moonlit desolation
tempered by the touch of
something of its opposite;
knowing I am anyway
to be let down, I pray
let me down easy.

By the Androscoggin

The Androscoggin flows, cliff-sheltered,
hidden by a thickness of great pointed firs,
so we cannot see it from our windows
though we know it's there. Sometimes we hear
after a freakish torrent of hard rain
its rushing over rocks — the ones we hop
when crossing — and we're sidelined for awhile.
The local ducks, deer, foxes, skunks
don't seem to mind; they let the river
have it's way — grow wider, deeper,
curving slippery as silk over the falls,
roaring down to swirls of sudsy turbulence
then calming to black pools of mystery.
Only the hand that winds the clock of thought,
the sleepless eyes that worry out the window,
know an urge to push the river toward the sea,
while among the firs, small bright eyes
caught on the dark like stars fallen to earth,
watch, and don't agree or disagree.

To a Tulip

You,
yellow flower
standing in a cobalt vase,
unfurling blades,
stemmed sacramental cup —
winter was hard

but now your simple grace
is green announcement:
things are looking up.
There by the window you
to sunlight are the antiphon,
beauty new as beauties past,
spring's insistence
life should carry on.
Yet you become
most beautiful at last,
when age and death are
what you must fulfill:
come that night
you can no longer
close against the dark,
you open wide until
you are all heart,
and every petal knows
translucence as it falls.
You could be hinting
how to do it, for us all.

Palimpsest

The earnest monastery scribe begins
to scrape: he must expunge, obliterate
a text of Archimedes. Tonsured pate
bowed over parched and pumiced skins,
stone bench stone-cold, to his chagrin
hemorrhoids, indigestion complicate
his task. But *laborare et orare*, so he meditates;
offers up his troubles in atonement for his sins.
Beyond clerestory walls descendant sheep
are growing new skins in a lilac breeze.
Fra Pennafolio envies how they graze
oblivious, while lately he's been losing sleep
fighting dark avengers of Hippocrates.
For help, he rubs his *cabuchon* of *chrysoprase*.
He must not let it faze him.
After all, in frugal fact, parchment is dear
and perfect skins are rare. He must persevere,

erase and rewrite without fear.
It is a holy labor, surely in the angels' care,
to cleanse away the pagans for a book of prayer.

Night Draws Near, Brother Ass

Night draws near, brother ass
pale sister moon ascends the dark
brother wind makes a chill pass
from long ago and far away
where Francis dogs still bark —
they echo sorry old beliefs
that make you lesser than
a thing that's called a soul.
As if some merciless sneak thief
has stripped you of your rigmarole
stolen all your oomph for dreams
of grasping the elusive carrot
and your fear of prodding stick
you slow a bit now, and seem weary
though you stubbornly as ever climb
the slope of each day, brick by brick.
You've been a good and faithful
servant — more than I can say
for parts that think and speak.
Yours is an understanding deeper
than all hope and pray. Are we perhaps
at last in sempiternal unison about
the moment that must come? Then
let's together bray . . . and bray…and bray!

Written when Cynthia Jobin knew she was close to death. Saint Francis of Assisi used to refer to his own body as Brother Ass.

Richard Brenneman

Richard Brenneman founded *The Rimrock Poets Magazine* with the educator, novelist, and poet Thomas Davis when they were both students at Mesa College in Grand Junction, Colorado. These days he is a Boston poet who has been published in a variety of journals in both the United States and Great Britain. These include *The Denver Post Magazine*, *The Muddy River Poetry Review*, and *Ibbetson Street*, among others. His avocation is genealogical research where his expertise has resulted in the publication of several articles. Now retired, he has returned to writing poetry, reading, continuing his genealogical researches, seeking kindred spirits, and observing the current Boston literary scene of which he is a member. He graduated from San Jose State University in California and worked as a library cataloguer until he moved to Boston and later retired from the Commonwealth of Massachusetts.

As in his poem, "Fish-Bait," Brenneman has a romantic, old-fashioned streak that keeps coming out. Sometimes the romanticism approaches the macabre, seemingly drawing inspiration from a world that ended when gargoyles fronted churches like Notre Dame in France. However, in some of his other poetry, such as "Heating Bill," there is a wry, contemporary voice:

> I sit here at seventy-five
> hoping to make eighty-five
> thinking, God, I'm not elderly, please!
> Spare me, though I know
> there's more gray in my hair,
> my bones creak a bit. . .

The most interesting part of Brenneman's work is that the poems of his old age seem to be getting stronger. Instead of being fanciful, striving for (and sometimes achieving) delight, they are more grounded, expressing the truths of old, and often his deepest insecurities, though we realize he is "not elderly, please!"

Fish-Bait

A silver fish swims
across the summer sky —
his eyes, stars,
and his scales
clouds thinly scattered,
glistening from the moon
as if freshly taken
from some farmer's pond.
What fisherman will come
to hook this prize
or even dream of catching him?
an impious feat of legerdemain.
Perhaps the moon is but
a silver bauble, bait
thrown into the midnight deeps
of silent sky, to entice
this giant creature to bite,
to swallow the moon —

and thin-skinned as he is,
lets the moon come burning through,
and dissipate the vapors
that caught my eye,
and let me see a silver giant fish
swimming in the sky.

Gargoyles

Thoughts of gargoyles on flying buttresses,
high above the human press,
ecclesiastical rote and ritual pageantry:
winged demons meditate the course
of affairs below stairs,
waiting for the elder days to return.

Now the demons sit on thrones,
are powers-that-be; these

do not think or meditate,
are not above the human press,
conform to civil majesty.

Only the gargoyles made of stone
can gaze coolly at the world below:
wink, leer, laugh and
point out the foibles of the race,
act them out. They wear
no masks in this heady air.

Heating Bill

On the radio, the announcer's voice proclaims
a timely message on the hour
after the sports, before the news.
Whether extreme cold, or blasting deadly heat
— weather is always banging at our doors.

"Be a friend, check to see
how your elderly neighbor is doing."

I sit here at seventy-five
hoping to make eighty-five
thinking, God, I'm not elderly, please!
Spare me, though I know
there's more gray in my hair,
my bones creak a bit;
I'm definitely afraid of falling,
a bit more fearful of risk.

I hate the cold, and I'm still waiting
for a real live person to call —
beyond the robocalls; those I'll hang up.
I sit here arranging the hours,
waiting to hear a voice on the phone
to ask if I'm still alive,
doing o.k., or a knock at the door
to exchange small talk, a laugh or two,
a sly remark or a pleasantry.

So whoever's out there, please,
please answer the call.
A smile would go a long way
to save on my heating bill.

Thin Ice

Going on forbidden adventures,
afraid,
yet full of expectation,
falling back in hesitation.

Like walking on the ice
of a pond on a sunny day;
is it thick enough?
Is it too thin?

Going slowly then,
hearing the crackle
beneath my feet,
running back to shore.
Wanting adventure,
forbidden adventure —
still, I can't swim.

Old Houses

Looking at the ruins
of old wooden houses,
slipping down to dust again.
Birds make their nests
in the gabled eaves;
the corners are littered
with cobwebs and dust,
and nuts, pilfered by the squirrels
some forgotten autumn.

Last year the wind blew

down the old kitchen;
next year — perhaps
the walls, termite-ridden,
will fall.

And in a few passing seasons
this old house
will return to earth again.
Grass will grow here on the hill,
blowing with the wind
in the sun.

Library Tour

I will not be sad because
the ones I want to check out
will not check me out,
turn my pages, peruse at leisure
my depths, my heights, my dreams.

They speed-read my works,
demand orgasm, or total unity
in only a moment or two.
They want to plug into me,
and get instant computerized replay.
They overdemand, only
skimming,
and I, I do the same,
because it's such shallow reading,
touching the pages,
smelling the ink,
caressing the volumes,
looking for love, deep love,
ownership perhaps,
looking for new publications,
wisdom, beauty, illumined with gold leaf
and lapis lazuli used liberally:
rare books, not portraits or yellow journalism.

I will not be sad because
the ones I want to check out

will not check me out
because I want to sit alone and dream awhile
as much as curl up like a contented cat
before a fire and purr away the night,
like a touchstone, a talisman,
a warm embrace,
but usually that call number
is out on interlibrary loan!

Haunted

All the shadows that have haunted
the yesterdays of my mind
return, beckoning.
Mists retreat awhile and return again.
What has been hidden is revealed
suddenly.

I start to look with some expectation
as the sunlight scatters the night aside,
but it is only strangers, shadows
from the past, ghostly presences
that disturb the balance of day to day.

I flee such shadows for real
present laughter, lightness, joy.
Dizzy heights have balustrades
to hold me back from shadow streets
below, empty without memory,
for there are rarefied crests above
where sun gold reflects true hearts' largesse.

Reflections

Ephemera of ages jettisoned:
images of the past look out
from broken faces
upon a world not their own.

Ephemera of the present —
neon lights blinking on and off
illuminate our broken shadows,
walking stealthily by night
in a world too much our own.

Chimeras, winged as if to fly
to a world beyond, rise
from the shards of this one,
tear-stained and broken
that line every highway. .

Statues, now broken ephemera
haunt the Western past.
Are their faces wiser than ours?
Are we reflected in shattered chimeras?

Our dreams glance out from billboards
in neon syncopation.
Shadows walking the night are broken
by a world too much our own.

John Looker

John Looker lives in England with his wife, although they are frequent visitors to New Zealand where two married daughters live. His poetry draws on the experience of forty years in the British Civil Service, chiefly in the Department for the Environment, during which he was engaged in European Union and international negotiations. In retirement he has been a board member of two charities and is currently Chair of a supporters association for a pioneering school that takes children with normal intelligence but severe difficulties with language. John Looker's poetry has been published by *Magma, Artemis* (USA), *Poetry Salzburg Review, Poetry Breakfast, Ink Sweat and Tears* and other print and online journals, and has appeared in two anthologies: *Indra's Net* (UK) and the Austin International Poetry Festival's 25th anniversary anthology. His first collection, *The Human Hive* (2015) was selected for inclusion in the Poetry Library of the UK's national collection.

Looker's poetry often sweeps through time, using images, symbols, and narrative to develop meanings that readers have to discern for themselves. He seldom uses private symbols in the way of a poet like John Ashbery, but instead works to be accessible to almost every reader, becoming demanding only in the sense that you have to think about the symbols of workmen, literary figures, incidents from the past, or the multiple time periods inside the poem to discover what he is exploring.

In a short poem like "The Day They Detected Gravitational Waves," he tells us

> Time was there were Han philosophers
>   standing on a hilltop at night
>   naming the Mansions of Heaven;
>   later, Galileo Galilei
>   weeping with joy at the moons of Jupiter.

then goes on to stun with the mathematics that describe how

> the Universe in its infancy
> had arched its back and roared.

Looker is one of Great Britain's most interesting poets, following up his extraordinary career in the British environmental service with just as extraordinary a career in poetry.

To a Winter's Day Also

For Frances

After Shakespeare's Sonnet 18:
Shall I compare thee to a summer's day?

... for isn't there beauty in a winter's day?
Not just the frail sunlight sparkling on ice,
the clear skies, the dark holly with those dear
berries; nor even the breathtaking lace
of trees in the cold air. Give these their due
but there is more — for all is stillness; peace.
    Walking, you take my arm, and I am yours.

On Your 70th Birthday

For Frances

I know it's up there, your Aladdin's box
high on the wardrobe, hidden from prying eyes,
a ready hoard of treasures for when Life asks
some little gift to bestow, some magical surprise.

When do you buy them? I never witness
the time spent choosing, the moment of discovery.
You must hover in the shop, considering this
and touching that, waiting inspiration, serendipity.

Now, planning your own present, I recall the party
when I found you among the drinks and dishes
all those years ago: my own moment of discovery.
You were the one answer to all my three wishes.

Violin (1778)

At the height of the rebellion of His Majesty's thirteen colonies,
while the *Resolution* was charting the unknown Pacific,
Jacob Ford master craftsman, St Paul's Churchyard London,
made this violin
and when it was complete
there he sat among the wood shavings, tools and pots of varnish
carefully tightening the strings
to set free its sweet young voice for time and the world to hear.

We look at it now and admire as he did then
its curves and glossy skin
and we lean into its song. Not long ago the bridge had broken
but that was easily fixed. Now there's a hint of a crack,
merely a hint, in the wooden panel behind.
That too could be repaired; it isn't the end.
Meanwhile the voice still sings
and Jacob Ford's gift to the world beguiles for another year.

In Jane Austen's House

This was her writing table, this her chair
('Please Do Not Sit'); two bijou items placed
here by the window where the light fell square
on her page from the horse-drawn world she faced.
In a cramped corner the public (that's me
and you) peer through glass at her neat handwriting;
or we squeeze into the bedroom which she
and her sister shared — until she was dying.
We visitors are whispering, withdrawing
from each other. We feel too tall, too loud,
navigating all this china, imploring
children to be careful. We're quite a crowd.
   We open a door (she would have opened it too,
   her skirts brushing the frame) and we pass through.

Made in Mesopotamia

When Saul was king
and his tiny kingdom of Israel and Judah
was beset by war, David was a boy
guarding the sheep from the wolf and the bear,
playing the lyre and
getting into fights, with fists or sticks or a sling.

It's the lyre that grabs our attention,
with its simple strings of gut,
its arms reaching up in graceful curves
like a woman dancing,
and its rounded belly,
its ample decoration.

Just how was it made?
Not: who was the craftsman,
how did he fashion the soundbox, the bridge?
But: who had the idea?
Long before in the ancient city of Ur
someone had pictured the thing, had puzzled it out,
had heard in the mind the ethereal singing of angels
if it were played.

In the Caves at Nerja

Nerja, Andalusia, southern Spain

As we enter the cave — the rocky floor
leading us down, and down again,
among the stalagmites and stalactites
— we are drawn to the deep past
where humankind
lived out its long, long infancy
by a now-forgotten shore.

The caverns are displayed by electric light.
So novel, so new.

For thousands of years
there was only the wavering glow
and the tricksy shadows
from a burning brand, and straining sight.

What might their lives have been like? Short
of course, with hyenas contending for the caves,
disease and the struggle for food:
pine nuts and snails, we learn, were big in their diet;
fish or meat when something was caught.

And yet:
and yet there was Art, or so we deduce.
Was it the women or was it the men
who splayed their hands against the cold rock wall,
blowing their pigments of black and red
across those templates of flesh and blood?
Who was it who painted these bison and deer,
these lifelike horses, these seals?
Who then stood back to admire the image as it set?

And although we look down, as it were, from above
we feel there must have been music and song.
Here in this chamber the stalactites ring
with discernible notes; some appear to be tuned —
that is scraped, or pared — for the ear.
Was there play? Was there laughter?
And, may we reasonably ask, how about love?

Summer Rain

There are certain summer mornings when the rain drifts
sideways, almost a mist, and all is doused
in a wash of silvers and greys: colours from a palette
of pebble and lichen, herring gull and trout.

Sun hats are thrown aside
in favour of anoraks. Plans
are revised. Do we miss the heat?
The primary blue, the glare? Well, yes.

But the air is fresh and sweet. Raindrops cling
to wires and glistening leaves, and snails inch
out from the hedges shining, while we just drift
idly: from breakfast . . . to morning coffee . . . to lunch.

Behold the Beetle

In the tangles of the garden undergrowth, long neglect
has left the stump of an apple-tree rotting.

In the soil among the roots is the pupa: imprisoned
in its cell, the pale grub lying squeezed and latent
waiting until time, DNA or the sun will summon it —

as the old lamp found in Aladdin's cave is rubbed
and the Genie, grotesque and implacable, erupts.

It is Other, it is Alien — neither human nor djinn —
and has lived to mutate. When it has remade its body,
is it astonished? What does it recall?

The Day They Detected Gravitational Waves

Time was there were Han philosophers
    standing on a hilltop at night
        naming the Mansions of Heaven;
    later, Galileo Galilei
        weeping with joy at the moons of Jupiter.

Now, in sightless tunnels
    beams from lasers have shivered
        at ancient astral events —
    and men and women around the world
        pore over computations

in awe at the mathematics:

the Universe in its infancy
    had arched its back and roared,
and they can feel
    the exhalation of its breath.

Julius Caesar in the 21st Century

In response to Shakespeare's play

In the Forum,
we stand among the crowd and lend our ears
to whosoever's rhetoric is balm.

Those men in togas! All so ambitious:
one is greedy to bestride the little Earth
like a Colossus;

another has a lean and hungry look —
he thinks too much
and this we do not like.

How hot it is. But some Mark Antony,
who always had our hearts, borrows our minds
and moulds them. Easily,

all too easily.
We run headlong through the streets
shouting, the dust rising beneath our feet.

RedWulf DancingBare

Ralph V. Greco, aka *RedWulf DancingBare*, is a poet, healer, photographer, and Ancient Way Café manager. He has adventured through much of the United States and now resides with his life partner, the poet and artist Standing Feather, in the Zuni Mountains of New Mexico. He has been a circus clown, a steward of a radical faerie sanctuary, a Lakota Sun Dancer. He has studied healing work at Kripalu Ashram and with various teachers, among other searches for self. Since joining the *Zuni Mountain Poets* in 2008, he has written poetry that reflects his travels, his healing understandings, his striving for gay acceptance, and his love of word play. His first book of poetry, *Waiting on the Monsoons for his Desert Soul*, was published by Four Windows Press in 2020. He has had poetry published in the *Gallup Journey*, the *Zuni Mountain Poets* anthology in 2012, and the mini-anthology *Querencia* in 2014.

The first thing to know about RedWulf DancingBare's poetry is that he is a storyteller. His words tumble down the page, as wild as a mountain stream splashing over rocks, but they always end up swirling into a plot with a beginning, middle, and an end. At one point he is telling about a witch and then suddenly we are meeting Jesus Christ through charged air. He describes a man tormented by his memories of Viet Nam:

> His eyes bulged downward
> into some abyss of captured soul wanderings.
> Something clenched around his body,
> as if a giant python
> twisted and torqued his torso.
> It trapped his breath until he clenched his fists.
> He cranked his head sideways and upward
> until his eyes puffed to tears
> and peered directly into mine.

And this is just the beginning of the narrative.

Healer, chef, mystic, compassionate soul, someone who regularly looks for ley lines of spirit and hope, circus clown, gay, RedWulf takes the reader on a wild ride that still, somehow, seems sane, and even wise. He has been compared to Charles Bukowski, but his stories, driven with a wild profusion of words, are his own.

Whale Songs

He couldn't recall
the song with which the old tent crew boss marked the rhythmic
     flow of time:
perhaps an old seaman's chanty,
mushed through the mouth of stained scrimshaw teeth
still clutching a half smoked unlit Cuban stogie off one corner.
The gruff bass voice
creaked out from his hulking vessel timbers,
connecting new tissue to ancient sound.
Especially clear, it rang the brash "clank" of his shiny gray sledge
as it walloped the wide head of the 3 feet long steel spike.
It had become indelibly etched in him
when the man 3 times as old as any man helping him
began to sing the stakes into the earth.
With his resounding cadence, the old salt
impelled the sledges of all six men in the chaining gang
to each deliver a loud telling blow,
each in perfect clockwise succession,
to the stake in the center between them all.
He would continue the chant as long as it took them
to drive it in until only 6 inches outcropped.
Then like a shimmering human octopus,
the six would move on to the next stake,
and the next,
and the next,
setting pilons deep
to the beat of his crew boss gathering-way song.

They moved enchanted, like one soul,
until all 120 stakes had been driven into the hard-caked earth
as the circus tent came to be soundly anchored in its new harbor.
The driving duet with the old man's eerie melody
against the haunting chorus of clank, clank, clank,
still bewitched him like whale songs connecting across oceans.

The memory of the elemental bonding of these six men
always returned him to that timeless sea.
Their great flukes of long hammers
stretched out from thick arms,
arcing out and up and over their bodies,

then swelling like a great breath taken
and driven downward to slap the surface.
It took him back to seeing Humpback mothers
teaching their babies to slap tails
against the waters.

He could still hear that clank, clank, clank and surreal song.
It always woke the town to the odd newcomers
who had mysteriously appeared to this out-of-the-way place
in its mundane routine of just everyday surviving.
The out of the ordinary sound
announced that the big top show of dogs and ponies
had come with exotic animals, death defying acrobatics,
and clown escapades:
an odd sounding that came with other world smells
of grease paint, cotton candy and dancing bear scat.
It carried an entrancing invitation that said,
"Come share our dreams and adventures!"
and then the next day would be gone,
a phantom ship in the mind's harbor.

But more than any of these,
he still could still see the sacred sweat
streaming off the grimy thick necks,
strapping shoulders, and dirty, bulging biceps
as they channeled their souls of whales,
saltwater rivulets cascading down
desert dirt smeared faces locked in ancestral ritual.
Lunar rhythms and solar wills magnifying force,
transcending self as one song,
one heart,
one beat
echoing across fair lots and fields
and into little villages nearby,
tent crew boss calling,

"Wake up!
Leave your small ponds behind
and jump into the ocean."

A Most Hate Filled Name

We were the bundle of sticks* thrown on as kindling post
to heighten the flame and burn witches to ghosts.
Stoned under rocks and burnished on fences,
"faggot," the curse with which it often commenced.

Along so many paths, the cry broke his serenity,
stole his composure, pushed him to enmity.
He never knew why. He didn't dress to look gay.
He didn't swish or flounce or even say "Hey."

But throughout his life he was often the guy
singled out by teen boys on testosterone highs.
Four or five in a car out of the blue driving by,
hanging out windows cursing, "Die faggot die".

From Pittsburgh to Portland, from Hawaii to Maine,
he always seemed faced with the blazing refrain.
As he walked peacefully along, minding his own game,
"We're comin' for you faggot," ringing out with sharp aim.

Sometimes he felt terror, and he believed they'd come back.
He'd hide in the bushes or try to hide his tracks
by turning on side streets or jumping over fences.
He could never be sure; he didn't want to take chances.

For a time though, he often would just give them the finger,
but violence to violence never seemed the right answer.
So, a kiss blown their way was a response for a while,
a wave, and a shrug, and an impervious smile.

But a wrench to the stomach was always there,
and sometimes all he could do was just stare
and trust in his gut he'd know how to run,
if the car turned around on that day with no sun.

That day never came, though at times it felt close,
and to this day he still holds that ghost:
that a simple loving man, who happens to be queer,
will still be that kindling and no witch need be near.

*It has been stated that many of the witch burnings of the 1400-1700's, used gay men as the first to be set aflame, before the fire reached the witch at the top. Hence the title "faggot," which means a kindling stick or bundle.

This is not just my story. This version of my story is mild compared to what others have gone through and continue to undergo. I have had my head pounded against a table, as well as countless anonymous gut punches while in high school and walking on various busy city sidewalks when I was in my 20's. I hid out of a fear of death when I was young. I and my partner continue to be taunted at times now. A few years ago, we even received a death threat. I am not that fearful anymore. The amount of freedom and acceptance we have gained in the last 40 years is amazing. Times are troubling again and I fear a resurgence of venom. But I am out and proud and not willing to go back!! I do fear for the transgenders, and the other GLBTQ kids trying to just grow up right now. And if this helps even one person who knows me to change their attitude toward anyone in our community for the better, then it is worth sharing!

For the People

(1)

One year he was invited to the Lakota Sundance
to dance as a "Winkte'."
That first day
the elder medicine man in charge of the ceremony
avowed to them,
their long skirts billowing out behind
toward the harnessed buffalo skulls
which still reeked where some old flesh still clung,
"You are Winkte!
You are holy people!
You dance with both sacred triangles inside of you,
one on top of the other.
One spins clockwise
while the other spins counterclockwise."

The Sacred Fire keeper drummed
out past the west gate of the sacred circle
and sang a soft smudging song
by the blazing just-past-dawn fire.
Soothing juniper essence saturated the breeze.
The elder continued,
"In this dance you can do whatever you need to do,

and go wherever you need to go,
if you feel called to do it in the name of healing.
You are asked to assist in those places forbidden to others,
like the moon lodge is for most men.
You have special duties that only Winkte's can do
in order for this Sundance to happen correctly.
And you may even enter the east gate
if spirit calls you to be there."

The 5 men all turned to look past the sacred cottonwood,
festooned with tens of thousands of brightly colored prayer ties,
to view where only the Winkte's, if divinely called, might go.
The east gate was where Ever-Changing-Mystery entered the
        ceremony,
and no person was ever supposed to be.
He felt an intense humility and responsibility flare within.
The medicine man added,
"What you are called to do in the name of healing no one can
        question.
Not me,
not even the Heyoka,
though they will try.
The mostly white faery Walks-Betweens' eyes darted back and forth.
Fear passed between them like lightning bolts
at the mention of the mysterious, feared Thunder Clowns.
"Have a good dance,
a ho metakuye oyasin," he finished,
shaking each of their hands heartily.

(2)

That year he danced mostly along the side,
under the sponsor's canopy.
Very timid to the new experience,
he carried a single small feather and moved in tiny steps
until "Chief Shellbone" appeared on the third day.

The mesmerizing man's presence was seemingly felt by all.
He wore pitch black leather chaps over the top of black pants
that stood out like no other dancer's attire.
His bare shiny chest cascaded down
to a wide-roving overhanging belly.
His thick silver mane hung down his back

held back by a medicine shield
with two long black feathers twisting in the wind behind.
Large, blackhole eyes,
seemingly void of anything,
bore out from the chiseled Ute face.
They threatened to suck all life into them
if one dared to look.
He brandished a long black bull whip in his hand —
even more of an excuse to not even dare a glance.

Chief Shellbone "corrected"
the hapless unwitting white Winkte'
several times that afternoon on "Lakota etiquette."
He chased him out from under the canopy
with a crack of his whip inches from his butt.
He chased him into the arena loudly cackling,
his voice crisp like a crack of thunder,
"Winkte',
if you're gonna dance,
then dance!"
Another loud crack as the whip came down again
within a hair of his backside.

All the while several men "hung"
by buffalo bone thongs poked through their pectoral muscles
on long tethers strung to the living tree.
60 more men and women danced, mesmerized
in the sweltering heat,
and 100 more watched as sponsors
from the sheltered outer circle,
as the wild eyed Heyoka hied
on the heels of the poor startled Winkte'.
Out at the heart of the ritual,
the medicine man used a scalpel
to cut into a prone dancer's chest
as he lay on a great buffalo skin robe.
Other leaders swung their eagle wing fans
and blew their shrill eagle bone whistles.
Suddenly some of the crowd erupted
in great gaffaws of laughter
when the wild Ute Heyoka swaggered
after his now high-tailed prey.
His sparking voice resounding over the crowd,

"'I'm gonna steal you off to Montana
and make you my wife.'
adding, 'You're gonna fix me a fine supper
and bead me some beautiful clothes
when I get you home!'"

But the roaring approval of the crowd
emboldened the once naïve Pennsylvania farm boy,
and he took off galloping like a giddy schoolgirl,
his skirt trailing in the wind.
A high leap in the air
with a queer twittering giggle erupted from him
every time a whip crack landed near his butt.
Some eyes flowed with amused tears,
except maybe for the Winkte's
which had a certain wide-eyed horror
blended with an exhilarated altered-world reality
that mixed with an ancient spiritual certainty.

At the end of that dance
the Heyoka came up to him
and handed him a turkey vulture wing.
He told him that he himself had once danced with it.
They looked into each other's eyes as the shimmering man said,
"You test me Winkte.
But I like it!
And I like what you do for the people!"

(3)

For 7 more Sundances,
where Heyokas bayed at his heals,
he danced.
Where traditionalists questioned his place
and even threatened to pierce his butt and hang him to the tree,
he danced.
And where the dancers continued to thank him
for his courage and support of them,
he danced.
Chief Shellbone's gift of the turkey vulture wing in his hand,
the seemingly out of place white Winkte'
never stopped dancing hard
for the people.

Waiting on the Monsoons for His Desert Soul

He hated the way June bore into him
like the dratted no-see-ums
that tangled in his body hair
and bit deep gauges that festered and pocked.
Desperation coursed strong and hard through his ragged veins
blistered by the sun's scorch,
throttled by the choke of his parched prayers.

He thought with exasperation,
"The Zuni's MUST be doing their rain dance by now."

A young mountain lion had come down a few weeks earlier
when the oppressiveness had already seemed relentless
It had easily leapt over the 5 feet tall perimeter fence
and snagged a couple of chickens roosting too low in the junipers.
He had to corral the rest of the girls
into the fortress solid chicken house after that,
so that the returning lion couldn't feast and would move along.
It had come back 5 nights in a row looking for an easy meal.

He prayed, "Drum hard Zunis.
Call the thunder beings to appease all that hunger"

He got a few more young chickens to replace some of the lost.
Old man raven broke through their enclosure,
tore their heads off, and ripped hearts out of their breasts.
Sickened, he had raced 60 miles to the nearest town
to build a better enforced cage for another start.

He pleaded, "Dance hard Zunis.
Call the water gods to quench all that thirst."

He answered, with resigned surrender,
his far away friends when they asked
if there was anything more that could be done.
"Just a few more weeks until the monsoons come.
Life is just this way here.
Everything goes on pretty normal until June

when the heat really starts to build
to bring the rain to the continental divide again.
It has been so long,
but for now we must wait."

"We build stronger enclosures.
We pay closer attention.
We use only as much of the sacred scarce water
as is just necessary to keep things alive."

"We know the animals struggle.
The people struggle.
The plants struggle."

"We are called to learn to trust in the course of things
beyond our control.
We have to work to hear and gentle
the inner reactions of our nature
because we know we cannot control
the nature outside ourselves.
Such is June here."

He kept praying,
"Sing hard Zunis.
Call the grandmother rain to comfort all of us."

He watched the heat get to his turkey hen.
She kept going out onto the old county highway
where she dared cars to take her on.
Her big breast puffed out and her body flared.
One car apparently took her on.

Her free ranging partner, the guinea hen,
now just calls and calls and calls.
All day long the shrill squeak,
like a rusty hand pump to an old well,
drills into all ears and all nerves.

He feels his own exhaustion.
He pushes against the heaviness in his own chest,
the thirst of his own spirit,
the grating squeak of his own nerves.

He chews some osha to break up the dry clot.
Takes an afternoon nap
because there is nothing else he can do out in the inferno.
He sips a little more water.

He can't watch the news
because all that he sees are oblivious chickens, cocky turkeys,
desperate lions, and cruel ravens.

He gets out his hand drum
and beats an unknown but familiar beat,
"Come on Zunis. Let's do this!"

If It Takes A Village

In his small village
everyone knew everyone.
If a man fell down
cursing his fate,
questioning his lot
in the middle of the road;
everyone would listen.
Drunk or sober,
in tongues or in tears,
they knew he was talking to God.
In his small village the people,
their hearts, would be open
for the wound
and for the wonder.

In his small village,
watching with leopard eyes,
there and not,
the people would sweep their porches
and reflect their paths.
The people would share their beans
and breathe their humanity.
The people would feed their verdant plants
as well as their dry, barren-soul patches
with the community waters.
For it was for all to use.

Such was their sacred trust of rain,
and of grief.

In his small village
the people would hold sacred witness
for that man or that woman or that child
who poured out onto the earth.
They would keen pleas at God's feet
for mercy, or sanity, or forgiveness,
    or love.
Patiently they entranced
until the god talker was spent,
wrenched empty,
surrendered like a lump of lifeless clay.
Then the people would pick that person up,
carry them to the river,
bathe them with silky yucca root,
gentle them with calming herbs and oils and caresses,
swathe them in rabbit pelt swaddling,
and place them in their clean bed.
All the while a feast was prepared
to honor the sacred communion.

In his small village,
the people were the balm of God.
The people shared their tears like manna from heaven,
so that each and every one was fed and comforted.

"My village is no more." he cried.
I heard his forlorn tale of how his small village
was smothered by a landslide while he was away:
how everyone was gone,
that he was the last one left,
felt how, now alone, he had the need to water his own trust.
I saw him weep in the cold sterile box of television.
I felt myself terribly saddened, wondering,
"Is there even a village left
that would bathe and swaddle any of us?
How could we forget?"

Tori Grant Welhouse

Tori Grant Welhouse just won the @Etchings Press Chapbook Contest; the prize includes publication of her chapbook book of "mother poems," *Vaginas Need Air*. She is a Green Bay, Wisconsin poet, misplaced from her Scottish heritage, whose poems have been recently published in *Adanna, Barstow & Grand* and *Stirring*. Her poems have also appeared in *Spectral Lines: Poems about Scientists* and *50/50: Poems and Translations by Womxn over 50*. She earned her MFA degree from Antioch International in London, England and has published two chapbooks, *Canned* (2014) and *Stashed: A Primer in Lunch Poems* (2019). Her delightful fantasy novel, *The Fergus*, won the Skyrocket Press Novel Writing award for 2019. She is one of the driving forces behind *Bramble*, a literary journal published by the Wisconsin Fellowship of Poets and is actively engaged in using her technology skills to promote poetry throughout that state.

Reviewing the book, *Canned*, Cathryn Cofell, another well-known Wisconsin poet, found "a whiplash of words: tight-lipped but curvaceous, somber yet sarcastic, poised but occasionally pissy…" All that, and more, can be found in the body of Welhouse's work. When she takes on the Scottish legend of Dark Beira in her poem, "Queen of Winter," a wild spirit explodes:

She is the mother of all gods and goddesses in the north.

her terrible hair, white and frozen, breaks from her head

in icicles. She remembers when the world was young,

and land was water, and water was land.

She wears a shawl that floats on the sea,

gathered up in snow and sleet, her teeth

red-orange, halation of a treeless horizon.

Sometimes she captures what it means to be a woman and mother in Twenty-first century America. Then she turns a phrase, and she is walking a Scottish landscape of legend and mist and exploring where the idea of eternity must really have been created.

Queen of Winter

Scotland's hag fury of bitterest winter.

Dark Beira howls across the moors and glens,

hewing the sea in great sheets of ice.

She is old again, old and weary.

Her one eye squires the light of a paltry sun,

wintertide a long night of desolation.

She is the mother of all gods and goddesses in the north.

her terrible hair, white and frozen, breaks from her head

in icicles. She remembers when the world was young,

and land was water, and water was land.

She wears a shawl that floats on the sea,

gathered up in snow and sleet, her teeth

red-orange, halation of a treeless horizon.

She is old again, old and weary.

On the night of nights, she searches for the drifting,

magic waters. She drinks. A sleep like

seasons, changing of the guard. She is the blossoming,

limb-legged one, fairer than any story.

We are pink with story. We like her mountainous

    sons. We like her conjuring hammer.

But for her, each day is a time bomb. She is middle-aged

    by summer, decrepit by autumn equinox.

This aging in fast-forward is the worst.

But for the Grace of Instant Coffee

Sleep is a bus that stops in the next village
Lhanbryde or Elgin, or maybe Dufftown.

He dreads the work, underground and
wet to his knees, laying block for airfield hangars.

Harrier jump jets spindle the sky with their fleech,
flying wheedle days, my Scottish husband is awake

with the milk float's escalating hum, past our
terraced house and the next terraced house,

dawn of pebble-dashing gray and mauve
and eggshell, maybe soft-boiled, maybe not,

solving cryptic clues without his workboots,
cups of tea and smokes, three sugars at least.

He folds the crossword exactly lap-sized,
gazing into a garden that's not a garden —

paving stones and circling white terrier —
until what might be sun hits the stove flue

chimney pot, and I hear his chair excuse
the whistling kettle, his tread measure

stair. He brings me a cup of instant coffee,
granules dissolving in boiling water,

splash of new cream. This blessing of coffee
is how I begin each morning, bidden or not bidden,

warming the air of our day's beginning,
his calloused hand slowly turning the cup handle

as I sit up with my sleep eyes, reaching hands,
and it's morning. And it's morning.

Bra Burning

Mother dismantled my argument
    to go braless,

twisting her lips, distrusting the story.

Why would a woman burn
    a perfectly good brassiere?

And if a woman wanted to be Miss America

shouldn't it be within her power
    to try?

She wondered if I got my facts straight.

"You will thank me one day,"
    mother said,

standing at the stove in her nightgown,

sautéing Hawaiian meatballs
    for a pool party.

Disappointment like the stomach flu

thumbed the soft underside
    of my jaw,
cruising in the backseats of cars with my two

best friends in their halter tops
    of macramé

and fringe. The catapult of breasts

as we ran around the car in a
    Chinese fire drill,

another phrase with a story problem.

We didn't know exactly
    who we might like,

so kissed each boy goodnight.

I stood on tiptoe. Boys tilting their chins,
    fanning their eyelashes,

holding their breath to make their chests broader,

less excited by the night air and the extra
    layers

between my breasts and me.

When I got home
women were changing

    in my bedroom.

Mothers of my friends, auxiliary women,
    women like mother

who were not bra burners,

but would like to surprise their partners
    their children,

themselves with what might be possible

if only they were unencumbered by
    expectations,

skewed facts. A neighbor woman

toweled off, bending from the waist,
    her pendulous breasts

hanging gruesomely to the floor.

Mother could be right
    sometimes.

There was no arguing with gravity.

Endocrinologist

Mother hugs her purse,
what she does.
Mostly unassailable
in her pressed slacks and blouse, matching jacket,
she makes me wear a dress
for the appointment. She is always making me
wear dresses. My legs stick
to the leather chair,
a drab teen in the psychedelic 70s.
The office is different
than the examining room of our family doctor
with cherry bookshelves and books, a globe.
I think of the places I would rather be.
Mother thinks I'm fixable.
Perhaps I am.

The doctor breezes in
as doctors do.
I sit in a chair and don't bleed.
He considers me over the rims of his glasses,
eyes full of bark and fizz like root beer.
Squares of sunlight fall on a leather reading chair and hassock,
plaid blanket spilling to the floor.
The doctor clears his throat,
unseals a jar of butterscotch from his desk,
ring of dime store glass,
smell of burnt sugar.
Despite myself, I salivate.

The doctor tilts the jar towards me, eyebrows raised.
His tweedy jacket and trousers don't match.
I unwrap a candy, golden cellophane crinkling,
calculating how much farther I will jog later.
The doctor asks questions.
Mother answers. I don't interrupt.
I do stash pork chop in a napkin at the dining room table.
I can subsist on an apple a day.
I run for miles at dusk, up and down our hilly suburban streets,
eternal light of the catholic church shining at my back.

I read cookbooks for recipes I won't eat.
Clothes hang on me.
The doctor paces behind his desk.
Mother balms her lips.
I'm good at starvation.
I don't know what else to do.
A boyfriend says he's through.
I take it as a sign,
an undeserving kind.

Enough, says the doctor.
See this? He points to a print in a frame.
I'm a doctor of chemical messengers.
What you see here triggers response.
Cells are activated.
How does this make you feel?

I see a bridge
and lilypads.
Private space of a gardener.
I could be the gardener,
foreground almost too verdant for words.
Being a woman isn't easy.
All that lushness, ripening.

Did a woman paint that?
I ask the doctor, my voice weedy.
She could have, he says,
steepling his fingers,
convinced of the body's elegancies.
Mother looks at me,
sets her purse on the floor,

her eyes the same intensity as mine
like dark chocolate
like urgency.

Flaming Pajamas

Cotton is the perfect

provocation.
Flame is in love

    with natural fibers.
Unsure of itself at first, heat gasps
the gimmick, slow lick trick, aberrant

breeze bellowing below stairs, pairs.

I am the keeper

of many flames.
I have an allegiance

    to shine, flash, burn,
having been sputtered by each in turn.
Oh, my ignitable heart, quinqua-

genarian phneuma, womb loom.

I awake to the nap.

My pajamas are on fire.
Blaze trapped in a cage,

    a lean-to of sticks
of my own making, knotted and
gnarled, spare and magnified.
Stirring catches the whole thing.

A spark must flourish,

lured by fabric, pattern, chronology,
burnishing the years

like a cautery.
I remember my two ribs, brittle
by now. They tell me: less is more.

I am the juxtaposition,

arms, legs, torso,
weight of experience,

brain incendiary.
Perhaps, unbuttoned,
I can dream better.

Spoons

For a week we live in the rounded belly harbor
of a cabin in the woods on a lake with a dock
and a tree-lined horizon, sandcastles crumbling
overnight next to bright pink shovels and a wet
towel turban left behind in a hurry for marshmallows,
chocolate and maybe graham crackers, the right
amount of sweet especially if my nephew roasts
them; he will be on his way to college this time
next year; he burns them a bubbly golden brown
like caramel, like his hands and face from working
in the boatyard, except for his feet which are still
whiter than whipped sugar; his dad palms him a
beer which he drinks slowly, holding it by the neck
like a bugle; water slaps the hull of a boat; a
descending mooniness fills the open spaces,
fluttering the birds on the branches which tweet,
rustle and chirp in the night kitchen where my nieces
and I sit at the polished plank table playing spoons;
twin girls aged seven they kneel growing bones on two
southwest chairs angled close together; my mother,
ever present at the table, helps with the rules which
they understand with propped elbows, fanned cards:
the game begins. Their eager blue-grey eyes wait
for cards passed one by one in the four-cornered
suits: clubs, spades, diamonds, hearts; upside-down
smiles the quick study way they sneak spoons, leaving

me spectacularly spoonless; oh, auntie, the nieces
and nephew say, acknowledging our connection,
the smooth shine slipped under the arms.

Maryann Hurtt

In another life, Maryann Hurtt worked as a hospice nurse for thirty years. From her youngest years, though, she never grew tired of hearing the stories folks shared. Now living midway between the Elkhart Lake, Wisconsin (USA) library and the Ice Age Trail gives her the best of all possible worlds. She is perpetually fascinated by smelling, tasting, hearing, and seeing unfamiliar worlds. *River*, a chapbook celebrating resiliency in the face of dying, came out in 2016. Her poetry has been published in mostly regional online and print journals and also in several anthologies including *The Water Poems, Ariel, Cancer Poetry Project II, The Aging Poems*. Dealing with social and eco-justice issues is important to her, and she recently completed a manuscript *Once Upon a Tar Creek: Mining for Voices* dealing with a place in Oklahoma where the water is orange.

Hurtt tends to write nature poems, but some of her strongest work comes when she talks about aging, death, the environment, and how war affects individuals. In "Forty Years After the War" she writes that

you work the graveyard shift
walk down long hallways
empty bed pans
turn old bodies side to side
soothe nightmares
but when the night is too quiet
the dark gives you time
to remember sirens
smoke and fire
bodies

eventually discovering that even though the horrors still exist in your mind, years later … "you and your family walk home/one more day."

There is a gentle nature to most of what Hurtt writes about, although there can sometimes be a hook barbed in the words that slices away from what you originally thought the poem was about.

Mother Shade, Mother Roots

when I was wise enough
to know
the importance
of walking with old women
my grandmother took me
to Columbia Villa
her old neighborhood
where a cottonwood stood dazzling and huge
but once had been a tiny slip of a tree
dug from along the Umpqua
on a picnic day where she reveled
in her status
as matriarch to a bunch
of hollering, wading, skipping stones kin
years later we stare at her tree
a kind of mother protector
the way old women
at least this old woman knew
this is what we are all
supposed to be

Doing Tai Chi, Becoming Mag Pie

on this rocky overlook
I *repulse monkey*
wave hands like clouds
even *bend bow and shoot tiger*
while three miles down
Wallowa Lake
stares straight up
I breathe in, I breathe out
my feet sink deep
granite rock grounds me
but soon I will be Mag Pie
hovering over a world
in absolute need
of laughter and levity

Forty Years After the War

you work the graveyard shift
walk down long hallways
empty bed pans
turn old bodies side to side
soothe nightmares
but when the night is too quiet
the dark gives you time
to remember sirens
smoke and fire
bodies
and the funny way a person remembers
horror not shared
in day-light
and how the whistles blew
your brother's broken leg dragging
the family slowly
to the shelter that would take no more
and how hope is lost
but still you run
till at last
squeezed into a faraway shelter
you listen as bombs wail destruction
and wait and wait
for the all-clear siren
you climb up the stairs
and pass the shelter
that did not take you
and witness its direct hit
while you and your family walk home
one more day

The Geometry of Love

you step off the plane
stand on what you think
is solid ground
just as your mother

defies gravity
and leaves behind
bones and blood and flesh
you start to understand
how at some point
we intersect
at amazing angles
continue on journeys
we don't quite understand
but have that measure
where we come and go
a touching point
that will always be even
when we slip
into places
strange to our senses
space and time
be damned

On a Crazy Fool Moon Night

a shiny-skinned possum
almost slips into the woods
undetected
when with one enormous
whoosh of wings
he is one last screech supper
the moon stares down
understands demise
for one
means full meal for the other
her lunar light
a kind of blessing
as both will fly in & out
this crazy fool moon night

Michael Kriesel

Winner of *The North American Review's* Hearst Prize and numerous other awards, Michael Kriesel's first full-length collection, *Zen Amen: abecedarians*, appeared in 2019 from Pebblebrook Press. A former President, and currently the Executive Vice President, of the Wisconsin Fellowship of Poets, his work appears in the 2017 anthology *New Poetry from the Midwest*. Kriesel was the poetry editor of *Rosebud Magazine* from 2017 to 2019 and a Guest Editor for *Bramble*. His poems and reviews have appeared in *Alaska Quarterly, Antioch Review, Library Journal, Rattle, The Progressive, Small Press Review*, and *Wisconsin People & Ideas*. His papers are housed in the Milwaukee Public Library's Wisconsin Poetry Collection. Kriesel served as a newspaper and TV journalist in the Navy from 1980 to 1990. He collects comic books, carnival glass, and original comic art.

Kriesel's work can have a strong vein of mysticism or contain his sense of everyday life, or become, in a heartbeat, as complex as one of his *abecededarians*, a verse form that is as difficult to compose as those used by the ancient Celtic poets. In a poem like "Grape Jam" there is a surreal quality as he and his grandmother make homemade jam:

That morning in September we made jam.
My job was keeping track of what was done
and what was next, while popping
wild dark grapes from their slippery skins,
then adding sugar and Sure-Jell
and cooking them so many minutes until
we poured their sticky darkness into jars
sitting on a scarred breadboard.

Each batch went to the living room to cool
on a warped card table by the TV
where a pair of planes in New York City
kept repeating the same scene
of bodies falling endlessly,
the way we do in dreams.

Every time she heard another lid's metallic pop,
grandma thought the Japanese were bombing us,
her brother's death in World War Two

still somewhere in the future,
Normandy a funny word nobody
in Milwaukee had ever heard.

Pouring the last batch of jam,
I tried to explain this was different.
"The dead are just as dead,
no matter what the TV says!" she snaps,
turning off the TV set like God
commanding darkness by remote,
knocking a jar off the table by accident,
both of us just sitting there a moment
watching darkness seep across the old linoleum.

In a poem like "Zen Amen," from his powerful collection of the
same name, the probing that is built through juxtaposition in "Grape
Jam" becomes a full-fledged spiritual search for identity, mirroring the
rigidity of the *abecededarians*, an ancient poetic form where, at the begin-
ning of each line, the first letter of the alphabet is followed by the
subsequent letter, with the sense of how time, the occult, and metaphys-
ics all interact with the physical universe and Kriesel's sense of himself.
Sometimes demanding and complex, Kriesel's poetry is always worth
reading.

The Washer's Bone Whiteness
Laid Bare

Kitchen necromancer, mom unburies
the washer each week from its shallow grave
of crochet magazines, Wonder Bread bags
of phone bills, coupons clipped and saved towards
some unexpired future dawn where Point Beer
doesn't trump groceries. She even saved

the washer box. More than once Maytag saves
me from boredom — cramped beige cave where buried
treasure hid, the way I did from dad's beer
rages. Make-believe vampire's cardboard grave
in the basement, stamped *Montgomery Ward,*
half hidden by newspaper towers, bags

of squirrel tails, severed ends salted. Bags
squirreled away like paper acorns, saved
for emergency beer money. *Howard's
Trout Lures* paid a dime a tail. Dad buried
the silver bodies in the woods, their graves
a quick kick of neon leaves. Later, beer

became my friend in the Navy. Barely
eighteen I'd cruise the back roads, no baggie
of dope. Just a bottle. Amber gravel.
While I'm in boot camp mom files for divorce.
Back home on leave we make wild raspberry
vodka, laugh at berries tumbling toward

nothing. I grip my grimoire and draw wards
to keep my father banished, start to bare
myself to me...young gay Wiccan buried
in a sailor suit. Mom starts burning bags
of romance books in an oil drum. Fire's salve
warms our faces. Smoke fills the sky's wide grave.

I lob a hair-spray hand grenade. Engraved
in dusk: its flash, the drum's red sun. Forward
thirty years: I own the house, father solved
by death. Mom lives in town, her barricade
of fear torn down, all the rooms of garbage
burned, the drum burned through, the ashes buried.

I dig a grave and pray and sip Point Beer
while light falls. Toward dark, I empty bags
of tails — gray tangle I saved to bury.

Aleister Crowley Lipogram

After Mark Zimmermann

I call a crow to steal its caw.
Soar air's aisles.
Eat scat.

A sorcerer's career is tears.
I salt a sea. Sow stars
across water's eye.

As Osiris, I see stars as tears.
As Isis, I see tears as stars.
As Crowley, I say we are stars.

As Eros, I call all.
Swallow Oscar. Wallow.
Lo, I attract Lolitas.

I start a Crowley sect:
writer, actor, satyr,
artist, liar, wastrel.

I retire to a twilit cell.
Create a tarot set.
Test astral laws.

Cast crystals at a cow.
I clear a way.
Stray.

> *Aleister Crowley Lipogram* is a lipogram, a form of writing that ex-
> cludes one or more letters of the alphabet. Wisconsin poet Mark
> Zimmermann has further refined the form by developing 1st person
> narratives using only the letters contained in a literary or historical
> character's name. My poem is an example of his form.

As Crickets Chip Away the Light

I quit the news, turning my back on the world
except for the weather robot on the radio:

chrome manikin sitting all day, all night
at a gray metal desk in a white broadcast booth

reading the page of our future over and over
into an old microphone big as a silver cucumber.

His monotone of highs and lows soothes me.
He's always there doing his job, not beating his

platinum wife or confessing some sordid affair
with an orange Cuisinart to the priest

who listened to our hearts for fifty years.
People don't want to grow up he confessed,

when asked what he learned in that dim cubicle.
I lotus too long on the floor and my foot falls asleep.

A frost advisory follows me into the kitchen.
I hop on one leg. This could have been heaven,

except for humans over-farming Eden's fertile plains.
There's always some Solomon cutting down Lebanon's cedars,

building a house for a God who moves on.
It's getting dark. I snag a beer and stumble out.

Crickets chip away the light, drowning out
the droning voice in the house behind me.

Squatting on the steps, I watch a line
of fireflies stream the interstate,

remembering a firefight a friend confessed,
a Navy buddy. We were drinking Mad Dog 20/20

when he told me how the tracers in
the river's mirror were an eerie beauty.

I press the sweaty can against my neck
and stare at a cattail's frozen explosion.

We're more than just a tribe of monkeys
writing angry haiku. It matters, what we do.

Secret Women

Anchors on chiefs' and officers' hats blaze
bronze, gold. Fear holds us, though technically
seamen are Navy property. But sex?
Dismissed. Inspection done. Red stripes. White crow.
Each left sleeve flies one. Our navy blue wave
falls apart. First night in Honolulu.
Girls love us. Gays too. I'm nineteen. My white
hat gleams like a seagull under streetlights.
I kiss another sailor. Don't bother
justifying it. Part of its mystique.
Khaki conspiracy of fear. A lip
lock in a bar. It's payday. Tabasco
moon, where witches send secrets. Wisconsin:
no one recognizes me when I'm home
on leave. Rednecks tell faggot jokes. I smile.
"Purple Kool-Aid sea," I say. They nod. Drink.
Quietly I work. No UCMJ
ready to jail or discharge me. Nights I
summon secrets from the moon. Bits of ash.
Tiny rain of flakes from mirrors. Once beg-
un, each secret summons another. Self
viewed in pieces. A broken vase. All me:
Witch. Sailor. Queer. My poetry unread
except by a few poets. Mosaic.
Y and X chromosomes balanced. Blowjob.
Zipper. Moon always broken on the sea.

Hidden Snow

Staring at the picture window's winter
yard, I focus hard and try to freeze time
from under the couch. Halt each flake of snow.
I'm six and watching *Twilight Zone* alone.
A silver flying saucer delivers
cancer and I know sooner or later

it'll find me. Now forty years later

it's late November. Another winter.
My uncle Dale and me, delivering
firewood. When we're done, there's still enough time
to cut red oak. The two of us alone,
his tumor in remission. There's no snow

yet, so our hands stay dry. Most years there's snow
before Thanksgiving. Each day it gets late
a minute earlier. Back home, alone
with my thoughts and a bottle of winter
bock beer, dad's old paperbacks kill some time.
"Swinging his broadsword, Conan delivered

a killing blow." Cancer of the liver
killed my stepdad. "Like twin piss holes in snow,
the wizard's eyes flayed his soul." The last time
we brought him home the clouds were bone. Later
I walked to Dairy Queen. It was winter
then, too. Two years ago. I drink alone,

thoughts looping down a logging road. "A lone
figure trudged the tundra where nothing lived."
Cancer just keeps coming back, like winter.
"Rolling downhill he grappled with the snow
ape — sheathing his knife in its guts." It's late.
I unsheathe my chainsaw, sharpen its tines

and brood on Conan's grim God, Crom. One time
he helps, grants strength at birth. My stepdad's one
gift. The scabbard's orange, plastic. It's late.
I sheathe my blade and rise; deliveries
tomorrow. I see where this all goes. Snow;
no snow. Banal repetition. Winter.

Trees. Time. Lives. The way my stoic liver
works. I drink alone, waiting for the snow
and a later season, beyond winter.

Zen Amen

Zen. Zero. Zilch awaits all afterlives.
Yet somehow we can't imagine nothing.
X marks the spot. X must equal something.
Whether math or death, nothing must be named.
Vending machine? Why not? Let X be death's
ultramundane, unknowable chrome-legged
toy dispenser. Souls sucked in, toy coffins
spit out — unless that soul is on a string.
Remember Lazarus, recalled by Christ.
Qabalistic texts agree how he was
pulled back from death like a coin on a string.
Oh, Jesus knew the secret would be safe —
no one who ever comes back recalls much,
mostly since there's nothing to remember.
Laugh if you want. It's good for the soul — though
killed, hope resurrects like dandelions.
Jesus knew all this. Still, he was right. We're
immortal, since mind can't survive its end.
How do I know all this? Easy. I died.
God wasn't there and neither was I that
first time in Madison, Wisconsin one
evening as I was leaning against a
dull red brick wall, chanting. And then I was
chanting, leaning against a red brick wall.
But there was a gap, and in my hand was
a toy coffin. Can I get an Amen?

Forgiving the Grass

Captaining a mower on a soccer field's green sea,
I leave a twelve-foot swath of sculpted sward behind me,

like writing my name in ammonia,
signing a fresh sheet of snow as a boy.

Same as God's signature under a clover in Eden's least corner,
small as a rabbit's pink bead of an eye.

The scoreboard blank above me as a teacher's summer calendar.
How I spent my summer: going blind while circling

a baseball field three times a week, harvesting myself.
Underground sprinklers rise each night to resurrect the grass.

One eye already blurry, I become my soul's meat-puppet.
Cut-rate harvest king. One-eyed kings are wild in cards.

I won the eyeball lottery. The VA gave me eye drops
and a magnet with a toll-free number on it.

Floaters swarm like no-see-ums against blue emptiness.
I hear the buzz of atoms big as bees behind the sky's wallpaper.

At least glaucoma's treatable, although what light I've lost is gone
and over time my eyes will fall from blue to loam brown,

a side effect, along with longer, thicker lashes.
I go back to writing poems and eating ice cream cones,

living in the land of *May Cause Drowsiness.*
Beats shopping for a bottle and a gun.

I could live with one eye. Just no eye patch.
Like Jerry Seinfeld, I don't want to be a pirate.

Odin sacrificed an eye for wisdom, swapping sight for vision.
Maybe the wisdom's in sacrifice. Maybe I'll get ravens, like Odin.

Instead of thought and memory, Hugin and Munin,
I'll name mine Heckle and Jeckle, past and future

perching on my shoulders while I mow a JV softball field.
Toward the end of my grandfather's life I came over

Saturdays to mow. He had a pair of John Deere riders,
both of us working our way from the road to the barn

while the silo's shadow fell across the lawn.
Later, we'd have a few beers in the kitchen.

I'd listen to him reinvent his life: *I could've been an auctioneer…*
but the cows were always there, needing to be milked.

Now it's my turn to remember he made nineteen cents an hour
canning string beans in a factory in Tigerton, Wisconsin.

Like driving a tractor, I loop at the end of each row.
A crow hauls ass. Craning my neck to follow its path

my blind spot gets in the way, and for a few seconds
that section of sky is bleached. I rub my eyes and see

my soul's albino crow, and for a while attain salvation.

Early in the Plague
(1985)

We call the antennas dinosaur cages.
Shaped like circus tents, they broadcast messages
to submarines throughout the southern hemisphere.
They're the reason we're all here.
The reason stateside beer is six months old
by the time the barge arrives from San Diego.
Most of the brands add formaldehyde
as a preservative. Every can holds a headache
waiting to bloom, so we stick with *Emu Lager.*
A shit-colored ostrich squats on the label.
No fence surrounds our base,
so real ones stroll freely, ignoring us.
Though once I got too close —
whipping its neck, it hissed like a goose.
The cable station plays tapes of old shows.
I'm the anchorman, broadcasting news
from a sea of red sand that may as well be Mars.
Everywhere you go, blowflies are
trying to crawl in your nose, mouth, and ears.
It rains a couple times a year:
pennies plopping in the dust, blood red.
Heat rides us from bed to bed.
That absolute blue staring down every day
makes it less real, when half a world away
people back home start dying of AIDS.
I remember two weeks leave in Thailand.

A sympathetic doctor discreetly
draws my blood at the dispensary.
I read the latest death toll every night
to sailors in the desert, live at five.
Spend two weeks sweating sand until
my test results come back from Pearl Harbor.

The End

The man who is writing
the end of the world
began like this: he sat down
in a chair beside a window,
closed his eyes and waited
for the steam to finish rising
from a cup of coffee —
pen and paper resting on
the windowsill, darkness
spreading from behind some
trees outside the window.
The trees are aquamarine.
What kind of trees they
are is unimportant.
What's important is the way
it's already begun: how
every night behind his eyes
a few less stars come out.

Feeding My Heart to the Wind

Emptying myself for winter
in a field of stubble
I'm a wind chime
made of bones

ribcage just a cave for wind
heart gone wherever
autumn went
and hope

that dandelion of the soul
a river in the air
that flows from me
like seeds

Sharon Auberle

Sharon Auberle is a poet and photographer who lives in Door County, Wisconsin, although she spent a considerable portion of her life in the southwest United States. She is author of six poetry collections, and her work has appeared in numerous publications and on-line magazines, as well as a variety of anthologies. Her latest book is a "poetry/sketch" collaboration with poet and artist Jeanie Tomasko, titled *Dovetail,* which won the Wisconsin Fellowship of Poets Annual Chapbook Prize. In April 2017 Auberle was appointed Poet Laureate of Door County, a two-year post through April of 2019. She has been nominated for several Pushcart Prizes. Her years of living in the spare landscapes of the southwest, and now surrounded by Northern woods and waters, along with her interests in Zen, music, and photography, provide, as she says, "endless inspiration."

There is both a cleanness and pastoral quality to much of Auberle's work. She is obviously concerned about the craft of poetry and is skilled at bringing each poem to a conclusion that contains both her sense of beauty and whatever emotion she is feeling at the moment. The Zen in her poetry, the enlightenment that comes out of meditation, is always searching for a moment that gives meaning to both her life and the lives of the people, woods, and creatures she is writing about.

Auberle also has a sense of significance that imbues her best language with an unforgettable quality that sticks in the mind long after the publication in which the poem appeared is put back on the bookshelf. In some ways, like the American poet James Wright, she has condensed her work into a series of intense perceptions that conclude with a sense of enlightenment.

In her poem, "Two Horses," she says,

> It's enough that there was a sunset
> in New Mexico one night,
> and a woman standing by a river,
> watching two horses, caught, as always,
> between shadow and light.

This passage sums up, in an elegant way, what a good portion of her work achieves, both its beauty as well as her sense of significance.

Angel Fire

the mystery of cornstalks
murmuring among themselves

a brown-skinned man
in orange serape
walking between them

the slump of his shoulders
tugging at my heart...

from any of these
a poem might grow

but today
there is only the man
light streaming down on him

he, who *could* be an angel
for all might be holier
than we know

his serape, fiery
in morning sun
the wind lifting it

like wings

Six Degrees of Separation

Only six people, it is said,
separate any person from another
anywhere on this earth.
I want to believe this.
I want to believe,
with just six connections
I could know an Eskimo,
an African tribesman,
a mother in Iraq.

I want to believe it would take
only six people to reconnect
with a gypsy I once saw —
the woman in cold rain
on the steps of the Duomo
in Florence, Italy.
I would find her again,
her feet knobby and bare,
her black hair tangled in dusty braids.
Begging, she would whisper again
for my bambino, please,
for my bambino

and this time I would take
her chapped brown hand,
place lira in it,
close her fingers around the bills.
This time I would get it right,
not turn aside
as her sleeve brushed my coat.
This time my shame
would not outweigh hers.

Praise for Dark Things

You run like a herd of luminous deer and I am dark, I am
forest.
> ~ *Rainer Maria Rilke*

on this bright morning
when light streams
into every old   cold corner
when sun warms each shadow
burrowing

whether we ask it or not
into our own darkness
we are   for a moment
assured
        that we will be saved

for a brief time we have faith
that the rolling wind
won't blow us away
and those sparks
that sometimes shoot
from our hands

   will not set us on fire

on a morning like this
we know that the crow
knows in spite of her blackness

   that she will resurrect

for it is fine to be
a dark thing   as well as a light

and even though
we are just passing through
we get to have all of this

    and love too

For Laila

In Memoriam: Laila Anwar Ghandour

Laila will never grow old enough
to have a doll or know the meaning
of the word *truce*

   or *peace*

or say as her first word *Mama.*
No one will see her
clap small hands in delight
at the dove singing
outside her window

or watch her dancing

beneath ancient olive trees.
There will be no one to adore
the laughter in her eyes
as they make happy love.

Made of lace and linen
her first fancy dress
will be a shroud,

but I hope there will be angels
and an olive tree
to watch over her grave ...

Forgotten

A music composed of what you have forgotten.
~ Jack Gilbert

Wouldn't you like to remember
the last time you made a snow angel
and don't you wish you knew
where that orange tree was
you sat under once
and how happy you were then?

Years have passed since I began
My Book of Important Things...

in it I can read
how one day I fed my love
cherries and wine and we laughed
as if summer would never end
and I skip the part where it does.

Once I wrote in it
the words *caprice*
solace and *rosary*
but not *death*
I crossed out *death*...

Still, I believe, every night

angels come down to us,
their arms full of forgotten songs
so that in the morning
we wake and ask ourselves

O what was all that sweet music?

Two Horses

after James Wright

There was a roan racing beside the river
that night, coat aflame in red light,
and another standing — black-clad and shy,
a shadow under cottonwoods.

I remember how they watched me pull over
and step out of the car, with hope in their eyes
that my pockets weren't empty
and how they waited, patiently,
as I stood there at the fence, dreaming
of riding one of them, being that small girl again,
heart open and unafraid,
every part of her body engaged
as only children and animals can be.

We write to know what we're thinking
someone once said, but I don't know why
this poem came to me now.
Sometimes there are things I'd rather not know.
It's enough that there was a sunset
in New Mexico one night,
and a woman standing by a river,
watching two horses, caught, as always,
between shadow and light.

Waiting for Manuela

Bent with harvest to the ground,
trees stand waiting for Manuela,
who walks the paths between them,
her mama's worn coat sky-blue
in the gray sunrise.

An apple-sack weights her neck,
and she stops to tuck dark strands
of hair into a yellow scarf.
The color of caramel, her skin
is warm as her southern home,
but in this place she feels only cold
and her bright colors can't hold
enough remembered sky.

Thin arms reaching upward,
Manuela climbs a ladder —
plucks apples, makes prayers,
and the unburdened trees
stand taller as she passes,
rain now shining the apples,
sewing the sky-blue coat
to her trembling back.

Betty Hayes Albright

Betty Hayes Albright has lived her entire life in the Pacific Northwest, where she is inspired daily by the beauty of trees, mountains, rivers, and the sea. She began writing poetry at age ten and is truly thankful for those who have mentored her writing over the years. Albright has published two books: a small chapbook, *Living Color* (1976) and *Skipping Stones* (Four Windows Press, 2018). Her blog, "Seasonings," at https://raindancepoetry.wordpress.com, has attracted a large worldwide readership for years.

Albright's poetry is invariably romantic, imbued with the scent of the Pacific Ocean off the coast of Washington state. Often it also, especially in the large collection of Mayberrie poems, which represents the strongest work she has produced, presents a universe filled with a mysticism that is just slightly blurred, both reflecting the world she lives in and the world of her imagination. A self-identified hippie from the sixties, she is especially concerned with Gaia as a living entity, echoing the scientific ideas of James Lovelock, but translating them into poetic, rather than scientific, expression.

In addition to mysticism her poems sometimes also bloom into a sense of joy that seems to be barely contained. This, of course, is the most difficult of accomplishments that grace any form of writing. Her poem, "Midsummer," represents this element in her work when it says,

Oh glorious!
I must sometimes turn away —

no wonder that the fly
needs a thousand eyes.

Joy is always a difficult emotion to portray in words, but Albright has a habit of making the reader feel good about the universe.

Journey

Crystal goblets ring
beneath my soapy finger
like the Tibetan singing bowls
and the ribbon
of the flute.

I follow to the Bodhi tree,
to the circles of Dante,
to Mary Magdalene
and her Lover,
to a footprint in the desert,

and there I find
the chalice of Socrates,
Blake's grain of sand,
a whirling Dervish,
the hem of a robe.

It is all present —
even Gaia herself
is not tethered.

Master, Master,
there are no words
on this journey,
no words at all —
hush, my Beloved,
hush.

Points of Light

Poetry is the well-worn sleeve
where she displays her heart.
Somebody said
the gods wear paisley, while
angels dip their toes
in velvet pleats,

but she likes best
a weave of silk
with lace crochet
around the edge.

Look closely
at the points of light
between the threads —
you'll see his face
and maybe even read his name
embroidered coyly
near her wrist.

Day after day
she sews anew
the fragile seam
that joins two dreams,
all neatly hemmed
and pressed —
or so it seems.

Fog

It softens the edges
of trees and crows,
blunts our point of view.
We can turn a corner
in the fog
and never know.

Do you see the old man
in the mist?
He is a Shaman,
shifting our perspective
with his white breath.

He knows that fog
is a giant, downy feather
which blesses our fever,
then suspends us

between all that ever was
and all that ever can be
in the alpha-omega soup
of possibility.

Midsummer

It's almost too much —
the bee in the center of the rose,

the hummer mating
with the hot pink flute of August,

puffs of clover in the honey
tied up in a bow,

scent of marigold
and the lion's yellow dandi.

Oh glorious!
I must sometimes turn away —

no wonder that the fly
needs a thousand eyes.

Caprice

Capricious one,
I often wonder
if, in truth,
our hearts grow fonder
longing for
the agate blue
of sky-reflecting
drops of dew,

of simple pleasures
on the skin

and tender truths
to wrap us in
fine threads of wisdom
knit with choices
weaving through
those distant voices,

firing up
our tender hopes
while mating in
kaleidoscopes.
Then shall we
consummate the sun?
I wonder,
oh capricious one.

To the Sea

And so I have gone down
to the salty, briny air
where the surf tumbles the sand
and the wind combs through my hair,

where the seagulls dip and squabble
and the pocket pools grow warm
and the starfish snuggle rocks
as the tide begins to turn,

where the sun lights through each wave
as it surrenders to the sea
and the sky steams into purple
and the night spits stars to me.

Anna Mark

Anna Mark lives in Ontario, Canada with her husband and two daughters. Intensely contemplative, her long walks in the Ontario landscape are where images are found and etched into a startling permanence. In the landscape, observation lends itself to contemplation, a deepening of both perception and meaning. Through editing, rehearsing, and searching, the tactile and metaphorical fuse to become the emotional eco-system of Mark's world.

In a poem like "First Death," meaning and emotional content tie in closely with the experience of remembrance, a child's reflection "on the tinted window."

I will never forget the day he died and I congealed,

became a still and hard world opposing an immensity,
an other-world, ceaseless and free of me — some kind of end.

The short poem, "A Circle of Red Chairs in Winter," has the concreteness of a poem by William Carlos Williams as the image of red chairs undergoes metamorphosis into the living green of earth, making time jump out of the poem.

As with other poets who achieve the intensity Mark exhibits, readers cannot always expect to simply read one of her poems once and "get" the richness that is actually there. Sometimes the value found in a poem is inherent in imagery that has private, as well as more universal, meaning. H.D., the great imagist poet, is a perfect example of this kind of poetry. Some of Ezra Pound's early work also reflects this particular poetic sensibility. More often than not, when reading Mark, the reader has to be aware that there is more than what is obvious on the first reading.

Mark also has a private aspect to her work reminiscent of Emily Dickinson's pursuit of poetry in her Amherst, Massachusetts family home. Mark's poems, with their particular landscape and unique perspective, often achieve universality.

First Death

The Death of a Soldier

When the wind stops and, over the heavens,
The clouds go, nevertheless,
In their direction.

Wallace Stevens

What you say of the clouds, what you saw over the heavens,
I saw on my way to remembering, in the ceaseless movement

of people in crowds, on the sidewalk firmament beyond the
autumn wind, when I and the crowd wrenched apart.

I faced his death and wished it complete, but the people outside
paid no notice, rushing by in streaks of light, marring the fluid

reflection of my childhood on the tinted window.
I expected the world to stop — with me — and when it didn't,

wondered, *Why not?* and thought it should, but didn't speak it.
I will never forget the day he died and I congealed,

became a still and hard world opposing an immensity,
an other-world, ceaseless and free of me — some kind of end.

Seeing Starkly

Winter's maple reaches long
to bare in her hand a nest,
a loose spiral of twigs, grass and mud,
coated with ice and snow,
her offering to me of a nucleus;

I believe the robin will return and gather her wings
within the verdant tines of a shimmering crown,
as I will never tire of finding something blue, whole or broken,

of newly hatched robins and the miracle
of their ability to lift their monstrous heads;

and today I've written in my notebook
about the mountains and oceans I may never see,
that maples, the old looming ones, are the closest I get to mountains,
as Huron's storm is the closest I get to oceans,
that both the tree-as-mountain and lake-as-ocean are truly wondrous,
considering a person is the closest, and see how close,
I dare get to a star.

The Timbre of Frost

I placed the kettle on the stove and heard
the steam's rising speed and pitch,

I felt the agitation of music inside a chamber
and enjoyed knowing, through sounds,

the moment to lift the stainless vessel
off the red spiral — just before the scream.

Later, I saw frost bloom across the window,
a spontaneous crystalline fire,

the fractals' perfect chaotic symmetry,
a burst of delicate flame-like ferns

— and traced their piercing cry.

This Cruel Winter

Can we imagine that a cruel winter, like this one,
melts softly into spring, a new warmth in the air?

Yes, but we can also see that spring gnaws winter down,
warmth rises from inside the earth,
bites into the layers of snow and ice

and dismantles it from within — winter collapses.

Surely, we know the difference.

I cannot walk through a winter field
without knowing the closeness of spring,
without sensing the fallibility within me, my need
for something like remorse,

for we become so hard, so mean-like,
so unflinching in our course.

A Circle of Red Chairs in Winter

A semicircle of red chairs tills the mind,
gathers the crescent moon with the cat's eye.

Though not a full circle, nor an essential red,
their broad backs fan into high summer!

Turned against the street, like silent pontificates
bent on epiphany, each their own lantern

illuminating the mystery, the half-circle
completes itself, vital and red, and so, also,

green all year 'round.

Ötzi's Cloak

Iceman, I see you facing the earth, found
with your back to the sky,
skin shriveled over the symmetry of your exposed ribs,
your protruding bones unnaturally stiff,
no joints comfortably bent and childlike,
no hands placed palm to palm.

Over the Alps a soaring eagle
circles the time before you were discovered
when only the elements swirled around your body

and laid you indifferently for thousands of years,
held you as they hold themselves,
saw you as they see themselves;

eyeing the parts of you as they vanish,
the moment your grass cloak turned to dust
in the winds of a new warmth, under a new sun,
when nothing tried to hold on,
when nothing tried to meddle
with that critical change of state.

Nothing more disappears into thin air,
yet, I have become your living expression,
your mirror, as fragile and as brittle
as your preserved remains and just as pale,
our spirits captured, you frozen in my time
with me lost in yours;

the weaves of your cloak are a woman's refuge,
her hands knot and plait the strands
in the graceful way she braids her hair,
her light weight and warmth embrace you,
she is the softness beneath and around you
for the everlasting night.

Memories of Fire

A hearth has the bony structure
of a woman's pelvis,
her pubic darkness — there,

and the framed pictures that lean on the mantel,
open to the room with laughter and tears,

bare the same womanly
shadow.

Colourful Child

for my daughters, Arden and Ravenna

I ran from you to the ravine,
to shed appearances on your behalf,
for your vernal understanding and ability to speak
outside of the moulds that guide you:

humanity's storehouse of axioms and old proverbs
you try on for size and consume like sugar.

I will go hungry for you and starve for the words
that dissolve in your mouth!

And the fountain, the cold spring that splits the rock
and flows to the river, will shower me
and wash away my clothes,

for I will always fail you.

Colourful child, you must release yourself
from the words you believe in.

Words, born from devastations
that are not your own — call you
to their dismantling clarity.

Angel in the Snow

She is our transference of heaven,
a stunning imitation of light,

with the moon and stars she fills,
gazes longingly at the sky and sings,

Freedom! implores, *Ignite! Ignite!*
and smothers the sparks with her wings.

Why such a mundane, carnal end
for one who dares touch the intangible,

express the inexpressible?
Serene, her angelic form, bound to earth

by our concave impressions, disappears
in the same mysterious way that a deer's

carcass isn't seen decomposing,
yet walking through the wood we know

green is the vibrancy of her decay,
white the sheen of an angel's reflection.

Before I Knew the Dream

Before I knew it symbolically,
or what it meant to him,
I asked him to tea; before I knew
what it meant for a person
to be *un arbre*, I called it forth
and it claimed me, a rapturous air.
Before I knew what a flower was,
what a bridge, what a horse,
what an eagle, what a shadow,
or what it meant to love him, exactly,
it was just there, all pouring
out of me, naturally.
And now, I am learning to the depths
about things like tea and flowers,
windows and curtains, gods and angels;
I'll never forget the moon I swallowed
like an oyster in the sea, pearl
of many pearls, the night.
I can't decide which I prefer,
the glorious spring fountain that came first,
or this deep well I lower my urn into
and draw upwards through darkness,
but knowingly, cautiously. Before
I knew the dream I dreamed it aloud,

and then the *real* I knew pixelated
into a *real* I didn't recognize, couldn't make
sense of. But now I know the direction
of my steps before I walk, as though
projecting ghosts, the direction of a thought,
even why I loved him, why the ardor.
A wider awareness, perhaps, has come.
Are these meanings cold? Do they rain
like sharp hail? I am wiser, and my heart?
It still bears a question, or something like one,
I know it by how it feels — open, and still foolish,
vulnerable, like a child's glee.

James Janko

Originally from Illinois, but now a resident of Albuquerque, New Mexico, James Janko has won the Association of Writers and Writing Programs (AWP) Award for the Novel for *The Clubhouse Thief* published by New Issues Poetry & Prose (Western Michigan University). An earlier novel, *Buffalo Boy and Geronimo* (Northwestern University Press/ Curbstone), received wide critical acclaim and two awards: The Association of Asian American Studies Book Award and the Northern California Book Award.

Janko's short stories have appeared in *The Massachusetts Review*, *The Sun*, and numerous other magazines. He won the 2002 Illinois Arts Council Award for Fiction. His first published essay appeared in *The Massachusetts Review* in January of 2020.

He says that he is ever grateful for the Zuni Mountain Poets of which he was a member for several years when he and his wife lived in New Mexico not far from the El Malpais and El Morro National Monuments.

During the Viet Nam War Janko served as a medic in an infantry battalion commanded by Colonel George Armstrong Custer III.

Janko's poetry is often as gentle, spiritual, and kind as he is in person. In "Gravity" he writes

> but a man knows more of gravity than flight,
> the weight of blessings and blood,
> the comfort of stones in their nests in the earth,
> and the fields of light
> wider than fields of Illinois corn
> that may visit us, welcome us,
> wherever we rest or wander
> in the flesh of the world.

As a Buddhist with a Catholic upbringing, he expresses the strength of his faith again and again, reflecting "the weight of blessings and blood" that seems to be central to who he is deep inside. He recognizes that "Fumes rise from factories, power plants, and burning fields./Yet," he continues, "even our poison longs for something else." He is always finding magic in the universe:

You can be the sky above
a rock, a twig, a leaf,
a small thing that becomes
unknowable as you
bend down for a closer look.

and even though war and turmoil exists, and it is important to
acknowledge the challenges that confront human beings who often cre-
ate dilemmas within a magic universe, the human qualities he has so
carefully cultivated through his faith that bends toward gentleness are
always present if only, as his poetry says, we reach out and mold our-
selves into what we can become.

This is not poetry that arises out of the stories of brief experiences.
Rather, Janko is a poet who reaches toward the eternal, running counter-
point to much of contemporary poetry, but always producing work
worth soaking into yourself as you try to get through one day after an-
other.

Morning

A lighted field —
gold flower, yellow flower, sun.

The veins of her wrists, her hands —
the blue I long to kiss.

Gravity

As a boy
running through Illinois,
racing deer,
I longed to slip
beyond the boundaries of the skin,
to leap over the herd,
over cows in fields,
over Mr. Malecki's farm,
over clouds shaped like
Jenny Brate
(I was too shy to speak to her),
and I flew out of my shoes

every summer
of my life!

No boy ran faster through farms and fields,
but a man knows more of gravity than flight,
the weight of blessings and blood,
the comfort of stones in their nests in the earth,
and the fields of light
wider than fields of Illinois corn
that may visit us, welcome us,
wherever we rest or wander
in the flesh of the world.

The Sea

The waves rushed in
and we had to leap,
bounding up over
the sand and rock.
I turned and saw
her white dress
in the wind,
a long dress like a sail,
and the great sea
boiling high enough
to toss a whale,
and I will remember
till I die and maybe longer
the way she sprang,
wave-like and reckless,
too young for wounds,
while over her sail rose
a brood of dark-winged gulls
between the ocean and the rain.

She found a broken shell
and held it to her ear.
No sound, she said. Nothing.
We were twelve years old.
She listened to my heart.

Poet

You can be the sky above
a rock, a twig, a leaf,
a small thing that becomes
unknowable as you
bend down for a closer look.

You can be the sky over
a poem, a story, a psalm, a song,
a weaver with pencils and moons,
sunlight and stars, and a handful of
rocks that brighten and spark —
the lightning that reads the page.

You can be the sky
opening long, blue arms
to gather seeds and wind,
the sky that bows low
and digs in the red earth.
You can be the rain that plows the earth,
that opens the caves,
the shapes and sounds of words,
and you can be the ear, the mouth,
the language of the world,
if you are humble enough
to move out of the way and
invite the stones to speak.

After School

8th Grade

Jeremiah walks along a curb in bright sun, kicks up dried leaves and twigs, whistles *Somebody Up There Likes Me*, and glances from the world in front of his shoes to the world of the sky. High white clouds give a sense of the sky's breadth, and its breath, too, its warm wind on his face and curling up the cuffs of his shirt and tickling his wrists. He decides most things are made of spirals, wriggly things like wrists and clouds and shoelaces and leaves and breath, and best of all a girl walking his way, a black-haired, black-eyed, black girl swinging her graceful arms as her lovely shadow, her face, drift by him, catch the light of the sky, and disappear.

Look.

This tree trunk wriggles toward a long branch the way her legs wriggle toward her hips.

Go ahead. Try and stop beauty.

Go ahead.

Breathing Out

People stand in line to buy water.
Fumes rise from factories, power plants, and burning fields.
Yet even our poison longs for something else.
Even the smoke smudging our lungs
may one day arrive again,
dark and essential,
a rain cloud over the mesa,
a shadow on a field of corn.

Long-Distance Runners

Running at twilight,
running through the shadows of the mesa,
two girls are watched by juniper and piñon trees,
by the growing dark that shelter the deer, the elk,
the lion and her cub, and a thousand nests for birds.

The night has blessed us for eons.
And now the heavens, the first stars, the new moon,
watch over the mesa as the girls run outward in a spiral, run faster and
with little effort,
perhaps tracing on the earth
an ancient pathway through the autumn sky.

Ben Naga

A well-known denizen of the poetry blogosphere at https://bennaga.wordpress.com, Ben Naga has lived in England all his life, apart from brief periods in France, India, and Scotland. Music is his greatest love, with England's Lake District not far behind. He has privately published *Northern Limericks* and *September Shadormas* and is working on two other collections. His poems have been published in several online magazines.

His best poetry is often short, succinct, profound, or simply funny. His blog is full of short gems like

COMET ALERT

His mind and body were discovered
During her ongoing extensive search
For objects that might at some point
Disastrously impact with her planet

His longer poetry ranges from a Buddhist ethos to explorations into contemporary culture. Well-read in philosophy, the world's religions, anti-war literature, and even physics, he often requires more than a little study from his readers. In "Dues for the Muse," as an example, his references come fast and furiously. If readers do not have a background in Greek mythology they will have to look up a lot of references. But then he will turn around and write a perfectly direct villanelle. This is the poet who wrote "Gaia's Offspring," asking

Are we any more then than shadow?
Cast by some greater light, then adrift
Wriggling fingers of a greater hand
Scratching for some miserly purchase
From endless oceans of fine ground sand

If nothing else, Ben Naga is a delightful poet who always keeps readers on the edge of their seats, wondering what is coming next.

When I Am Old

When I am old, do you suppose
That hairs will grow out of my nose,
And, as I count the passing years
Will tufts of it sprout from my ears?

When arms and legs are thin and frail
And memory begins to fail,
Shall I recall those days gone by
When passing women sought my eye?

When face is wrinkled, fold on fold,
And summer heatwaves leave me cold,
And teeth are gone, and eyes are weak,
Shall I lose all desire to speak?

When I have lived my lifespan through
And found at last a perfect view,
Will others see there no more than
The mumblings of a mad old man?

When I am always far away,
Too deaf to hear a word you say,
Your feelings — will they be the same
When I keep asking you your name?

When mind's decayed, and flesh repels
And speech no longer casts its spells;
When I am old, then we shall see
Just what it was you loved in me.

Poem on His Birthday

This morning I reflected
That today I am the same age as you were
When I was as much younger than you
As you are now older than me

This just goes to show
The kind of thing that happens
When you start calibrating
What you should be celebrating

So what's to celebrate
What of worth then
Gathered from the years?

That it's not what you see
It's the way that you view it
It's not what you do
It's the why that you do it
It's not what you've lived
But the way you lived through it
And that's what really counts

That you should neither judge nor aggravate
The turmoil that surrounds you
And everything is already perfect
Whether you like it or not

Why rush around in pursuit of pleasure
When you could simply enjoy
The suffering you already have?

That there's more to the I
Than meets death
And even if you're dead important
You're not important dead

Of course I forget most of this stuff
For pretty much of the time
But I wanted to make my birthday
A day to remember

IYOUMEUS AMAREBEIS

I

In all the time of breaking fast together
only chance decided how the food was shared,
what became the eye looked into,
the hand the other held.
And so we are as one
and yet by chance divided.

How so near?
How so far?
Ah love,
for whom else should I eat?

II

In thoughts that turn to love and loving
(the eye looked into):

A sphere
whose circumference is nowhere,
whose centre is everywhere;
a panoply of nodes;
an exercise in isometric tensions
(the eye looked into).

The sleepy snake is opening
(the eye looked into)
and you will meet me again at last,
here where the four winds dwell

Alas: A Villanelle

Alas, I bring no stardust home tonight.
The sky is overcast and all is maya,
For I confess I see no hope in sight;

Where once each daybreak promised fresh delight
We only found that time had proved a liar.
Alas, I bring no stardust home tonight.

These poor neglected coals cast little light,
So place another log upon the fire,
For I confess I see no hope in sight.

The wind is chill and bitter; hold me tight
And stoke the fire till the flames climb higher.
Alas, I bring no stardust home tonight.

Let's not apportion blame or rue what might.
How can we but accept the trundling gyre?
For I confess I see no hope in sight.

In impasse let us yet remain polite;
Offer comfort, even as our dreams expire.
Alas, I bring no stardust home tonight,
For I confess I see no hope in sight.

Upon the Shoulders of Giants

Sweet juicy jazzy jackanapes
Crusading king of Fairy Hill
Immortal motley troubadour
Breezed into town with time to kill
To put the free back in free fall
Peal forth the vow in disavow
Ah, but I was so much Adler then
I'm Junger than that now

TV sophists spewed skewered truth
Cut Ethos, Pathos, Logos dead
No musketeering buccaneers
But lame tame talking heads instead
With propaganda for proper geese
He cackled at their sacred cow
Ah, but I was so much Adler then
I'm Junger than that now

Provincial ham let figments strut
While stuttering beneath his breath
"Wh-wherefore art thou Juliet?"
His sad performance died the death
Outrageous fortune took the blame
While it was she who took the bow
Ah, but I was so much Adler then
I'm Junger than that now

Soon leery learned the golden rule
In prison's schoolyard hide and seek
Found respite from the siren call
Played truantly eight days a week
With John and Paul, and Pete, and Bob
Unlatched the lightning bolt of Tao
Ah, but I was so much Adler then
I'm Junger than that now

Embraced the peaceful warrior's way
Through battlefields of poison dust
Explaining to the deaf and blind
"In heinous blasphemy you trust
Cool off your mumbo jumbo jets
'Thou shalt not kill' and that means thou"
Ah, but I was so much Adler then
I'm Junger than that now

With righteous anger, sanctioned style
Refusal to be compromised
By inchworms who would take a mile
Their dress sense, world view, he despised
"Stomp out the unacceptable!"
His motto and so solemn vow
Ah, but I was so much Adler then
I'm Junger than that now

Loose Change

Endoscopy opens to a hush, closes to applause
Dramatis personæ stride and snivel in between
While the playwright owns up as simply the you
In disguise and of course vice versa — All change!
Newton, Einstein, Erwin and his imaginary cat
A different sounding at each fresh embouchure

Bringing light, demolishing the old — All change!
Revolution on revolution yet nothing changes
Ancient foolishnesses replayed ad nauseam
Minotaurs and dinosaurs strut the halls of power
External, internal weapons of mass distraction

Eternal, essential the pulse the pulse the pulse
Distorted persists, breathes through every pore
Where would we be without our surroundings?
In a flash flood, a roar and a blaze of lightning
The walls of the citadel quiver and fall — All change!
As Alice tiptoes lightly through her looking glass

Boundless waters surround us as above so below
Rivers linger not and carry our bread away
A true love that will neither fade nor wither
Memories drift like leaves torn from a book
Even as the moving hand writes on — All change!

Evenings herald nights overburdened with
Dark eldritch dreams peopled by eerie voices
"Wake up at the back there! Pay attention!"
I look around and find myself looking around
"Ninety-eight, ninety-nine" — "All change!"
"At the third stroke …" "At the third stroke …"

Buy new improved, ditch the old — All change!
Rapine of the earth is not a spectator sport
Advertisements invade us twenty-five-seven
More and more of less is what and all we need
Emergency! Emergency! All hands on deck!

Gaia's Offspring

Are we any more then than shadow?
Cast by some greater light, then adrift
Wriggling fingers of a greater hand
Scratching for some miserly purchase
From endless oceans of fine ground sand
Or pen and ink with which to stake claim
In truth no Shelley nor even Smith
The core of us barely substantial
Yet strut our stuff and nonsense at will
As self-appointed lord and master

Wild histories strained through calendars
Fuzzy snapshots back before colour
Ghost spirits captured in black and white
Beckon ever further inward yet
Moments, centuries, millennia . . .
Taurus, Scorpio, Aquarius
Join hands with Leo — a circle dance
To comfort those who seek for shelter
From the icy blasts of Fenrir's howls

Parasites biting the hand that heals
Imagine that, a serpent with hands
Mythic conjurations down the years
Coded missives handed soul to soul
Like wormholes threading through the fabric
White with black within and black with white
Future yesterdays in present time
Before the confluence was broken

Who dreamt who dreamt before this head show?
Way back before the Word was spoken
Paradise captured in rhythmic rhyme
Across the darkness, "Let there be light"
Though not enough to read the rubric
Revealing the journey as the goal
Triumphs and failures, laughter and tears

Roaming eyes and hands mocked wedding bands
One for his nob and two for his heels
Reprobates disguised in monkish cowls
History's course runs helter-skelter
Manifestation a game of chance
Your turn to despair, Ozymandias

Borne on see-through wings, ephemera
Born to dance one graceful minuet
Knowing too well death comes before night
In denial beneath the pallor
Masking the stench with sweet lavenders

The blood rushes faster and faster
The time approaches to pay the bill
The evidence is circumstantial
Time to see what hides behind the myth

Mayhap just a game — no blame, no shame
A pageant being played out as planned
In some realm beyond thought of purpose

Fresh blooms revealed all across the land
A new day emerges as mists shift

Wildflowers nodding slowly in a meadow

Diane Denton

Novelist and artist DM Denton is a native and current resident of Western New York. She studied and, subsequently, lived in the United Kingdom for sixteen years. She has published three full-length historical novels. Two revolve around the 17th century composer Alessandro Stradella: *A House Near Luccoli* and its sequel *To A Strange Somewhere Fled*. The third, *Without the Veil Between, Anne Brontë: A Fine and Subtle Spirit*, offers an intimate portrait of the youngest of the 19th century's literary Brontë sisters. She has published several Kindle short stories and an illustrated poetry journal, *A Friendship with Flowers*. She is currently working on a novel about the Victorian poet, Christina Rossetti, sister of the painter, poet, and Pre-Raphaelite Brotherhood founder Dante Gabriel Rossetti.

Her poetry has echoes of the nineteenth century women writers she chronicles in her novels. She is modern in the sense that she writes free verse rather than using traditional meters or rhymes in forms, but she has a tendency to write about birds, flowers, stars, and, sometimes, aloneness, topics that Anne Brontë and her more famous sisters, Charlotte and Emily, often brought into their poetry.

The reader has to be a little careful, though. In "Lavenders," for instance, the footnote to the poem tells us that "In Medieval and Renaissance Europe servant women who washed in lavender water, placed lavender in linens or draped laundry on lavender bushes to dry became known as 'Lavenders'. The lowliest of these were sometimes reputed to be prostitutes." She is a close student of history, and often her poems refer back to the work of some of her favorite poets from the era where she has the most expertise. A poem about a flower or scent is not exactly what it seems when it is first read.

This poetry seldom contains a mystery or contemporary symbols. It is popular in the same way William Wordsworth was popular, because it is romantic and filled with life's wonders. It reminds us of a magical time in a much different era. Like the work of Betty Hayes Albright, this is a poetry that can make you feel good about the universe.

Troubadour

There was music on your breath
made softer
but not stilled by death;
the bright greeting of your eyes
lost, but for
reminiscing sighs;
the quick smile that found each one,
a star with
the warmth of the sun;
a playfulness in your hands
extending
songs from foreign lands.

You moved many through the fairs
and left them
mourning you in prayers;
those times past and present, too,
with all your
audience to woo;
mine a quiet memory
not to let
fade and thus bury —
when neither too sweetly soon
nor too late
you sang for the moon.

By A Thread

So small
hanging on a thread
of its own making,
hesitant
to go up or down,
caught in a
movement larger than
its life,
taken for a ride,

let down so gently
after all.
Flattens out then gets
up again,
delicate and brave
as it
decides its next move.
Tiniest spider
I've ever
seen, slowly sliding
through the cracks
where it's safe.

The Lavenders

A sprig on the wrist
a spell for a plague
is worth two
in the bush
where the Lavenders
lay their cares.

Such a fair flower
stolen like sinning
sweeter than
forgiveness
scented from heaven
lost on earth.

Found to be useful
for washing and cures
of body
and heart ache
lullabying sleep
and madness.

Such ladies at work
their laundry to air
for rumors
to ruin them
unless modesty
can save them.

All through the ages
a toiling to some
and leisure
for others
somehow a likeness
in essence.

For how they do grow
Well drain'd in full sun
or covered
in winter
with still enough breath
to live on.

Clusters of secrets
that beg to be kept
in sachets
and strewing
their hopes to the wind
and a way.

Note: In Medieval and Renaissance Europe servant women who washed
in lavender water, placed lavender in linens or draped laundry on laven-
der bushes to dry became known as 'Lavenders'. The lowliest of these
were sometimes reputed to be prostitutes.

Like a Nuthatch

What wouldn't you give
for that peanutty feast —
something of your shyness
at the very least?

For you have valor,
obvious in your stance,
blue-gray caped crusader
eyes fixed in a glance.

Long-billed and short-tailed,
you observe from your perch,
impatient for my hand
to shorten your search.

While head over 'heels'
you see nothing absurd
in making a descent
to reach what's preferred.

And then there are times
you also move sideways
with strong toes and claws that
gravity obeys.

Your voice is distinct,
tiny horns on the wind,
red breast hardly counting
your breaths out and in.

You have a technique
that seems topsy-turvy
but finds more delights than
others more nervy.

Tapping each crevice
you find grubs and insects
that many high climbers
routinely do miss.

Despite your short wings
you lift off with some pluck
to prove, after all, you
know which way is up.

Eire

I traveled there a woman
and came back a child
with my eyes full of the clouds
coming over the mountains
so I could never tell
how high they were,
the rivers going on
forever,
the irises
floating down to the sea,
the fuchsias so wild
but not really.
All along the way
cowslips lived
where meadows survived
and milkmaids didn't mind
the rain
so sudden
as suddenly gone.
The fields were greener than any
in France:
through the glass of our visit
going down to the sea,
everywhere surrounding,
only my heart brave enough
to go on
into the waves,
a lonesome boatman calling me
to come live with him
forever.

Clearing for Bluebells

I am long gone
from that small coppice
where one man's purpose
was all I had.

His saw, his scythe
cut through the clutter
to shed some light where
the ground was soft.

Fires were set
to burn away brash
and warm us at last
on such cold days.

We'd stop for lunch
and speak of nothing
except the birdsong
leaving winter.

He loved my hair
and constant silence
and woman's promise
to stay for hope.

My hands, my heart
wanted to be his
working with nature's
way of growing.

Clearing the way
for sunshine and rain
growing love not blame
from what was past.

Bluebells, bluebells
in sight and fragrance
I have come back since
just as he thought

I would.

Jim Kleinhenz

Jim Kleinhenz graduated from Hofstra University with a degree in philosophy. Then he received his Masters degree from the C. W. Post campus of Long Island University in Library Science. He has been a building superintendent, a handyman, a finish carpenter, and a maker of fine wooden boxes. He started writing poetry for a blog he launched in 2009 (*extrasimile.wordpress.com*) and has been writing ever since. You can read his poems and see many of the drawings on this blog. Later on he taught for a number of years at City College in New York City. He now lives in New York City, right in the heart of midtown Manhattan, in an area known as Tudor City.

Influenced by Wallace Stevens, Kleinhenz's poetry can challenge those not willing to work at understanding his poetry. Most readers can pick up the energy in his stanzas, but the tangle of references to literature, mythologies that can come from anywhere in the world, and history, wrapped into the rigor of his training as a philosopher, can leave casual readers scratching their heads.

Still, the reader who is willing to ask the question posed by John Ciardi in his book, *How Does a Poem Mean?*, can discover both the entertainment of a puzzle as well as deep meaning in nearly every Kleinhenz poem. A good example is the first poem in this selection of his poetry, "Pangaea."

The first thing the reader has to understand is that Pangaea was a continent that broke apart 175 million-plus years ago. It is also, in Greek mythology, a mountain where the Greek gods fought against the tyrant god Cronus, who had earlier been put on the Titan throne through the wrath of Gaea against her husband, another tyrant god, Uranus. Isaac, the subject of the poem, was one of the few people named by God in the Bible and was the miracle son of Abraham and Sarah when Sarah was past the age of childbearing. To find out how the poem means, the reader has to also listen to the poet who keeps breaking in and saying things like "

> So let's call him Clement Cliff and let's say that he's
> an actor and distant cousin of Montgomery Cliff —
> that he's a stage of sand, a progression of the beach

as if he's giving directions for a stage play.

All of these elements together, including the reference to a thousand ships which goes back to Homer's *The Odyssey*, combine with the poem's Isaac's story to place the writer of the poem, and by extension the reader, into a contemplative state that considers the meaning of our time on Mother Earth and conjures both powerful emotions and complex explorations of thoughts.

When Kleinhenz was fifty-nine he was diagnosed with Parkinson's disease. The most powerful poetry he has written was produced after that diagnosis. This is not poetry you are likely to find in your local poetry group that uses prompts to generate poems. It is a poetry concerned with the big questions of existence as a poet tries to explore what he really means as he leaves "on a singing ship."

Pangaea

It's evening. Isaac walks to the beach as if he's lost.
He climbs through artificial dunes, through false ramparts
pushed hard against the ocean's erosion — cliffs of sand.
So let's call him Clement Cliff and let's say that he's
an actor and distant cousin of Montgomery Cliff —
that he's a stage of sand, a progression of the beach.
Blind, he walks to the beach each evening now
because I make him walk. He hates the water's soul.
He feels its fear. He goes because I make him go.
He does this now (we do this now), so I can walk;
walking, it seems, is very bio-mechanical.
So-bio, so-mechanical: the brain's music.

We call this beach Pangaea, for it looks to be
a map of early earth; it looks a plan for earth cut by
the tides before the continents were torn
asunder. (My, how Biblical, my dear, 'asunder'.)
It looks that way when I stand on the cliffs —
like lands formed in jest. I love the air up here.
I love it that these cliffs are not a place
for sacrifice or suicide. Jump and you will
take a tumble. Jack fell down and broke his crown
and Jill will land on the soft sand of Pangaea.
Pretending flight, they fall. Don't cry, honey. It's just
a bruise. Give it a kiss. Isaac, he laughs.

It was right that he should die before me.
Every night we stand right here among the cliffs.
(Prominent among the bluffs.)
We watch and listen as the ocean sings.
The ocean is alive. Pangaea is where sun and sea
must meet. Pangaea, the sea, the soliloquy.
We go down to the sea in ships.
A thousand must set sail every day.
(All launched by your face, my dear.)
Tonight we sit and listen.
The ocean makes its music.
I leave on a singing ship.

Grasslands

The way the world sways. Every leaf left
in place, its stance chiseled to each blade,
an iteration of time; each tassel of seeds,
thy bread, thy handmaiden;
as breath on the brink of disappearance,
becomes a wave become water; proportions so
large so as to stagger the seasons —
one winter questioning another.
We listen. We listen as if musical crabs are tracing a
giant sine wave across the dark mud flats.
We watch it as if a rotted rowboat, its oars like two hands
at prayer, is signaling a gesture
of permanence towards the sky. The grass
has turned from gray to blue to green.
The tide washes in. A bell is rung.
It's as if the merry-go-round has turned it's calliope on.
What Lao-tse has said is true.
The earth is a bellows. Use it.
The grasslands bellow and glow.

Chapel of Words

Again, we see a cloud of seals — as if by their mating,
they join the land with the sea and sky.
Sit here, sir, on the edge, out of their sight.
Sit and let their words sit inside you.
In this darkness, they look like mounds of sand,
a crust that must form in the tides.
We of the Earthcutt, we
will bury a loved one here today
among this procreation.
We will ask it
to take its breath back,
its voice back, its words — that speak
so valiantly for him — back.

We will write his name. We will write the verbs
as the tides let us — in a kind of prayer
that unites the near-living with the near-dead.
We will continue to listen
even as the words empty,
as they crash inside the beach.
We know we lack body. We lack substance.
In what will emerge, we will find our place.
May the peace of our home
stay with you and your absent family.
May it stay in the sand.
May we bury the words we write right here — as
the sea will take all of us —
my friend, our many eyes, myriad friends.
Life is prayer.
The Earthcutt send you blessings.
We wash away.

The Halloween in Harlequin

Such Thought—such thought have I that hold it tight ...
W. B. Yeats, Oxford 1920

The Harlequin Circus comes back to Harlequin
each year for Halloween. The elephants,
the Flying Whistler Boys, some jugglers,
Madam Sosostris to read your palm to you,
Captain Mighty spouting mighty flames: all here
for one day only. They pitch a tent,
put on a show, we have a nice parade.

This Halloween in Harlequin the twins
will dress up as a circus clown. Ben will
be on bottom; Betsy up top, on his shoulders.

They've been practicing for weeks now,
I understand, so as not to fall.
Since the accident, Betsy can no longer walk;
Ben can't be her legs forever, though.

Imagine you write a poem to find a subject
and all you find is this.
You write a poem to find a self and all you find is this one.

Betsy,
You are the gasp of air I can
only breathe one day a year. They say
you should have died instead of me.
They say I saved you on a narrow skid of road,
a clown in a town called Harlequin, a clown
for one performance only —
on a beach full of breath,
O my chevalier! —

Ben,
You should only
blame God when you're ready to blame yourself.
A daddy is like a god, and
this daddy, he blames and blames and blames
enough. It's more than I can say.
Your mom tells me you cry to go to sleep.
Let me try to find the ground for you, okay?
Just be Betsy's little man a little longer.

Just keep the ghosts away another year.
This Halloween, this All Saints All Souls Day
and Eve, I'll walk beside them on parade,
Betsy and Ben. I'll catch them if they topple,
I'll try to hold each one's hand.
Then like the one-day circus that I am
in the town of Harlequin, like
a clown made up of crippled kids, with crippled
little bones,
I too will leave —
We're all here to give just one performance.
We pitch a tent,
put on a show.
We have a nice parade.

Evening's Everything

•

Each baby glows. Wings unfurled,
they spring from a crease of clouds.
They can't know what it's like to see
them flying overhead, to see
their diapers peel away, their bodies
so hairless: to see so much energy,
so concentrated in what are,
after all, immature muscles.
Yet they move more like falcons than kites.
To be what must be a fractal of yourself
as it forms amid the clouds: to feel
in each beat a wing of your own expansion:
to be produced from clouds every evening...
all sweetmeats, incense, gold leaf, everything.

Postcards, Unsigned

The First Card

An adventurous 'hello' from Hollow Head
Island! Apologies about the penmanship.
It seems the postcards shake these days,
not the volcanoes, not the earth.
So far we've been to the Stalactite Park,
the Gotterdammerung Grotto, hid in
the Hidden Caves, got lost in the Lost World.
We even walked some of the Infinity Trail.
No one finishes that, I guess. Ha-ha!
Abandonment *in extremis*. Ha-ha!

The Second Card

Another 'hello' from Hollow Head Island!
Yesterday we took the 'Journey to
the Center of the Earth' tour. Down, down
into a deep crevasse, two miles to see
the Rorschach Sandstones! I shall have
to write to you about panpsychism,
about the 'antecedents problematic'.
It was like being inside a volcano.
The tremors remain inside of me. How can
I even think at all? Remind me. Was it
Protagoras or Pythagoras who jumped
into the volcano? The antecedents thing
suggests 'he jumped' sufficient, precedent
enough, enough to be a god.

The Third Card

A hollow 'hello' from Hell! Yes, from Hell.
Where do names come from? This Hell is
a sleepy fishing village and the best
spot that we've found on Hollow Head,
a Sleepy Hollows, so to speak.
We are in the 'Bridegroom', a little Bed
and Breakfast, run by a Rip Van Winkle
wise enough to know it was Empedocles
who jumped into Mount Etna. Empedocles!
Is my face red! Yet it will glorify
my pronoun to perfection — 'he jumps'. Yes,

both poetry and philosophy ought
to have the same antecedent. They forge
a world that's capable of consciousness.
The self, per se, remains vestigial —
the voice of the volcano, not its source.
Your pronoun is the antecedent, not
your noun. Problematic resolved. Perhaps
I will go for a walk in Hell, perhaps
I will take the air, take the breezes.
A wonderful day in Hell! Ha-ha

The Last Card

You ask no questions; I provide the answers.
Greetings, my friend! We have moved on from Hell.
Today I stand in surf up to my knees.
Imagine: liquid rock, a steaming sea,
the battle of fire with water, land
like iron being forged, the earth refreshed.
We must make this moment a postcard from
infinity. My friend, I need your help.
This message, like our hope for life itself,
must be left unattributed. It must
be left an unresolved antecedent.
Think of Empedocles poised at the mouth
of that volcano, Etna's edge. He is
about to enter this world's soul. He is about
to die. We are all thrown into the world.
Empedocles, the poet philosopher,
must hear a voice from far into
the future, a voice from today that will
insure his resurrection, one
to clarify his immortality.
Write something in the sand for him to see.
There was something more,
something more divine,
more bestial…
Write that. Leave it unsigned.
For I have been here now a boy and a girl,
a bush and a bird and a dumb fish in the sea.
Write that. Knowledge will come.

Penelope on the Beach

It was only day. It was Ulysses and it was not.
—Wallace Stevens, "The World as Mediation"

When Penelope bathes, she wades
into the wake of the wave he has left behind.
Her hands still shake remembering that his hands
had grasped nothing, nothing of her mind.
She'd said she must hide so as not to seem
to be bidding him goodbye. Transformation
would be her suitor now, not her guest.
He'd said, if she went swimming in the sea,
her mist would complete a marriage vow,
one made to him and to the approaching sun.
How bright the morning is.
How brisk the wind.
Penelope was on the beach
when the light flashed
and the earth cracked apart.
Ten thousand birds lifted her into the air.
Who or what was out there?
Was it the mist or Penelope's whisper
he heard throughout the stars?
 I will be a different person when
you return, my love.
I will still be your fate,
but I will know you only by your scars.

Echoed

A shout shouted, a gunshot shot —
each echo echoes the plea
for a new silence.
A car crashes, a flight turns to violence.
A belief is lost in the night,
the night itself, a state of fright,
an act of active imagination,
a kind of poet's poem sung to music —
music that you used to play, my dear.
Isolde, say. From one chord to the next,
the discord of love, by a man-god who
changed into all the harmonies
your child-soul could take.
A baby crying all night,
a cry just to keep alive the twilight
as twilight echoes dawn —
as twilight echoes dawn.
Shouted.

Sheet Music

Me too.
I too switched to
the trumpet in fifth grade.
It made a lot of sense.
I rode a bike to school.
The trumpet case fit on the handlebars.
I could learn to play things like
THE FLIGHT OF THE BUMBLEBEE and
WHEN THE SAINTS COME MARCHING IN.
My mother's fave was Harry James
(and not Mr. Armstrong. Strange).
Just listen to the sound a trumpet makes!
And so I left the sousaphone behind.
Too bad.

How could I know its acoustic world
echoed so deep—in waters that
went so far beyond the lake?
So far into the sea the whales could hear?
It could be like the wind Vermont stirs up,
come November, but in July, like an
old sheet blown off a clothesline, and then
the clothesline snaps, as both tensions
leave earth. Things do disappear, you know.
Both rot away, both are left behind.
I set a music stand up on the dock.
I serenade the lake all summer long.
I play the balls off Harry James.
But whales don't come up through the rivers.
And come the end of August, Uncle Bill comes back
to close the camp and we go home,
that last sheet still flapping in the breeze,
the one I will never take down.

Is Near

If I left the ending
which is the air you wished for
—Jesse Seldess

The old attic is near.
Where he lived is near, the old man.
Where the string pulled taut,
had left his eyes bulging in pain,
his mouth a bowl of salvia
he could not swallow.
Where he almost drowned.

Say. The lake is near.
Say, the lake is on fire.
The swamp is full
of ooze, monochrome darkness.
So still. These balls of air,
too black to wear,
too sharp to capture.
The balls of hair.
Is near. Dear.
Is near

Margaret Gross

Margaret Gross was born, raised and educated in New Mexico. Associated with the Zuni Mountain Poets, she has spent most of her life working for either the Navajo or Pueblo Nations. She currently lives in her hometown of Albuquerque where she is fiercely a New Mexican with Coyote heritage.

Gross's poetry often either sizzles, celebrates, or screams on the page. A lifelong Catholic, she sees both the human and current condition of the American dream as a violation against basic human rights, especially the rights of women and children. At the same time she has an enormous pride in who she and her family are within the borders of her native state:

> i am from coyote red blood
> from this and that people
> wandering
> through the *rio abajo*.
>
> from blue mother,
> earth mother,
> corn mothers,
> mother maria
> my own mother.

Her poetry is not always comfortable, especially when she is writing about what has happened to so many women, especially young women, just south of the U.S.-Mexico border. "In the other side of the border" she writes:

> the filth that murdered my daughter
> stand around the streetlight laughing
> pulling at their crotches and smoking
> *mota*.
>
> in my dream, the one i have every night,
> i see her hand laying on the sand.
> nails broken and the dark marks
> around her wrist.

She seems to be saying over and over again, we can be better, this country can be better, we can live better, healthier, more compassionate, lives.

and i am from

i am from coyote red blood
from this and that people
wandering
through the *rio abajo*.

from blue mother,
earth mother,
corn mothers,
mother maria
my own mother.

from the aroma of roasting green chile
and red chile browning
in my cast iron frying pan.
from the hands
of my grandmothers
patting out tortillas.

from summer clouds
and virga swishing
her skirts along *los volcanes*
and the aroma of a dark storm
off in the distance.

i am from mesas
outlasting snow, rain, sun.
from gramma grass
golden in the cold sunlight
of a winter morning.

from clouds spilling
over the sandias
moisture pouring out
over the alluvial plain
and flowing toward the rio.

from rich dirt
shaped and formed
like an adobe brick,
lasting for years,
but not forever.

i am from *la milpa*,
old as my hands
new as the thought
that just skittered by.
from the frothy
green and the hidden
ears, bursting
blue, yellow, white.

most of all
i am from rain
and heavy bottomed clouds
from thunder tumbling into the valley
and lightning popping along
the llano to the west.

and i am from those summer nights
years ago
lying on pink sheets
at gramma's house,
dozing off into the cool.
night air
moving
over my skin.

The Desert, Heuesos and So On

I came here and didn't know
I would be stripped to my very bones,
she explained.
All I knew was I had to
get out of suburbia
and off grid
and out
into the desert

alone.

Be where no one
knows my phone number
or where I buy my groceries.
Be where the sky is limitless,
the sun persistent,
and the endless wind
buffets the tin roof.

People come here,
you know, to divest
down to their most
authentic selves.
It is painful,
she said,
to lose pounds
of flesh
and tissue
just
to get
down
to
bone.

Those of us from here,
I replied,
were born
bones
and spend
our lives
putting on
flesh.

the table wine

i sip on a zinfandel that has
a memory of the back porch
of the old house on 4th street-
dust motes lazing in a shaft of fall light,
the ring of the old-fashioned door

bell, steep concrete steps.

an old coke box cooler
filled with water and wine bottles
behind a wood table.
small glasses for a taste stacked
up for a taste of the table wine.
the cash register that fascinated
our little fingers.

the wine making came from
france, but the sun and the sky
were something new Mexican
that cannot be named.
old pete called my grandpa
"old man" in the later years.
where would we all be without
pete who so understood the land
and us?

the remembering of scents
of old adobe dust, dank leaves,
and the lingering smoke of a lucky strike
enfold me into powerful arms-
the fermenting of my small self,
still holding on to grandma's hand,
with the grapes into the rawness
of the wine that is us.

she was born early

she was born early.
underneath the lengthening shadow of solstice.
what is unseen lingers there for a moment,
shivering in the cold.

she was born early.
between night and not yet morning
and into a wordlessness
echoing throughout the world.

She was born early.
just before the wintering geese
rise above the dormant fields
carrying her high into
the burgeoning pink and purple sky.

taos men

it was like
the Father, Son, and Holy Ghost
descended early one morning.
emerging from the shadows
on the north side of the Plaza.

the men stand
in the bright morning sun.
their tightly wrapped,
white cotton blankets
emanate light.
the very Light.

in 1967 she knew
about mystery and the unknown
and how it wrapped around her
eight year old body
all the time.

she knew it in the plaza
that early morning,
looking at those men
and sipping at yesterday's
left over rain
on the moving air.

the other side of the border

the filth that murdered my daughter
stand around the streetlight laughing
pulling at their crotches and smoking
mota.

in my dream, the one i have every night,
i see her hand laying on the sand.
nails broken and the dark marks
around her wrist.
even in the dream i cannot let myself
look any farther.

they found her among the garbage
and tumbleweeds blown up against
a barbed wire fence.
they told me how she died,
but i cannot remember nothing
except the words rape and beer bottle.
i screamed then and i scream inside
when i let myself think too much.

the filth that done this,
the police do not touch,
not on this side of the border.
not with them american masters
running them factories.
running drugs
and running the streets.

but me, i don't care no more
about what is right or wrong.
i find the sharpest knife i have.
the one my daddy used to slit
the throats of pigs.
me, i finger the blade
and head downstairs.

chingate, i think when as
i walk out the door.
chingate, i whisper as

i stomp down the sidewalk
chingate, i scream as
i run at the filth,
blade raised above my head.

fall to earth

he was a drunk looking man/he could see wounded hands/a dog sleeps next to him in the alley/pain never makes him cry/night clouds burgeon/the son of man dies with a wordless scream/a storm of stars fall to earth.

Third Heart

Hear coyote calling to the wild dusk? Cottontail shivers and scuttles into the carport. In the growing darkness, in the warmth of my bed, in the folds and crinkles of my brain i wrestle with the ripped veil in the temple. Was it the third heart, creaked shut that creaked open? Or just a weaving torn apart and left sagging, hiding nothing with nothing to hide. Coyote is joined by his pack and they shrilly cry out, as Jesus did as he died. This wordless scream that drives Cottontail into his hole and ricochets in every gust of wind, opens my third heart, beating bloody and true, just before sleep overtakes.

Annette Langlois Grunseth

Annette Langlois Grunseth has published widely in journals and anthologies in the Midwest, New York, Oregon and Nova Scotia. Poems from her chapbook *Becoming Trans-Parent, One Family's Journey of Gender Transition* (2017) were nominated for a Pushcart Prize. She has received awards for her poetry from *Wisconsin Academy Review, Wisconsin People and Ideas,* and the Wisconsin Fellowship of Poets. She often writes poetry on the bike trail, or in her kayak on northern lakes, where, she says, "her muse tags along, just for the exercise."

Her best poetry often comes from her experience of having her son come out as a daughter, or from the days when she was a student during the Vietnam War at the University of Wisconsin–Madison while her brother served as a soldier in the jungles and rice paddies of Vietnam. In Vietnam he faced some of the war's most vicious fighting. Both experiences have led to reflection and turnings in her life that come out through her poetry.

In "Pears" she reflects on her brother as a child and a Boy Scout.

Growing up in the shadow of WWII my brother
grabs a pear from the *Green Stamp* fruit bowl,
pulls the stem out with his teeth, pretends to throw it,

making hand grenade blasting sounds.
He arranges green army men on the floor for attack and retreat,
plays war games in a foxhole dug into the empty lot next door.

But then he is in Vietnam, and

His graphic letters detail how a bursting mortar
sprays a buddy's brains across his own helmet.

My brother writes of helping amputate a soldier's leg that is
pinned inside a mortared APC. He tells me, *You have it easy because
you're a girl, you weren't forced into war, or that kind of fear.*

Her poems about her daughter describe the day her son announced his decision and what happened the first time mother and daughter went into the women's restroom together. Experience is behind Grunseth's poems. The sanity she finds through those experiences make her poems worth reading.

Pears

Growing up in the shadow of WWII my brother
grabs a pear from the *Green Stamp* fruit bowl,
pulls the stem out with his teeth, pretends to throw it,

making hand grenade blasting sounds.
He arranges green army men on the floor for attack and retreat,
plays war games in a foxhole dug into the empty lot next door.

As a Boy Scout he learns survival, camping out
on weekend bivouacs. With Dad, he hunts pheasant,
partridge, and sometimes deer. He becomes a good shot.

Like his father, uncle, and grandfather
he grows up to serve in the military.
His draft number comes up at college graduation, 1967.

After Basic Training, he flies off to Vietnam, barely prepared.
He writes home of government-issue weapons that jam,
won't fire properly; they have no rain gear for monsoon season.

My parents buy a rain suit and mail it to him. His letters tell of
living in an APC as they sweep the jungle, bulldoze through
rice paddies and level farms, dodging snipers and ambushes.

Scouting and hunting skills keep him alive in that jungle.
His graphic letters detail how a bursting mortar
sprays a buddy's brains across his own helmet.

My brother writes of helping amputate a soldier's leg that is
pinned inside a mortared APC. He tells me, *You have it easy because
you're a girl, you weren't forced into war, or that kind of fear.*

Maybe I have it easier, but whenever I eat a pear now,
I feel his burden — my guilt ignites
as the taste of pear explodes in my mouth.

In the Bloom of the Moment

"...Live In the bloom of the moment."
                                    Henry David Thoreau

This is not the life she imagined
after fifty-eight years of marriage.
They should be off on some cruise to Alaska
watching ice calve into the ocean,
eyes fixed in silent awe on whales migrating to Mexico
their massive tails gracefully slicing through the icy ocean.
Instead she visits her husband of nearly six decades
at the home where residents pace the floor
randomly trying to remember, who, what, or where.
She brings foil covered kisses, hidden in her purse,
and to his eyes this wonderful stranger
carefully peels each delightful, chocolate morsel
pops them, one by one, into his mouth.
"Mmmmmmm", he says, *"That's such good candy."*
Every day she repeats her visits, bringing him kisses.
Every day he smacks with delight of the newness
of such good candy. Envious residents watch,
one in a loud whisper tells the group
"how sweet — she comes every day."
Gradually, walkers line up, join the concealed audience
at the far end of the room, fixated on the unfolding
of foil after foil. *"Mmmmm"* they hum in unison,
twenty pairs of eyes watch with the same grace
as whales diving, tails descending,
following their instincts.

Fish for Flowers

Rural Wisconsin economy
runs on the ingenuity between
Amish and English women.
One has a pond with Koi
in need of marsh plants
for her multiplying fish to hide.

The other has delicious gardens
of marigolds, glads, water plants
tomatoes, cabbage, lilies,
parsley and peppers.
They meet at market to barter,
fish for flowers.
Pond plants and pansies
purple petunias and a pasture of asters
in trade for darting koi in orange, white and speckle,
an exchange of gills, not bills.

At the Back Steps

Marie Ruud Bergh
Madison, Minnesota, 1930s

During the Great Depression
they rode the rails,
knew where to get a meal.
They'd jump from freight cars
into this little prairie town.
They'd look for the white house
with the big porch. At the back steps
she invited them in, two or three at a time.
They ate meatballs rolled with nutmeg,
ginger, allspice and clove, swaddled in gravy,
with mashed potatoes and green beans,
snapped fresh from the garden, and pie.
Yes, pie! Resting on crust so flaky

it melted comfort on their tongues.
She fed them in late afternoon,
men with sad eyes. Hoboes -
probably with children of their own
somewhere back across all those fields of dust.
Great Grandma filled empty bellies,
asked one favor, that each do a chore
in return before they hopped
the clacking wheels again, riding the
wail of the whistle into the distance.

Becoming Trans-Parent

We were gathered in the family room
the day our son told us,
I've got an announcement that's a long time coming,
handing us a letter in an envelope.

The day our son told us
we read silently, he watched anxiously,
handing us a letter in an envelope.
I'm transgender, I identify as a woman.

We read silently, he watched anxiously.
Going forward I will finally live openly and fully as a woman.
I'm transgender, I identify as a woman.
We feel time-stopped shock, at the word woman.

Going forward I will finally live openly and fully as a woman.
After years of turmoil and questioning, I finally feel right.
We feel time-stopped shock, at the word woman.
I've begun to understand myself and discovered what makes me happy.

After years of turmoil and questioning, I finally feel right.
I've got an announcement that's a long time coming.
I've begun to understand myself and discovered what makes me happy.
We were gathered in the family room.

When Your Child Comes Out

I often think of the day you were born when
I held my sweet boy for the first time,
marveling *where did you come from?*
It's a lot to take in, when your child comes out.

As I go upstairs to bed I stare at old photos in the hall,
your short-cropped hair, striped shirt, toddler jeans,
that little-boy smile. I walk past you in a suit and tie for
graduation. At Christmas tears still well up as
my fingers trace the "old" name on the stocking.
It's a lot to take in, when your child comes out.

But now you walk with confidence,
meet new people with ease,
get together with women friends.
Your skin is soft like pink on a peach,
your blue eyes sparkle, your child-like humor has returned
and your familiar expressions are back.
You are the same person
only now that doubting discord is gone.
You live through yourself, instead of beside yourself.

You are the daughter I always wanted.

My Mother's Moon

Her day was not complete
until she stepped out to see the moon.
It might be an orange ball rising
or a white turtle egg hovering.
More than a thousand full moons
shadowed my mother.
She studied the moon when Neil Armstrong stepped upon it.
She cried for her son who saw the same moon rising
over rice paddies and incoming mortars in Vietnam.
There was the empty nest moon the autumn I left for college,
but the loneliest moon was the August my Dad died.

The moon of selling her house changed the view,
rising to different walls. Yet it was always her moon at bedtime.
She loved the strawberry moon, harvest moon,
eclipses of the moon, Indian summer moon.
And finally, a full moon rising on her last night,
crickets in the grass singing.
I held her hand, bed pulled close to the window,
moonlight falling gently across her face.

Elizabeth Herron

Elizabeth Herron is also the Reverend Elizabeth Herron, an ordained minister in the interfaith Creation Spirituality tradition, which is usually associated with the theologian Matthew Fox. In that practice she integrates psychology and spirituality by "listening deeply to the soul's calling through mental health symptoms and finding practical, creative and spiritual solutions." Since 2010 she has been a psychology professor at the University of New Mexico, working at both the Gallup campus and with the Pueblo of Zuni A:shiwi College. Herron has had two books published, one on feminine psychology titled, *Fierce Beauty, Feminine Fire*, and a book of poetry, *Poetry for the Ear of God; Healing Trauma Through the Music of Words*.

Her poetry comes out of the spiritual traditions that her background suggests. The universe she depicts is intensely alive and dynamic. There are "night mares," frogs "Crazy happy to be alive," "cricket drone" and "coyote howl," and a world that is wailing, beating, and ceaselessly moving with the pulse of life. At the heart of everything is a search for healing, even when "There are some pains that cannot be changed." When the miracle happens, though, when

> You may stumble onto an island,
> Cloaked in mist-ridden veils,
> Where you are welcomed
> As the long lost relative that you are…

the spirit shifts, and the universe becomes a welcoming place filled with warmth and well-being.

To Herron the stories of trauma have to be told if the wounds from trauma are to be healed. Her book of poetry is dedicated to exploring both the wounding and the healing, often relying on the magic environment of the Zuni Mountains and Zuni Pueblo culture to help reach a place of safety as she explores her universe.

Winter Solstice

The storm rode in
On wild horses,
Fearsome night mares
Carrying northern winds
That shrieked and swirled,
Cold seeping under doors
Penetrating cracks
In well worn adobe,
Shaking the foundation
With such ravenous abandon —
We were all taken
Down to the bone.

Huddling around
Juniper fires under siege,
We drew close
Into one another
In precarious defense
Of our smallness —
Made evident by the
Vast uncontrollable night.

The Old One

I saw You one day
On a bus in Mexico.
We rode side by side,
seeming strangers —
You in your black rebozo,
Worn hands fingering rosary beads,
And me in my tie-dyed shirt
Carrying a backpack of dreams.
Your dark eyes looked into me
As if you knew the
North star of my soul
And I became humble
And listened to a
Deeper truth.

I saw You again one day
In the Gallup Walmart —
Your turquoise jewelry and
Crimson skirt vivid against
The sterile shelves.
Across eons and carts of groceries
Your ancient eyes beheld me,
And I marveled that You
Could find me
In the far reaches of this
Scattered world.
Held in the gaze of your infinite smile,
I knew with startling clarity,
        You were never gone,
                It was me that left.

Frog Noise

The rain came down
And woke up the frogs
Who slithered out of
Hidden places and,
Crazy happy to be alive,
Began to sing, a wild noise
That filled earth and sky,
Turning the air into playgrounds,
A radical testimony
To resurrection —
That made us feel small
And only barely there,
Because we had forgotten
The rhythm of cycles —
And the
Inevitable turning of wheels.

And now in my secret
dark quiet places,
I weep,
wondering what lies dormant,
and when the rains will come,
holding the carved stone frog

close to my heart,
my own salt tears moistening,
that which waits
to be born.

Through the Rabbit Hole

Go willingly into the night,
Dear friend.
Tumble down the rabbit hole
Into that secret realm
That lies waiting.
Let yourself fall
From one world to another,
Riding on the ghost winds,
Like a ship sailing
On an unknown dark sea.

And even as you plunge,
Kicking and screaming
In abject terror, all bearings lost,
You may stumble onto an island,
Cloaked in mist-ridden veils,
Where you are welcomed
As the long lost relative that you are.
And as you awaken
From fear-induced slumber
Into this place where
Falling becomes flying,
Weeping becomes ecstatic song,
And your howl of anguish,
A peal of laughter,
Your heart will be in awe
Of all that you have forgotten.

Of this I know little,
Only the smallest glimpses,
Like a small orphan child
Outside in the cold,
Peering through a window
Into a room
Warmed by a crackling fire,
Resplendent in brilliant colors
And soft rugs.

Midwife

I would wrap around you
like a softly woven blanket —
color, heart and warmth,
holding strong
against the wind.
I would wait at the edge
of the crucible of your pain,
holding vigil while you do
your holy work,
and then in the long night
when hope thins
to a gossamer thread,
I will bring you tea
sweetened with wild sage honey,
remembering the inevitable dawn.

There are some nights
that were never meant
to be born alone.

The Wailing Time

There are some pains
that cannot be changed,
resisting all healing,
unmoved by
the wind in the trees,
sunlight on water or
even the laughter of children,
but sit, hard,
with ragged metal edges
snagging and tearing
fragile places of heart healing,
defying time and
annihilating epiphanies,
until,
exhausted and bereft,

she slid out the cracks
of her mind
and found a perch
up in the boughs of a tall pine.
Comforted by aloneness
and the crisp smell
of pine sap,
she watched the
flight of a kestral,
weightless with hollow bone,
finding her sweet delight
carried upon the evening breeze

Weather Maker

I slipped into the dusk,
riding on cricket drone
and coyote howl,
a fresh wind hailed from the south,
scent of swamp and secret memory,
and I, already alight on night sound,
rolled effortlessly into storm cloud,
rising cumulus — moist, dark and ripe,
I rose bigger still
until thunder rumbled
from my belly and with a
mighty roar and arms raised,
let loose with
the crackling lightning fire
that was always
mine to offer.

.

Jon Marshall

Jon Marshall was born in East Texas on the western edge of the South and near the lowlands of bayou country. Finding himself within the mixed cultures of the American South, the American West, and the Louisiana Cajun country, he experienced childhood and teenage years balancing all three of them. From encounters with the KKK and genteel Southern charm, canoeing through the deep bayous to attend Cajun festivities, and raising Hereford cattle on a family ranch, he managed his way through the turbulent 1960's. Such an upbringing provided ample experiences for his later writings. Through the years, Marshall has taught at one university and two colleges. He has published poetry in several local and regional publications. Currently, a novel is in progress.

Marshall's life experiences in the South and perception of the human condition are frequent dynamics showcased in his poetry. He emphasizes regional narratives about people, and the relationship between people and nature. Within his poetry portfolio he has created a sophisticated web of characters, many of whom become acquainted with each other through auspicious means. In "Grief," he allows the reconciliation of human events in our karmic wheel to manifest through such meetings.

> Uncle Bill, driving at dusk, hit a Mexican on a tractor
> running no lights. They say he didn't know what hit him.
> Maybe. Maybe we always know what hits us, eventually.

In addition, he approaches our relationship with the supernatural as a personal human journey always unfolding before our feet. In "Old Road"

> I enjoyed sitting on the ground in the middle of that road,
> pine canopy hiding the sky
> muffled silence loudly pressing upon my ears
> sometimes.
> I heard the long-haul freighters approach:
> tired horses straining, pulling heavy load,
> weary drivers singing lonesome songs to absent ladies,
> unconscious habitual whips snapping in the empty air

Quilt

When I step softly into our intimate room
and your love-woven quilt throws its brilliant colors into my eyes,
I hear the past grow serenely quiet
and feel the future become ineffably still.

Grief

It's like that train rumble
rolling around Joy-Wright Mountain,
off way in the distance;
so lonesome,
makin' a body want to sit and cry
til the Saints think to call us home.

Sometimes I still hear that bull gator
under Silvy Bridge
where Bobby dared me to sneak'n grab his tail.
How does he do it?
Livin' in that holler,
no other gators around,
all alone?

The folks passed years ago.
Them being so much older, seemed natural.
Both vanishing like starlight in the dawn.

But not the others.

Grew up playing with my brother, sister.
Faded away: she first, stubborn to the end;
then him, denying, how all could be so wrong.

Thought they'd always be around.

Years later, felt that about my grandkids, too.
Now, gone to the four winds;
I, to a fifth,
heart baked bare by a dry Southwestern sun.
Once I wandered deep into Tiawichi Creek,

becoming lost in those ancient thick woods.
Stumbled upon an old cabin
now forgotten by everyone who ever knew it.
A feeling of loss drifted about that place
like an early fall fog over Mill Pond Bayou,
just laying itself over the smokey water,
like my dog Dori used to drape on me
when I laid upon the cool ground
staring at a night sky wanting me to fall into its infinity.

Used to drive out Afton Thrash road with Brad,
way off in the east county,
where we could ride'n drink beer with nobody carin'.
Ten years later, he was gone: snuffed out. Don't know why.
I still think about the way he always had my back.
Some said he held no moral fiber, but I knew better.

Uncle Bill, driving at dusk, hit a Mexican on a tractor
running no lights. They say he didn't know what hit him.
Maybe. Maybe we always know what hits us, eventually.

Older sister has that Alzheimer's. Barely knows me.
But always asks where've I been.
Always say I'm back now. She smiles like that's a comfort.
Didn't know she missed me til a part of her was gone.

Where'd they all go?

Thought they'd always be around.
Never gave it a mind they wouldn't.

Not even once.

Old Road

barely seen when a teen
that old road through those abandoned piney woods
beyond our farmhouse where my brother was born
    I wasn't around yet

ran between the big trees

ditches hardly visible
smaller pines in the bed
raked the straw aside: wagon-wheel grooves, cast-hardened ruts
    a hundred years forgotten

ancient slave-shacks rotted under a nearby big oak
iron-rock stones circled for long-begotten fires
perhaps they waved at weary travelers up from Nacogdoches
    or hid their faces, avoiding notice

Father said the gold-seeking Spanish built this roadway
Camino Real toward Louisiana
for Spanish troops defending this abandoned frontier
from a Neutral Zone of bandits, renegades, and the gluttonous French

oh god, protect us from the French!

I enjoyed sitting on the ground in the middle of that road
pine canopy hiding the sky
muffled silence loudly pressing upon my ears

sometimes
I heard the long-haul freighters approach:
tired horses straining, pulling heavy load
weary drivers singing lonesome songs to absent ladies
unconscious habitual whips snapping in the empty air

cracking upon nothing
nothing beyond anything
but Time

Angel

The Angel decided she had enough
of the demands by God.
So she left.
God didn't miss her for a million years.
By then, couldn't even remember her name.

She hid within the lives of Creatures
when called by the Force of their good Intent.

So many beings, so much marvel.
When another finally came around,
she found humans the most fun.
So many conflicts, she never got bored.
Then she discovered Alice and fell in love.

Alice believed she talked with angels.
One in particular.
Especially when standing on the banks of the Little Muddy
beneath Shelby's Bluff
where one could find seashells buried in the strata.
Something about this spot
made her feelings peruse a million years back in Time.
Many moments forgotten, unnoticed,
as if God's attention lingered elsewhere.

Often she found herself speaking to the air
as if the elements listened,
responded in sensations,
played in the sunlight above the Little Muddy.
A hidden Bliss within a carnal world.
Souls delight.

One day a name settled.
Francis.
Of course.
Her angel needed a name.
Even God couldn't remain nameless forever.
Could he? No.
Is there personality without a name?
Difficult to say.
But she'll name her angel Francis
and they'll speak to all the times of the world.

Francis felt pleased by this naming.
So pleased she hummed a favorite tune
from the Sumerians,
one created by a princess escaping the wrath
of an angry father wishing a loveless marriage.
A favorite tune for her Alice.
But Francis knew Alice's life must be too short.
All humans lives sparked too brief
against the backdrop of the Universe.

So sad.
But today she'll hum her tune
and allow Love to flourish
however short.

Even angels have their limits.

Word

I seldom say it
that one word
nor do you
even when our mountain vanishes into the wilderness night
and your hand
reaches over to mine
certain of its welcome

Ralph Murre

Ralph Murre considers himself a jack-of-all-trades, although he was, before retirement, a working architect, and, "as any good Jack must, he's tried his hand at writing a few poems and has met with some success in that endeavor." He's published several volumes of poetry, among them, *Crude Red Boat* (2007) *Psalms* (2008) *The Price of Gravity* (2010) and with his poetry partner, Sharon Auberle, *Wind Where Music Was* (2013). A man of the Great Lakes, Murre served as poet laureate of Door County, Wisconsin for 2015-2017. He also "considers himself something of a dabbler" in the visual arts, having had his art presented in galleries and published in magazines.

A master at presenting his poetry, his gravelly voice, gray hair and beard, and dramatic flair bring those of a certain age back to a time when poems were read in smoky coffee houses as listeners riffed on the rhythms of the words. This is the voice that clearly comes through in his written work:

> The morning, yes
>   but in the dark before it
>   the four-thirty dark
> the sleeping cock sleeps
> and no crows crow
> and the prayers
> are yet to be prayed
> as the woman, aging
> gets up and comes down
> as she starts weak coffee
> in the pot
> of timeless enamel
> as she toasts
>   the potato-bread toast

he writes in "Agrarian, A.M.," the clauses stretching out into a chant. To hear and see him present his poetry is truly an experience.

The themes in his work usually swirl around everyday experiences and sights that encapsulate a comment on the human condition. About half the time he manages to make the universe seem humorous even as he delves into a truth that, more often than not, deserves a shake of the head — or maybe a bucket-load of despair.

Agrarian, A.M.

something and everything beginning once again —
August Derleth

The morning, yes
   but in the dark before it
   the four-thirty dark
the sleeping cock sleeps
and no crows crow
and the prayers
are yet to be prayed
as the woman, aging
gets up and comes down
as she starts weak coffee
in the pot
of timeless enamel
as she toasts
the potato-bread toast

The morning, yes
   with one forty-watt hole
   in the five o'clock dark
where another day can pour in
and the zees of the snoring
get out
as she's out
to the barn of the cows
and their lowing
and chewing and hungers
their quick switching tails and
their great plopping droppings
the slop in the straw
of their droppings

The morning, yes
   and the milking begun
   in the five-thirty dim
now run in to tell him
that it's day
and run back to Bessie

and Bossie and Minerva and Grace
and coo to the cow
whose bull-calf has gone off
for veal for a meal
for a family still sound asleep
and dreaming
The American Dream
a scheming of ease and plenty

Now six o'clock's gone
and six-thirty
the old man's driving down
to his job in the town
and the kids should be up
should come 'round to help
to shovel and scrape, to sweep

The morning, yes
   there's a truck on the road
   a howl of its tires at seven
the coffee's reheated and
for a minute she's seated
paying bills, reading verses
giving kisses as the schoolbus
flashes its red and red
on a bluegrass blue hill
and she's alone
to begin thinking of more work
to be done and of supper
and sewing and sowing
and reaping and mowing

and always, another morning

Like This Morning, Crazy with Wind

Or just the other day, the bad roads
Even that time, and maybe it was long ago
When we all danced in circles

Take last night, what you said
Take the fire in the ring of rock
Take sun and rain, finally
Pulling frost from earth. A garden

Like falling in and out and in, again
Since the beginning and until
We are very, very old and
Maybe falling in and out, even then

The seasons, I mean, the leaves
The greening and the turning to gold
The rush of it like the sea pulling
The ice and streams of high mountains

Think of that water in the Pacific
Or the rain in Spain if you prefer
Or the little cloud that you are, driven

Like this morning, crazy with wind

Odds

On the off chance
that we should meet again
given that there are billions
and, let's say, in a different life

On the off chance
we'd be attracted to one another
and were of the same species
that is, I hadn't come back

as your dog
or you, God forbid, if there'd be
a god, my cat
(not that there'd be anything

wrong with that)
On the off chance

we'd be on a planet
with breathable air

and we'd survived acne
and alcohol and atomic
annihilation on that globe
circling a star, somewhere

On the off chance of love

what do you suppose
would be the chance
we two could get it right
learn the steps, dance the dance?

Cantata for Woodland
and Orchestra

There, just there — where the first cellos
of March come in, before the oboes
or the ides — there, the brooding

before budding or cranes return,
before clarion brass of calendar spring,
the thing made of maple and ice,

there, that dripping, the ripping of the long,
white garment, there, the giggling
of flutes, perennial roots waking in cold soil.

At last, a roll of timpani just
before this symphony season's end,
a thunder of freeze unfreezing.

Cymbal crash of lightning tightening senses,
there, the tension as a hundred violins go wild,
waking your lover, waking your child.

Crescendo!

Innuendo of greening in the plop
of that first drop of the applauding rain

and it's over again — there's a silence
so profound we can hear the stirring
of the deep unknown, and underground.

Portrait with Contradictions

You'd want to call him
a rattletrap of a man,
though shorter than that.
A loose collection of ideas.
Solemn as smoke.
Sullen as snake.
Then not. Then again.
Creaky as truck.
Crazy as eights.
In love with luck.
Dishonest, no lie,
then true, I guess.

You'd want to paint him
battleship out of water,
and as gray as that.
A look-out scanning the horizon.
Distant as dove.
Instant as shove.
Then here. Then slow.
Steady as rust.
Heady as stout.
Half-and-half lust.
Happy-go-lucky,
but blue, nonetheless.

Sing him old as stories.
Now sing him new.

Prayers of Old Men

I'll bet you think the old men
are praying to be young men
with young lovers, but
they kneel now beside your bed
and pray for the things young men
haven't heard of yet —
the high plateaus of you
and the rivers rushing
to the deep sea of you.
Old men pray for height and depth
and the quivering leaf of your ear
touched by a tongue,
for that quiet cove of you
where they may lie sheltered
for one more evening.
They pray for the light
of sunrise in your eyes
and they pray to believe
in whoever they pray to,
for they want to believe in everything,
because believing in nothing didn't work.
And they pray for the touch of you on me.
They're all praying for you and for me,
the high ground of you towering
above me, and the river,
they're praying now for the river of you,
and they're praying for me
to go adrift in the river
　　to the sea of you,
　　to the sea of you,
praying I'll be lost at sea in you
and they're secretly praying
that this storm will drown me
in the depths of you,
because they are old men
and they know I am a sailor,
and they know that drowning
is the only way for sailors
to get home.

The Price of Gravity

How much of this life do we own?
   Payments are always coming due.
We are the ones who signed the papers,
   but there's something more,
there's something that can't be helped.
   You and I look different
than we did in morning light.
   Now we wade in lead boots
and gather no speed
   away from this dead center,
or toward something brighter.
   Which is to say away from here,
where the embers have dwindled.
   Which is to say we can fly only
with the creatures of dreams,
   if we can fly at all.
The dreams will become family,
   the dreams will become clan,
scattered like dust among stars
   in the cages of our ribs,
in the cages of our cries,
   in our breath in the night.
Sometimes the dreams may be of falling
   and cold earth rushing to us,
but, travelers now,
   they'll call us travelers,
amid the dust
   and the stars
where we've known the dark eclipse,
   and we've flown with
those creatures of dreams
   between galaxies.
We won't be in lead boots
   once we've started to dream.
We'll no longer make payments
   on things that hold us down.
This is not the end of this poem —

   something pulls at us forever.

The Sky is Full of Bluebirds

but not everyone can see them
so they think it's just a blue sky,
and at night, when it's all crows —
well, you know.
And early and late
come flamingoes,
the cardinals and tanagers,
but don't try to explain that
to just anyone.
There are gray birds, too.

Vacancy. Inquire Within.

ask again
and yet again
is this the place
the time
could you be the one
in all this black
this white
this winter
of the wolf
could the hungering
wind
fill your lungs
could you shout
the height
of the city
could you sing
the frozen river
the milky
way
could your belly
hold the salt
of the sea
the clean-swept
sea

ask again
of the cockerel
crowing
is this the time
of the shells
of the shore
is this the place
ask of the bells
their ringing

What is Given

The likelihood of finding strawberries
tiny and wild and sweet
around your ankles
on any given day
in any given place
is not great
but sometimes
people find strawberries
right where they are standing
just because it is their turn
to be given a taste
of something wild and sweet

NICK MOORE

A master of traditional verse forms, the English poet Nick Moore has written poetry for as long as he can remember. Classic English poets of the countryside such as Thomas Hardy, John Clare, William Barnes, and the great American writers, including Robert Frost, Wendell Berry and Billy Collins, influence most of his work. Having worked variously as a farmhand, groom, journalist, PR man, college lecturer, and corporate trainer, he turned freelance as a copywriter, journalist and consultant in 1999, which means he hasn't had a real job this century. An almost obsessive road cyclist and mountain biker, he published a non-fiction book, *Mindful Thoughts for Cyclists*, in 2016.

Moore's mastery of the sonnet form is especially notable. Both his meter and rhyme are so unforced that they seem a natural part of speech. Read out loud, his poems sing from a skill that has been honed over decades of hard work. Also unusual, especially among contemporary poets, is the range of traditional forms he uses. He can pick up the almost impossible form of the ancient Celtic *droighneach* with its triple rhymes, sprung meter, and restrictive rules for alliteration, then produce a sestina, and then neatly turn a Persian *rubha'i*.

In his poetry Moore harkens back to the historical stream of poets that have found meaning, solace, and danger in the pastoral earth and its human and animal inhabitants. Over and over again he works to find the traditional beauty discovered by Homer or Wordsworth. In his *doha*, "Late Frost," he writes

> The frost hits late; a hard bright scattering of crushed stars;
> A white fallen sky, lit by daffodil suns.
>
> A slow-waking winter, gripped with sudden jealousy
> Snatches back the earth from spring's warm, outstretched hand.

This could have been written a thousand years ago, and the beauty of it is that this sense of poetry, of the earth, of the place humankind has found within the living pulse of the earth still can be found in the contemporary world.

Blown Away

A restless wind -
South-west, heavy with salt
And smells of seaweed, storm-stripped from far-off islands -
Sets my mind flapping like luffed sails,
Every thought straining at its shrouds. Holding, just.

But
One rogue gust
And all could be torn loose,
Sent madly swirling miles inland
To wind up wound around
The cracked, barbed boughs of a gale-wrought pine
Way out of reach
And shredded beyond repair.

Called In

In Wellingtons and waterproofs he stands,
A lonely lighthouse in a sea of grass,
To call the cows in: whistles, claps his hands,
Cries 'Hup' and 'Go on then, girls' as they pass:
Unhurried, rope-veined udders swinging, large
With milk, the smells of warm crushed turf and dung
Surrounding them in their slow-motion charge
Towards the gate. Their names are on his tongue
And they obey his summons. What do I
Bring in from my own forays in the field?
No milk or meat, no crop to justify
My time; and yet my labours have their yield:
When nothing's left of this land, man or herd,
Their memory will live. You have my word.

Deflation

Poplars hiss displeasure
At this out-of-sync dishwater sky,
Clouds on the ground.
Draggled wheat fields darken,
The shocked land losing hard-won riches
Laid down and laboured for.
And in the leaves' wind-silvered sibilance
I hear the slow escape of summer:
A punctured season
And a long, slow road ahead.

Doha: Late Frost

The frost hits late; a hard bright scattering of crushed stars;
A white fallen sky, lit by daffodil suns.

A slow-waking winter, gripped with sudden jealousy
Snatches back the earth from spring's warm, outstretched hand.

I could rail, resentful, against this cold selfishness;
Point to all I have endured, hoped for, dreamed of.

Yet with this day's unlooked-for sting comes a clarity:
A sharper sense of all that is, and might be.

Droighneach: Harvest

High summer heat. Out here, the pressure's palpable.
Sun-shimmer on the wheat, and yet we're worrying
About the weather, praying it's possible,
To keep running hell-for-leather with harvesting.

The tractors creep beside combines crawling ceaselessly.
Night brings no sleep for now; we're hauling heavyweight
Trailers gorged with golden grain, and checking constantly
For news of rain; the threat we don't care to contemplate.

Days drag, dredged in dust and diesel fumes. We're wondering
If we've edged ahead. The work consumes us utterly.
From dawn to dew the big rigs roll through, thundering
Scorn at forecasts and fatigue. The heat builds brutally.

One last load. Black battlements brood high overhead.
On the road, racing back beneath a sky suspended
Like an executioner's axe; throbbing thunderheads
Prepare to strike. The first cracks come. Dark, distended

Clouds tear open; an electric ecstasy
Ignites the bristling air too late: the storm's defeated -
The fields stand silent; tyre-tracks the only legacy
We've left. The land exhales. Another crop completed.

Homeland Security

From the hot road
I watched combines make wide-wale corduroy
Of gasping fields cast in bronze and gold;
Racing balers trailing fine brown dust
Build their fleeting henges and tight-rolled scrolls of straw;
Felt the fat, satisfied summer -
The goodness and greenness of the place -
Wrap itself around me.

I come from here. That can never change.
Its deep rhythms are my heartbeat;
By its moods and seasons, I measure out my own small days.

In these dark times I cannot look upon it as I did:
Forces far beyond these gentle hills conflate
A love of one place with a hatred of The Other.

But this country is deep-grained in my hands, clings fast to my boots:
I am bound to it, and it to me
Until I too am gathered in, and finally ploughed under.

Letter of Wishes

When I am gone, do not lay me to rest
In some town-council cemetery: my bones
Would ache for all eternity, distressed
By unfamiliar soil and serried stones.
Don't bury me at sea: I've no desire
To haunt the deep with Davy Jones' crew;
Nor box me up and feed me to the fire:
The planet doesn't need my CO_2.
No. Take me to the woods: the trees will keep
A vigil, that you need not lose your years
In watching me. On rainy days, they'll weep
For me, that your sweet eyes may know no tears.
But now, the sun is shining. No more thought
Of this: there's much to do, and time is short.

Love and Marriage

There's not much left now. All that stuff, brand-new,
We unwrapped, gasping, twenty years ago
Has faded, been passed on, expired, worn through
Or simply vanished. Little did we know
That toaster would explode, those shining pans
Burn black, the glasses chip, the gleaming knives
Turn dull, plates end up mismatched. Some grand plans
Got mislaid, too, somehow. But what survives
We had no need to list; came with no box
Or owner's manual, spares or guarantee.
It's just kept right on working, stood life's shocks
And daily labours; quietly, constantly.
A gift we gave each other with no strings.
Still ours when we have lost all other things.

Field of Dreams

He parks the truck, then takes her by the hand.
They walk together round the field. The bright
March sun strikes silver from the sward; his white
Lambs, soft as new-baked loaves, awake the land
And hope within them. He shares all his grand
Schemes for the flock: she leans on him, the light
Of love strong in her eyes, and holds him tight,
Mind filled with home and children she's got planned.
Does it occur to them that they may see
Their cloudless heaven ripped by sudden storm,
Their high ideals hurled down and smashed like glass?
No thought of this. Not here, not now. They're free
To dream. The sky is clear, the sun is warm
And smiling on the lover and his lass.

Man in the Mirror

Who is this man? I knew him once, I swear,
But though he seems familiar, I can't place
Him. Did we meet out on the road somewhere,
Drink beer, load hay, play music, ride bikes, chase
Loose cows (or ladies)? Something in his face
Speaks of things as they were long lives ago;
Of half-forgotten dreams and days of grace.
He's lithe and quick; makes me feel stiff and slow,
Set in my ways. The world is his to go
And conquer still, while duty, age and fear
Have vanquished me. We could be friends, I know,
But time is short: some day, he'll disappear
And leave the mere remembrance of his light
Until it, too, is taken by the night.

Sestina: Midwinter

So. Winter's chill attendants walk the earth
And starveling days die young in mist and fire.
Above the leafless trees black rook-bands wheel:
Their raucous evensong laments the sun
That sinks behind the sodden, shadowed wood
And night spreads like a sickness through the land.

How long it seems since Spring smiled on this land,
When wild flowers bloomed on banks, and long-cold earth
Stirred in its sleep, awakening the wood
Where bluebells, like smoke from some unseen fire
Swirled round the birches' feet; the lusty sun
Bent cheerfully to turning heaven's wheel.

For months to come the soil will know no wheel:
The rain has made a mire of this land
That, back in summer, cracked beneath a sun
That breathed its heat upon the gasping earth.
Did we once walk bare-limbed in fields of fire,
And crave the shelter of the drowsy wood?

Hard to recall how Autumn dressed the wood
In gaudy gold and copper as the wheel
Sent summer southwards. Then Orion's fire
Blazed higher, and the warmth seeped from the land.
The birds felt mystic stirrings in the earth
And took their mapless pathways to the sun.

And now we stand our furthest from the sun:
The twilight settles quickly in the wood,
And in the tilt and aspect of the Earth
We reach the moment where the ancients' wheel
Begins its long roll back. They blessed the land
And filled their twelve Yule nights with feast and fire.

And still we're drawn to that ancestral fire;
Still counting down the days until the sun
Returns to drive the darkness from the land
And set the new leaves bursting in the wood.
Still following the slow spin of the wheel
That drives the deepest engines of the earth.

I'll leave my fire to stand watch in the wood
Await another Sun, as night-birds wheel
Above the land, and Winter claims the earth.

Penny Hyde

Penny Hyde is an Registered Nurse working with the elderly in the remote landscape of NW New Mexico where she navigates her Subaru over dirt roads that tunnel deep into the Chuska Mountains, through the Bisti Badlands where the bones of dinosaurs have been found, and around the mesas near Chaco Canyon. This geographic region includes the Navajo Nation and Zuni Pueblo. Her poetry helps meld two worlds; modern-day medical care and the traditional ways of medicine men, shamans, and *curanderas*. Many of her clients have no running water or electricity, and English is their second language. She states, "I want to remember spirit when I stoop to enter a Hogan and carry grace with me as I work among the suffering. And sometimes, I find myself writing to give voices to the poor and forgotten."

Hyde's poetry consistently endeavors to infuse compassion and humanity as spiritual answers to the healthcare limitations and financial constraints facing Native American elders living in remote locations throughout Northwestern New Mexico. Laced between her powerful physical images are introspective and often tender moments that attempt to make sense of the telling differences of available resources between each family.

> I talk in a soft, slow hum, dodging promises,
> dishing hope, a gentle predictable rhythm.
> As if stroking her hair, as if caressing away all that's been dumped.
> As if my briefcase carries an endless supply of possibilities
> and I can whip them out, lay before her a banquet.
> She whimpers, she cries, yet all the while,
> from the rickety chair I know I'm nursing myself,
> tending my own sad fragile bones.

Many of the poems demonstrate Hyde's awareness of shamanic healing practices and ancient ancestral traditions. Her poetry beckons the reader to feel deeply into their own bodies so they may discover the healing possibilities that reside underneath their trapped anxieties.

> Keep the lantern of your own light near your bed.
> You will be called now to grieve, to bless and to resurrect.
> Called to suck the marrow from your own soft hip,
> To stir and tend to your own spiced broth.

This is the liminal time where moons drift without direction
and lost strands from the songs of our ancestors
whisper their names from the hollows between the stars.

This is the long season where each of us sets out by foot
upon the unmarked path with our herbs,
thermos of bone soup,
our walking stick and flickering lamp.

Head Injury

This week a heavy man,
a unsteady trailer with steps
shifting from left to right under
the weight of any person entering or leaving.
Space so small and dark, I must stand
near a small window with my clip board
resting on the edge of a dirty sink.
It takes me an entire hour
to ask the questions he cannot answer.

I am in a world of one small bed
a chair, make shift desk,
ancient big box computer,
these things only inches apart.
Near the door,
a broken down bench where cans of beans
wait in a pile for a can opener, a hungry mouth.
On a shelf a sack of potatoes, fresh and out of place,
he will eat if he can find someone to peel them.
Both arms in braces now.

Are you ever sad I ask,
working my way down the list
of required assessment questions and check boxes.
No, no, never sad, he says
but sometimes I wish I could go fishing,
problem is, I have to wait
for somebody to come and take me.
I'd like that though,
to go out to the lake and catch some fish,

his words trailing, as if he knows
he will never see that kind of blue again.

I will try, I respond, in a voice already fading,
I will try and help you.
I fall through time, into his other life
before the engine fell on his head,
before the moment when the lake dried up.
I leave the trailer,
step back into the sun, feel my heart
as it sinks into that lake,
knowing there are no fish.

Going to lunch at a Downtown Cafe

They are sprawled next to each other
against a graffiti door,
tucked slightly out of the wind.
Their legs extending into the walk way
just far enough that passersby take an extra step
avoiding the possibility of tripping or touching
the men's boots. Boots torn up,
one toe on the right foot of the smaller man
ragged beyond repair.

The larger man is leaning into his companion
crouching really, without standing
patting and patting the smaller man's heart.
Moving his hand in circles
and then again the pat pat pat.
He leans very close,
whispers as a woman approaches.
Says something to him she cannot hear,
does not want to hear.
The smaller man lies motionless
does not open his eyes
moves just a hand
from the concrete to his thigh.

She is past them now,
a little breathless,
a little heartsick herself.
Does not remember
if she slowed her pace or quickened.

There is an open space
adrift in her compassion
colliding with fear,
her own internal wasteland
that lengthens her strides
pushing her away.
But there is the echo too
of the soft words
and the pat pat pat,
the haunting.

The Bowl

When I found her
she was sitting on the kitchen floor clutching
the brown bowl, excavated unexpectedly
from the back of a lower cupboard.
She was crying, weeping and rocking with the empty bowl
filling now with years of tears.

She remembers her casseroles baked in the old brown bowl,
warm concoctions served to her children through all their years.
Baked for their blooming hearts,
sleeping and growing under her roof,
served to their mouths, that in the beginning
before the bowl, she had offered her breasts.
Her life so contained then, all of it a meal,
slow baking and bubbling softly in a brown crock bowl.

She wonders where it unraveled.
How, when the final meal was served upon the last plate,
it went unnoticed.
Each of them wandering onto the edge of their page,
shredding themselves as they reached the horizon, disappearing.
The bowl, no longer necessary, finds its way, empty and alone,
to an abandoned shelf in the dark of the cupboard.

Outside trees stand naked in the winter night.
She carries the bowl into the falling snow,
places it under the moon, stands motionless,
trying to hear the sound of a single snowflake
as it settles in the hollow of her heart.

Inside her chest the snow piles up.
She is buried into the winter of her longing,
holding an empty bowl, under the trees, below the moon.
She is howling, I tell you,
She is spilling everywhere.

A Nine Year Old Girl

1.

Here is a girl on a stairwell suspended in her descent
from the room where it happened
to the rooms where it doesn't happen.
The rooms existing in their own separate seas of blindness,
connected now by this tunnel of silent contract
where she will wear her masked and broken face.
Walk with it most of her life.

The man upstairs, who stole from her, has been given the gift
of silent agreement. He is already bloated with confidence
anoints his own greasy hands.
The people in the rooms below her, chattering away,
cocktails in hands in an endless celebration of patriarchal bliss,
will be given the gift as well.
The girl does not yet know she's been discarded,
will move like a cloud of un-belonging,
caught in the folds of a family.

Already she understands the gun-metal color of exile,
the weight of a speaking gun.
Already her own color is turning gray,
and she understands it is not the act itself that is the greater pain
but the silencing, the loss of her own sweet budding song.
Already she understands how one secret chases another.

2.

She is on her knees now, digging through hard dirt
on the longest blackest night,
searching for her original face, for the stones and bones
she left discarded in the stairwell,
for her true mouth that comes to her in dreams,
wanting to speak.
She has brought with her a brown bowl
where she will place the waiting bones,
a few night stars she has hidden near her breast
and the song of a meadowlark.

Season of Lanterns

In late November darkness settles into silence by 5 pm.
It is the season of lanterns.
The time we are called to carry our own light,
step onto the path when the dream wakes us mid-night,
the bones in our flesh having tossed
themselves into the cave of wandering.
our hearts beating with the breath of remembering.

Keep the lantern of your own light near your bed.
You will be called now to grieve, to bless and to resurrect.
Called to suck the marrow from your own soft hip,
to stir and tend to your own spiced broth.

This is the liminal time where moons drift without direction
and lost strands from the songs of our ancestors
whisper their names from the hollows between the stars

This is the long season, where each of us sets out by foot
upon the unmarked path with our herbs,
thermos of bone soup,
our walking stick and flickering lamp.
We make our way back to our own belonging.
To bless the frozen ground with her buried seeds,
spin the starlight into the snow,
stand under the sky and breathe in ice.
Finally to surrender, lie down, sleep till morning light
beneath the evergreens and spruce.

Last Exit

Somewhere in Michigan my mother's friend
lies asleep in a pastel room atop a hospital bed made soft
with a fluffy stuffed dog and a thick down comforter
salvaged from the last few items of her apartment.
There are a few cards on the windowsills,
small vase of flowers on a small table,
a Hospice nurse at the end of a button at the end of the hall.

It is a long road from Alabama.
The online source says 13 hours and 1 minute, to be exact.
The tires slap, slap along the highway
as the SUV pushes through the spring wind,
headed north, headed eventually to a final exit.
My Sister is driving, while my mother directs from a frayed
paper map she has used 100 times, folding and unfolding
it into 4 inch squares. Watching for mile markers, familiar towns,
commenting on nothing at all as they lift over
the hills of Tennessee, glide across Kentucky valleys,
and the flat lands of Indiana.

They are going to have lunch with their friend on her 88th birthday.
They have been friends for 70 years,
threw down anchors in 1948, but began to drift by 1989.
Two families set to sea on lifeboats drifting to opposite shores.
My mother moving from a tiny apartment, stuffed with 3 daughters,
to a comfortable white carpeted home in Florida.
Her friend from her plush blue living room, suburban home,
to a smoky subsidized flat, their conversation dwindling year by year.

Yet here they are, still searching for blooms in their lonely hearts.
Mother driving, then eventually being driven 13 hours and 1 minute
every single year and back again to take her friend to lunch in the spring.
What happened to those pretty girls, slow dancing at the YMCA
with their future husbands? Each of them now long divorced.
What broken pieces can they not find?

This time, they will actually touch. Hold hands tight,
knobby hands with blue veins, while mother sits on her bed
her friend beams, a broad smile birthing from her sunken face,
her eyes, behind her mammoth glasses, singing.

They will sit like this a long time, my sister, quiet in the shadows, listening to the music of that post war dance.

Albert DeGenova

Albert DeGenova has published four books of poetry and two chapbooks. He is also the founder and co-editor of *After Hours* magazine, a journal of Chicago writing and art, which launched in June of 2000. He received his MFA from Spalding University in Louisville, Kentucky and leads several writing workshops throughout the year, as well as an annual writing week at The Clearing Folk School in Ellison Bay, WI. He hosts the monthly Traveling Mollys reading series in Oak Park, Illinois, now in its 22nd year. He is also a blues saxophonist and one-time contributing editor to *Down Beat* magazine, a publication about jazz. DeGenova splits his time between Sturgeon Bay, Wisconsin, where he has a writing shack in the woods, and the metro Chicago area.

Reading DeGenova's poetry is like listening to a jazz concert as words become notes that riff up and down the scales of meaning and emotion. There is always a rhythm to the lines that, when read out loud, sound like a jazz chant of images, characters, and incidents conjuring up the feeling of a half lit stage at a venue filled with most of the emotions a human being can feel.

If you read DeGenova out loud, which is highly recommended, sounds dance, sear, laugh, become so sensuous you half wonder if you really should be involved with them, and then twist into a moment or story that makes you remember you are a human being. There is beauty, ugliness, and the panoply of the human condition that makes readers look into themselves and wonder, who is this describing anyway? Me? My best friend? Some alien that's slipped into human form? All of us?

We are the ancient dirt beneath our feet,
are the Nazis, the Popes, the Michigan Militia
all the hot dog vendors of Bourbon Street,
we are the President, we are the bombs,
the dead babies, the homeless garbage eaters,
we are history —
the waiter delivers our fathers' tabs,
and we pay, we pay.

DeGenova can swing between poems so sensuous they almost burn on the page to a poetry that contains insight into the human condition that still manages to be a song.

Thanksgiving Poem

Young buck drags
  his hindquarters —
eyes wild for escape —
   across the unlit road.
The car ahead
   had swerved, pulled
 off the road
our friends out of their car
   shaking, pacing, *Oh Jeez! Oh Jeez!*
in a field, behind
   the struggling, the useless
legs. *Call the police.*
An accident. Flashlight. A shot.
Heaving steamy breath. Second
shot. To the head. Silence.
  Policeman pulls
the carcass to the gravel shoulder.
   Highway crew's morning pick-up.
Again the moonlight, white
   frost, empty fields.

Farther up the highway, a country tavern,
our friend's son, bartender
and chef, serves us
whiskey, no
ice, no flourish —
his friends go
   for the carcass, the precious meat
cannot be left
   to spoil. Out back
the buck is dressed. The tenderloin
removed and fried with onions
and carrots. A white plate is
passed along the bar
for sharing, thinly-sliced dark-colored
venison, one communal fork. The plate
   reaches us, we hesitate
a moment. The taste
is wild, it tastes
   like running.

Black Pearl

I hear a faraway cello
legato tone as long as life itself it seems —
the horsehair bow turns
on edge, the timbre winces
to the wind, to the thunder.
The Pacific reshapes miles of beach
overnight, sometimes in minutes. Waves,
their sucking recoil, the salty tumult
teases me today
with nothing more than a bruised hip —
how dare I rest against a rock.

From within the splashing crash
I hear a muffled baritone's tempt, what
waits for you within the churning wave?
I've heard love sound like this. My god
is not this heaving brute of sea, but a quiet
black pearl in the shell of my heart.
I feel the hair on my arm move as it dries,
the flies bite my ankles. Too much love
in my one stormy life to ever deny god

A Good Hammer

Blessed are the splinters, the little
cuts that never bleed, the dark
blue-black fingernails —
at 53 you long
for more hours as a carpenter
nailing and planing, a pencil
behind your ear, sawdust
on your shoes, the clean
sweet smell of fresh-cut lumber
in the basement, the backyard,
in the new attic bedroom —
eager for that brief moment when you close
the toolbox and exhale the good

and strong of completion, something
your sons can sit on, climb up
or walk under. What is
a marketing manager anyway?
A son should see his father's work, see
that a sound joint fitted in the wind will hold
against rain and hail and time, should
remember his father's sweat.
Learn the only tool he needs,
finally, is a good hammer, love
he can hold in his hand.

One-Sixtieth of a Second

He is almost out of the frame. Maybe he is hesitating, trying not to step into the picture, leaning on the backdoor with one hand, the other hand in his pocket, looking down, not at the camera, not at the aging woman in the backyard of this four-flat apartment house. He may not want to interrupt her. The woman is sitting on a simple wood bench, surrounded by potted Easter lilies and hydrangea, which she is cutting. The flower-pots are decorated with foil and bows — perhaps leftovers from her church. The kitchen windows are open to let in the late spring air. She wears no sweater over her plain apron and short-sleeved housedress. She is busy, careful, focused on her work.

He is young, 19 or 20, already dressed beyond the means of this simple backyard, this working class home in 1950 Chicago. His white dress shirt hangs open, tails out of dark dress pants, sleeves rolled up. He isn't look-ing at his mother, or at the photographer, who is probably his older brother. She is at the center of the picture, unaware of the camera. She can't see the son who keeps his distance, waiting to walk through the frame, he could easily reach around the corner of the building and touch her.

Black and white, shadow upon shadow, a frozen one-sixtieth of a sec-ond. What little illumination there is. He is my father. This is as well as I know him.

First Love

You, who loved me first,
gave me words. Now,
I offer them back.
You forget
sometimes, so I
complete your sentence.
You were nineteen-years-old
counting my toes, your firstborn —
we've grown up together.
I was in the backseat as you
learned to drive. With no one
on my sidelines, you sent
my uncles.
        Today, at 57,
I have friends your age. Time,
that elastic measure
so much living between us,
your life, my life — the slant rhymes
I've left out. We've an unheard language.
No need to read your yellowing journals,
the passions you couldn't say out loud —
I understand, and maybe
our living is enough, you
just a few steps ahead, reaching back
to take my hand.
Look both ways you say again and again.
You, who I loved first,
to the last word.

Refuse Pile of Mortal Sins

Tree limbs, plastic water bottles, unfurled condoms,
Lake Michigan sweeps with steady strokes —
its refuse neatly piled against smooth stones
in quiet corners of its sandy beaches.

Freeways too, though lacking wave and tide,
collect what's left behind — hub caps, broken tail lights,
a small blue jacket — all piled high against
cement lane dividers under dark overpasses.

My front yard accumulates its own
leftovers in that neglected corner between
stairs and house, under some shrubs —
washed-out window cleaning flyers, soaked and crumbling
newspapers, the lost homework of passing kids.

This is the way of discarded things once
valuable, once practical, once desired —
there is a place behind my third rib
on the right side where I'm sure
I've tossed my first kiss and a long-winded lesson
from my grandfather on making crosses
out of long green fronds on Palm Sunday.

But under my heart's back porch
where no one dares, so many shredded photos
and scratchpad scribblings and silver napkin rings
dropped between wooden slats, underneath
with the spider webs and raccoon droppings
is the place of mortal sins, the buried
evidence, the fall from grace — sometimes, on gray afternoons
in November or warm mornings in May, I'm tempted
again, to reach
to touch what is gone, that once-known resurrection
that one turn of the hour glass so much more threatening
than that last bite of chocolate rum truffle
spoiled as it is
still wrapped in a napkin, saved from then, a gift for me
from then, way down there, never quite
out of sight.

              Some acts
are simply unforgivable —
no matter how strong the hunger.

Living History

Hemingway's breath still lingers
here on this street, my street,
his street.
Did he ever walk across
my lawn, sit on my porch
on his way to school, the same school
my sons sit in now?
I walk past his boyhood home,
look up to his third floor bedroom.
The light is on tonight in that center window.
Whose 17-year-old shadow
contemplates the glory of war?
Do those old floorboards still hold
the crescent moons of his fingernails?
If matter and energy can never be destroyed,
then history is a fishbowl —
we share this same water for eternity.
The song Hemingway hears
as he runs to catch a football
is my voice, my son's piano from our open door —
then, if it's all true
I swim in the same salty Mediterranean
where my grandfathers wash their feet.
I touch the skin of the dead then,
when I write my name in the dust
on my brother's Manhattan bookshelves
and the dead know me, know I am
here — now — trying to taste
their history like a ripe plum
like sour mash, like
all the lovers who've kissed my lover's lips.
We are the ancient dirt beneath our feet,
are the Nazis, the Popes, the Michigan Militia
all the hot dog vendors of Bourbon Street,
we are the President, we are the bombs,

the dead babies, the homeless garbage eaters,
we are history —
the waiter delivers our fathers' tabs,
and we pay, we pay.

Family Album

These are pictures of my family —
smell the garlic sautéed in olive oil
and poured over blanched escarole greens,
the stale air of trans-Atlantic steerage
fused with the sweat and bad breath
the rotting teeth of *Napolitano* poverty,
the oily coal smoke that replaced
sea air, forever,
the long train ride New York to Chicago,
one way.

These are pictures of my family —
fading color slides in plastic sleeves
that account for a decade, the 1950s
the fulcrum years
when my family teetered between
the slum streets of Naples and
Southside Chicago unpaved alleys and
suburban subdivisions.
My grandparents with enough English to
play with their grandchildren, my young American parents who
never spoke their parents' language to each other.
We are the babies.

These are pictures of my family —
eating and smiling, singing "*happy birthday day*"
preserved in plastic just like Grandma's sofa . . .
the sofa that discolored anyway, the streets that were paved,
we grew up, those who remembered Ellis Island
have been buried.
We are no longer guinea dock rats, we are no longer
sweating dark-skinned immigrants, we no longer
dig the ditches for Chicago sewers, no longer
lay the bricks of the city's skyline.

These are pictures of
my family.
I breathe these pictures into my lungs
and smell my grandfather's cigar,
his wine press and the emptied oak barrels.

My sons read this family album like a text book,
the dry branches of a family tree, the sterile history
of lineage.
My sons will never know what an Italian smells like.

We are become
Americans with Italian names
tossing old country phrases
bocce balls that
miss the mark.

Among Friends

I pour the red wine —
to each guest a personal
toast, the eye to eye
Salud, the glass to glass
clink, the dull sound
of full crystal to full crystal
that does not chime. This

night, the wine is
dark, a fine vintage that asks
ever so discreetly, between
the laughs and stories:
who here this night
has ever hated the morning, who
among this group of friends has thought,

Tonight I step over the line,
in front of the train? Whose chair
sinks into the carpet having slipped
your mooring; easier to drink
in silence pretending to listen staring
into the eyes of your friend's wife

than to resist the nagging urge
to watch this repartee from the top of the stairs.

Who steps into the bathroom to stare
into his own wine eyes? How many bottles
between dinner and morning? There are those
among us empty already.
Red rings stain the white satin tablecloth
so many distant planets.

We Thought We Could

I'll hold the umbrella, your arm
in mine, we'll walk through
the looking glass through the ink-filled rain
through what's left of our meaningful dream
peer back at our scribbled vanity.
We hide under desks and behind
our tailored cloak of connectedness
and precious handmade chapbooks, it's all
too much lettuce
our reality sandwiches are rubber playthings,
those old and dry manifestos.
The barren, poison-tipped
bullets of privilege
are forged of synthesized metals —
where is blind Cupid's golden bow
gone like so many mythic dreams
ended, the alarm clock
BuzzBuzzBuzzing
our awakening out of reach.
We've put the pillows over our heads
with easy posts and angered shares,
outstretched fingers that hope
and fail to touch more, more than
this — this wasted, bombed out Camelot.

Transform malaise, our bourgeois curse,
squeeze wine from intoxicating poems
exalting, exhalted
taste the prophets

of jazz, of rock 'n' roll
of benevolent science
their golden-ruled breaths
and know again
the black and white of sin's responsibility.
The alarmed alarm shakes
the Yes-We-Can dream that was
America,
no poetry to this dark morning
no trust for a rising sun, I've nothing to offer
but my own confusion caught
between the singing Buddha
and the hot smoking barrel of the dark dyanmo
menacing in the machinery of the night.

Chris Moran

Chris Moran, an English poet, began writing poetry in 2011 after a diagnosis of Progressive Multiple Sclerosis "violently rocked the boat on my reasonably calm sea. I fell overboard where I stayed floundering for a good few months while I did my best to come to terms with this news, splashing around from shock to denial, to acceptance and back again, until I was rescued by what I guess was my muse."

At first Moran did what most beginning poets do and simply wrote down thoughts and feelings, Initially her poems were related to herself and her illness, but then "I tried to write in a universal way so that maybe it could help others going through difficult times in whatever area of life." In 2013 she joined a writing group called Adventures in Creative Writing led by the British poet James Nash, and the world of poetry opened up for her.

In the best of her poems there is an honesty that can be almost painful as she writes about her disease or her earlier victory over addiction. Sometimes, as in the sonnet "In Between,"

My body searches for an in between,
Not winter's gelid wind or summer's heat
But where the birds dip wings into the gleam
Of liquid warmth and air is fresh and sweet.
I long for daylight hours and newborn hearts
Where buds break free from safety of the womb,
A place where life begins, where journeys start
And fears abate as flowers begin to bloom
Whose joy is so infectious, so sublime
Their small hurts barely touch them, peace abounds.
I'd love to share this calm throughout springtime,
Spend hours alone just listening to the sounds
Where I, at last, feel free to breathe, serene.
My body craves this precious in between.

In other poems the pain is closer to the surface:

From the corner of my eye
I could see it — disability
sitting on the sidelines
gloating, large as life
with a smugness I could have slapped.

But often, in both free verse and sonnets, she has something memorable to say in language that sticks in the reader's mind, letting the reader know what courage is really like.

I, Myself and Me

I search the nooks and crannies of myself
and find me huddled, cold, a frightened child,
afraid of every ounce of life, the wealth
of confidence bestowed upon me, pride
and self-assurance, head poised way up high,
tall enough to reach the glowing Milky Way.
Oh yes, I owned it once upon a time;
I could tease the stars and lead the sun astray.
So now I sit beside myself and smile,
compassion healing all the wounds that bleed.
We linger quietly, me, myself and I
and feed each other love, our only need.
If this is what it takes to set me free,
we'll eat and drink our fill, I, myself and me.

Dancing with Grief

Grief devours her face; an icy waterfall
gushes down her neck, her shivering breast.
It's not the loss of loved ones she recalls;
the loss she feels is simply for herself.
If only it were over in a flash,
a firework's fleeting glory blaze - then calm
and equanimity restored at last,
but grief clings hard, a limpet to her arm.
I won't let go, says grief, you need me here;
I have a purpose to fulfil - you'll see -
Just fall into my arms, forego your fears;
just fall into my heart; come, dance with me.
With open arms she lets him take the lead;
with swirling skirts she lets her colours bleed

Dad's Hat

It sits on the kitchen table like
a huge bird, motionless,
protecting its young,
a light brooding patch
where it has worn thin.

Its been there for three weeks now.

I pluck a small feather of courage
from the anguished air,
ask if I could perhaps put it away.
Her sharp-edged words pierce
my sleeping loss and it stirs.

I make more tea;
she sits squarely on his chair,
knits a few more ounces of grief
into the last few stitches
of a sleeve,
as a vagrant star peers
through the window
at the close of another
wounded day.

Past Lives

He takes his tiny brother by the hand;
they sit by the window,
browse family photos on the sill.
There is no one else here.
The room seems like a deep secret
they both promise to keep.
That's you when you were a baby,
says the older one,
that's what you looked like.
And that's mummy when she was small.
Its almost as if they have been here before.

They stare at the sudden rain
pelting against the glass, silent,
recalling past lives.

New Year's Eve

The house is quiet now; they have strolled
into the darkness of a passing year,
each to leave their footprints, fresh and bold
upon earth's floor; a newborn path to steer.
Sometimes it's hard to bid a fond farewell;
we'd rather scream and shout the old year out,
forget about it, crush it's brittle shell
as if it never mattered, didn't count.
But if we search among the fragments there,
we're sure to find some long forgotten gold
glistening in an ancient sunlight's glare,
a silken thread of strength, perhaps, to hold.
I hear the thrum of a new year's life begin,
so I dust myself down and stumble in

Owl

It has to be the owl, it's the eyes I think;
they draw me into a hypnotic depth,
pools of luscious darkness where I can sink
inside myself at last, no burdens kept.
Beneath crepuscular wings I take flight
to newfound freedom, (sadly only dreamt),
until the dawn creeps through this purple night
and leaves me fearful of the new day's scent.
But this wise creature, or so the stories flow,
lulls me into an unexpected peace,
where I feel a welcome sense of letting go
and shackles of disquiet are strangely released.
I weep into his feather duvet wings;
his warmth embraces me and numbs the sting.

Lost and Found

I long for what I can no longer be,
strong limbs that move and never question how.
I long for who I can no longer see,
the one who disappeared and left me now
to tread life's path a very different way;
a stranger in a world that I once knew
where land and sky just seem to fall away
and raging, rolling seas, my soul imbrue.
Until a shaft of light somewhere appears
and lulls the tempest to soft whispered waves
that ripple on the shore, allaying fears
restoring peace and hope my spirit craves.
The sun, the moon, the earth now realigned,
and I am who I thought I'd left behind

Crying Over Spilt Tea

I spilt a full cup of tea
over the bed;
my hand simply gave way.
It happens.
Everything soaked through
including myself, and

you, the stoical carer
already overloaded with
extra chores, and a time schedule
that used to belong to me,
rose calmly to the challenge,
stripped the bed,
placed stained linen carefully to soak
and went out of the door
to collect our grandson
for the day.

From the corner of my eye
I could see it - disability

sitting on the sidelines
gloating, large as life
with a smugness I could have slapped.

Sometimes I feel like a child.

But unlike a child,
I watched your face as you
cleared the mess;
the pursed lips, unassailable truth
in the extra crease on a forehead,
that said
this wasn't on today's list.

We said nothing;
silence grew louder
until we both heard it -
the sadness, sobbing softly
for our loss.

Bruce Goodman

Bruce Goodman is truly a renaissance man, a former Catholic priest and a retired school teacher, he likes to catalog his writings: 1,700 stories to date, more than 160 piano compositions, 60 produced plays for children, teenagers, and adult groups, and, well, "a number of poems." He has also written a novel, *A Passing Shower*, and an autobiography. He currently lives in Stratford, Taranaki, New Zealand, "slap-bang next to a volcano that hasn't erupted for several hundred years and is yonks overdue."

A master of traditional forms, like Nick Moore, Goodman's poems tend to be graceful, musical, and clever. In "I Cannot Love the Sky" he not only has fun with the scientific names of things:

I cannot love the sky
until I know the scientific names for all the clouds.
Look! how dramatic is Cumulonimbus!

I cannot love the garden
until I know the scientific names for all the flowers.
Oh! such lovely Lobularia maritima!

I cannot love the song
until I know the scientific names for all the birds.
Hark! to the rapture of that Turdus philomelos!

But he turns it into a love poem with the very last line, a practice that flavors much of his poetry.

As with his compositions, stories (many of which are flash fiction), and plays, he loves to count and catalog, and then give it all a little flip and turns the poem in an unexpected direction.

I Cannot Love the Sky

I cannot love the sky
until I know the scientific names for all the clouds.
Look! how dramatic is Cumulonimbus!

I cannot love the garden
until I know the scientific names for all the flowers.
Oh! such lovely Lobularia maritima!

I cannot love the song
until I know the scientific names for all the birds.
Hark! to the rapture of that Turdus philomelos!

I cannot love reflections in the water
until I've checked for giardia,
those anaerobic flagellated protozoan parasites of the phylum Sarcomas-
    tigophora.

I cannot love you
until I have dissected your opinions
tested your resolve
verified your good faith
and checked that you don't have a Daucus carota stuffed up your
    Sphincter ani externus
like some overcharged know-all who

...cannot love the sky

The Meaning of Flowers

The path from my front door
is lined with maybe more than flowers;
each bloom bud stands somehow
for love, or joyful vows, or truth...
Since ancient times virtues
lived nestled in a blue or red,
pink or white, petal bed:
love felt but never said, for fear;

the grace of rue; the cheer
of daisies; phlox that cares, adores!

And yet my pathway walk
is lined with silent thoughts, harsher
than thistles of a marsh;
despair that wilts and lasts; bereft
of hope, since when you left;
footsteps fading, heart cleft, too late
to lock the garden gate,
too late to hide the hate that seethes
along the path, in trees,
in flowers, in seeds, from my front door.

All day I think my ears will catch
the lifting of the latch.

Sea Waves

Sea waves! Kinaesthetic
   masterpiece! The earth's trick to shine
     hefty stones into fine
       marble and, over time, transform
         dull rock. Beauty is born
       not in fierce forceful storms but slow,
     quiet, gentle to and fro,
   wave on wave, stop and go, hard grit.

Children ever question,
   perpetual in their din and quest
     to know. They prod and pest.
       Their parents never rest at all;
        but as the breakers fall
       on stony shores to maul and grind,
     Mum turns into diamond,
   and Dad, wave-worn, refined forged iron.

Frog

The frog
a tad too old
to hop from log to rock
content to sit and bathe in sun
croaked

It Just Seems That Way

Swaying grass in wind
teaches me to dance in one spot.
It makes the hillside waltz
but really not.
It just seems that way.

I wait, stuck in corners,
dumped in old folks' home.
He's long past it, so they say.
He dribbles in his chair.
He wheezes in his air.
His mind's not very clear.
His bank account is bare.
He won't see out the year.
His end must soon be near.
This place has a bloody waiting list as long as your arm.

And yet

Swaying grass in wind
teaches me to dance in one spot.
It makes the hillside waltz
but really not.
It just seems that way.

Blue

Kingfisher waited near fish-filled stream and flashed blue fire.
Distant thunder grumbled to a scream and flashed blue fire.

A welder melded into shape tough unbending steel;
this artist's arc launched one steady beam and flashed blue fire.

The frantic horse's metal shoes on stony gravel
broke the silence of the morning's gleam and flashed blue fire.

Massed irises turned their heads towards the rising sun;
yellow, purple, peach, rose, rust, white, cream; and flashed blue fire.

And Bruce, patience at an end with this and that and things,
saw a growing mound of stifled dreams, and flashed blue fire.

Gary Jones

Gary Jones is a writer and teacher who summers in Door County and winters in Platteville, Wisconsin. He has published a memoir, *Ridge Stories* (Wisconsin Historical Society Press 2019) and a book of poems, *Gently Used* (2017) as well as poetry in a number of small literary journals and magazines.

His poetry usually has the same wry humor as his prose, looking at the world a little cross-eyed as he storms through a variety of times and cultures with a dollop of cleverness and a definite flare for language. He often hankers back to a sensibility he learned in Wisconsin driftless country on a windswept ridge when times were, like they still are, for farmers determined to wrest a livelihood from the land. His sensibilities are not those of the highly cultured academic learning their craft from large tomes of books hidden in the vastness of a forever library. Rather, they are those of a man who knows his literature, but also knows how life is just not quite what it is cracked up to be by those of a more serious nature.

> Yes, I have been inappropriately touched by literature;
> I have been fondled by Shakespeare's sonnets,
> And once, in the back seat of a car,
> By one of Elizabeth Barrett Browning's;
> (Her nude iambic feet look quite lovely in the dark!)

he writes in "A British Lit Teacher Tells All." Such are life's O La Las, and "you've got to be kidding mes."

This does not mean that Jones is never serious in his work. That is definitely not true. What it does mean is that he comes at that seriousness with a little tongue in cheek and looks askance about how he approaches what he is telling us. If you are entertained a little while showering at the YMCA and seeing that "au naturel satyr tinted olive by Mediterranean sun," that's okay too.

Dressing in Darkness:
A Writer at Work

Like a clandestine lover I dress by Braille in autumnal darkness,
searching fly-down boxers in a yesterday's lasagna of clothing
draped on the seat of a black Windsor chair, a tag-up tee-shirt,
zipper-down jeans, buttoned plaid flannel, sock-stuffed shoes.

With arms extended in a foggy dimness, I find my way to stairs
and ease my way down, an ancient Romeo racing the tardy sun,
leaving behind me a vintage Juliet, grateful for added bed space,
and flip the switch on the coffeemaker that sets about its work,

gurgling and sputtering, coughing and hacking, like an old man,
clearing his throat in preparation for once again meeting the dawn,
retired not for the night, but for morning, searching out words,
like loose change, a ring of keys, reading glasses, a worn wallet,

spilled amid the debris gathered on the surface of an antique desk,
hoping to find the oracle, gently awaken him, and listen, patiently.

Looking for Christopher Robin

The trail was back-lit by the morning sun,
like the flame-colored light of a distant fire
filtering through dew-damp leaves of trees,
the implied warning of a red-sky morning,
a stillness, a hesitation on the leaf-mold path,
a search for the elusive Christopher Robin,

and I thought of the others that I'd traveled,
evocative Old Stage Road, lost Wagon Trail,
the puzzle of paths that veined Pen Park
and running them with other Christopher
harriers that I had known, foot and fancy
free, and I one of them, almost boy at heart,

like the author I met at a writer's conference,

Walking Home Ground, his published book,
In the footsteps of Muir, Leopold, Derleth,
and we forge trails in our old-growth woods,
mine a quarter-mile long, adorned with masks,
with totems, with statues, with religious icons,

and occasionally we look up at patches of sky,
bits of blue pushing through the tops of trees,
a view that lets us see forever, always hopeful
that the red sky at night will still bring delight,
and that the paths we pave with all our words
will be happy trails again, finding Christopher.

My Friend, Tom

smiles from his perch on a curly maple lowboy
sitting in the hallway at the bottom of the stairs,
the regal bust of president Thomas Jefferson,
only plaster, but with the white sheen of marble,
like his famous words, All men are created equal,
inspiring for us to behold, but ultimately hollow.

The Monticello gift shop offers the bust for sale
with a lofty price tag of several hundred dollars,
but we picked Tom up at a resale shop, a bargain,
a fanfare for the common man, our noble guest.
Come and see us, we had wished at Monticello,
and here he has, and as I pass, I smile back at him.

When old age and new politics make me frown,
I welcome any opportunity to allow myself a grin.

Still Waters

Do not lead me beside still waters,
unless planning my burial at sea,

but rather let the chosen waters fall,
like those of Frank Lloyd Wright,

gurgling and burbling like naiads,
bubbling in sudsy anticipation,
journeying from purest springs,
boyhood creek, developing rapids,
slowing into the muddiest of rivers,
arriving at an old salt destination.

Still waters are for churchy folk;
fizzy waters for people who party.
Keep me safe from stagnant waters,
their empty promises to run deep.

Tall Trees

That I had become long of tooth
and gray of beard was inevitable;
but the towering trees around me,
pines and maples, quite unexpected.

They began young Tannenbaums
and willowy optimistic saplings,
soft of green needle, callow of leaf,
at play in an expanse of new lawn,

now piercing the sky's clearness,
standing on their very tiptoes,
hoping for an even better view,
and I rock back my head to look,

fighting vertigo, stiffness of neck,
and I'm not praying, I tell myself,
only remembering to breath in,
and out, the rhythm of gardening,

an evolution of all that's vegetable,
a revolution of that which is animal,
a resolution of this becoming mineral,
these tall trees, busy, keeping watch.

At the National Gallery of Art

for J. Alfred Prufrock

His back to me he showered at the YMCA,
and unobserved I watch him from my falling water,
as if I were standing alone in the National Gallery of Art,
this au naturel satyr tinted olive by Mediterranean sun,
butt-parted fur down to backwards knees, thin ankles
spreading to cloven hooves, and I knew, should he pivot,
I'd see horn stubs amid curls, tangled whorls of chest hair.

I worried over what mythic magic I might have missed
with my ghostly smooth skin and undivided feet,
scrubbing myself with anti-bacterial soap, rinsing,
shivering beneath cooling water, the giggling of nymphs
drowned by the counter-clockwise swirling of the drain,
disappearing silently into the ancient bowels of earth.

A British Lit Teacher Tells All

Yes, I have been inappropriately touched by literature;
I have been fondled by Shakespeare's sonnets,
And once, in the back seat of a car,
By one of Elizabeth Barrett Browning's;
(Her nude iambic feet look quite lovely in the dark!)

Yes, I have been inappropriately touched by literature;
I have been groped by the work of the carpe diem poets,
Abandoning myself to their shallow promises,
Plucked rose buds by Suckling, Herrick, and Lovelace,
Poetry that often seizes more than the day.

Yes, I have been inappropriately touched by literature;
I have been caressed by the silky words of the Romantic poets,
The naked crooning of Lord Byron, Shelley, and Keats,
Alfresco romps through sensual diction and syntax,
Verse adverse to more than one-night stands.

Yes, I have been inappropriately touched by literature;
And I have been gangbanged by the poetry
That my students have written for me,
But I was a willing victim, I confess,
Seduced by their innocence and youth and hope.

Snow Falling

A snow falling on the pines sort of day,
windless flakes sifting down from leaden skies
black sentinel crow frozen to an oak limb,
in the distance, the scrape of shovel on cement,

the sort of day when long novels beckon,
forgotten quilt pieces call for stitches,
hickory nuts await the hammer and picks,
overdue letters ask to be written and sealed,

a well-made bed on this sort of day, invites,
accepting no regrets, warm bare skin pressed,
the past rediscovered between flannel sheets,
buried under fragrant layers of vintage quilts

a day of sorting, of sifting, of searching,
when questions aren't answered, but forgotten.

The Dark Ages

Learning came to a standstill during the Dark Ages,
Mrs. Laufenburg told us at the Wheat Hollow School,
eight grades gathered in one room to learn about the world,
and I imagined a locked door and boarded windows,
a year-round summer vacation, but without sunshine.

Not until I was fully grown did I realize Dark Ages
come and go:
sanctioned beatings of labor organizers,

interment of Japanese-Americans,
kangaroo court trials of un-Americans,
blood of young men shed for dominoes,
or carelessly spilled for crude oil,
the triumph of oligarchy over democracy,
the need for xenophobia and miscegenation,
the justification of bigotry and racism.

And now, long past middle age, I see public schools,
metaphorical locks on their doors,
sheets of figurative plywood nailed over their windows,
children of small rural schools, like the one I attended,
clustered refugees in the new world of education,
a climate change during which the sun doesn't shine,
and Mrs. Laufenberg worries about her teacher retirement.

Son of Adam

A son of Adam, my father killed snakes
while his wife my mother baked apple pies.
Bitter about his father's condemning curse,
compelling him to sweat and toil in the dirt,
he vented his frustration on innocent snakes.

A New Testament son, I made reparations
for the sins of my father, shooing sunbathers
on my walks into the safety of roadside ditches,
and waving occasional laundry room visitors
back to their mouse hunt in the cool garage,

and once, when I found a tangled fox snake
caught in the length of a bunched grape net,
I came to his rescue, leather gloves, scissors,
and gripping him behind his ears, while he
coiled and recoiled, snipped until he was free,

and I, an Androcles, waved goodbye to him
as he parted grass during his slithery escape,
calling softly after him, Till we meet again,
rolled the nylon netting, stuffed it in a bag,
and closed the garage door on my new friend.

Ina Schroders-Zeeders

Ina Schroders-Zeeders has served as the Island poet of Terschelling in the Netherlands, where she has lived most of her life, since 2018. She has published six volumes of poetry in English. Mostly, however, she has written and published over 400 novels in Dutch, some of which have been translated into other European languages. She is also a prolific short story writer. Her poetry has appeared in Great Britain and European magazines and anthologies that publish in English.

Recently widowed, Schroders-Zeeders poetry is often concerned with the complex agonies of contemporary life, leavened by a sense of acceptance and peace inside the turmoil of love, loss, anxiety, loneliness, and experiences that range from moments in everyday life to the supernatural. There are times when poems are clearly not written by a native English speaker, but they are nearly always coherent, sometimes beautiful, and often powerful.

In some of her poetry she masters meter and rhyme in the traditions of English poetry. At other times she uses free verse. A poem like "The Thought" represents the metaphysical reach found in a lot of her verse:

She feels the thought as physical,
a growth under her skin, it glows in her bones,
yet it occupies the room she sleeps in,
walks with her and keeps her company
while her mind wanders off to the day.

Chemist

Words have been used for other sentences,
but even if they are the same
those were not written in her name,
not meant the way she means them,
as the receiver of her words is another person.

Her worries are that he will never understand.
She tries again to make the formula work,
holding sentences to light

and slightly shaking test tubes,
admiring crimson and violet merge.

She omits acids and bitter substances, adding salt,
knowing she might as well throw it away; she is aware
he does not share her idea of sugar into chemistry.
He can not see her newly made colour, not appreciate the taste.
She writes him her best letter, and he will never care.
Irony to do

Emotions put in words, then stored
in corners of the cupboard also known as heart,
unfold as linen. I can see the stains
of where too much was spilled,
where mould has taken over blood.

There is a silent moth
escaping in the blue of day,
and you are gone, and I am left
in dust and feather bed,
with heaps of irony to do.

The Balance

She weighs the thought by the weight of her child
as she carries him up the stairs —
the boy seems lighter —
but she won't speak of this with the father.

Slowly she reaches the landing,
where she forces her thought over the balcony —
as it would crash the bed of the little one,
as it would shake the house on its base,
and the walls be tumbling down.

The Thought

She feels the thought as physical,
a growth under her skin; it glows in her bones,
yet it occupies the room she sleeps in,
walks with her and keeps her company
while her mind wanders off to the day.

The thought lives in her arms and wants to possess her,
and she lets it enter, time after time.
It enters, stays and yet enters in new proportions,
new appearances — this overwhelming thought
that she could be herself again, and finally be safe.

The Lodger

Death moved in with me some years ago
and will not leave.
He pays his rent in ticking clocks,
I hear him sigh in squeaking floors and howling wind,
and dust reminds me he is here to stay.
He sits opposite me at breakfast in a silent, grumpy mood.
I put a brochure of a cruise on his plate today,
hoping he will take the hint
and pack his stuff and go away.

Making Memories Fly

Our thoughts hanging over us,
invisible text balloons, colliding, flirting,
some of yours mating with mine,
and new thoughts are born.

They will once set off into life,
freed cage birds,
no longer intertwined in our speech, gone
with more and more blue skies in between.

You have a way with words, I say,
and I think you know what I mean,
as your hands are a bird now,
flying silently, fluently, away.

Felinelle

The cat is always shitting on the floor.
We tried to educate him, but no luck.
He runs away, and we just close the door.

We do not want this shitty cat no more.
We are fed up with all his nasty yuck.
The cat is always shitting on the floor.

The neighbour once declared us war.
He stepped in shit and told us that we suck.
He ran away, and we just closed the door.

We used to like our cat, but now? What for?
How could we know this cat was such a schmuck?
The cat is always shitting on the floor.

The neighbours moved, the street is as before.
We'll never get rid of the cat, so we are stuck.
The cat is always shitting on the floor.
He runs away and we just close the door.

Estella Lauter

Estella Lauter had a distinguished academic career both at the University of Wisconsin-Green Bay and the University of Wisconsin-Oshkosh where she was Chair of the English Department. She has published two influential studies, *Women as Mythmakers* and *Feminist Archetypal Theory: Interdisciplinary Re-Visions of Jungian Thought*, among other scholarly works. Since she has retired Lauter has reveled in the writing community, publishing four chapbooks and enjoying membership in three writing workshops. Her poems have won awards from WFOP, the Wisconsin Writers Association, *Fox Cry*, and the *Peninsula Pulse*, among others. She has also published in several literary journals, including *Bramble, Midwest Review, Stoneboat, Free Verse, Verse Wisconsin* and *Wisconsin People and Ideas*. Two poems were nominated for the Pushcart award.

She was appointed Poet Laureate of Door County for 2013-2015, during which time she founded the Door County Poets Collective that published an anthology, *Soundings: Door County in Poetry* (Caravaggio Press, 2015). The Collective is now, under her leadership, producing a second anthology, *Half Way to the North Pole*. She co-edited the 2017 *Poets Calendar* for WFOP with Francha Barnard on the theme of water.

Lauter's poetry can contain traces of her life as a scholar as in "How I Met Pablo Neruda," or the historical details in *You Never Said. We Didn't Ask: A Legacy from World War I*, which tells the story in poetry of her father-in-law as he and a group of soldiers from Battery B, 306th F.A.—77th Division experienced World War I. However, her current poems have taken on a sharper, more political edge, especially fiery when she considers the Age of Trump in the United States, or explores the significance of spirituality in contemporary society. In "Pray Tell, How Will We Know Him," she takes the message about Jesus Christ from a billboard and then points out that

> His skin will likely be dark, and since he spoke
> for the poor and lame, the hungry and sick
> he may be poor himself, one of those who visits
> the food pantry under the cover of night,
> humble, perhaps humiliated.

Both her commitment to community, human survival, equality, love, and justice and her long academic practice make for a poetry that is meaningful, passionate, and interesting. As Alicia Ostriker said of her first book, "the poems sting and soothe."

How I Met Pablo Neruda

It was by accident.
Walking in Mexico City
I saw a poster about a reading
at the National Stadium.
A tribute to Pablo Neruda.
Like something that might
happen in a Greek ruin
not in North America.
I had to bear witness.

My Cuban friend guessed
from their dress and speech
that people came from all over
Mexico and South America,
and they knew their man.
When the readers spoke his lines
a steady whisper surrounded us
as if the poems were a rosary.

Suddenly from the center came a chant,
Neruda esta aqui. Neruda esta aqui.

In New York, Security would have dragged
the visionaries out of there in minutes.
But no. The readers waited. People wept quietly.
When the voices hushed, the program resumed.

No one was frightened by this spirit.
Neruda was there. He was expected.
We were glad for him.
Esta bien.

Incubator

Anna Hooker Lawrence, 1880-1938

Her third daughter, premature, was born
at seven months, three pounds, with hernias
in her belly wall, intestines bursting through.

The doctor said *now Anna, don't you fret,*
you can have more. But she called her sister Nomi
from upstairs and asked her for clean cloth
to bandage up the baby's gaping wounds.

While the untimely child hung on, she sewed
buttons on cardboard, lined them with cotton, cut
strips from old sheets to hold the organs in.
Then, lifting the baby between her elbow and palm,
she nestled her broken treasure in a box for boots
and kept her on the oven door of the old wood stove.

All that hot summer and a year, she changed
the dressings, nursed the fragile body, sang,
canned, churned and cared for children late
ever so late into the night with her sister.

In other times, she might have been feared
for witchcraft. The numbers prime: her third
girl, born in the seventh month of nineteen-
o-seven. But she knew neither medicine
nor magic, only the steady, ragged rhythms
of pressing a life together by hand.

How to Pray

Just say what you love.
                    Julia Spencer-Flemming

Then poems may be a form of benediction
to save from harm the people and places,
voices and feelings that appear there,

the humble cowbird,
the dog who learns to say *amen*,
a river in Zimbabwe, the woman who sends
a photo of her hands to the Secretary of Defense
after her son is killed.
                    And paintings may be
vespers in *plein air* slants of natural light
for children who live indoors, on-line.

Words and images like these
belong to the web that connects us,
whether we see it or not,
from the home the spider spins
at the highest corner of a room
to the litanies that come
from ancient books.

Go in peace, we say, and take
these tokens with you.
No one can save the world,
but together we can make visible
more of what we love.

Pray Tell, How Would We Know Him?

A Public Service Announcement: Jesus is coming very, very soon
From a billboard in Green Bay, Wisconsin

His skin will likely be dark, and since he spoke
for the poor and lame, the hungry and sick
he may be poor himself, one of those who visits
the food pantry under the cover of night,
humble, perhaps humiliated.

We may have put him in jail
for his color or some imagined transgression
like those of his inner-city brothers.

We can hardly expect to match his DNA
to shroud or bone. Besides, we don't trust science
unless our hearts malfunction or melanoma forms.

Maybe he has already come and gone without
notice, say in the person of Martin Luther King
or one of the dedicated nuns who travel together
on a bus to troubled places where people have lost
the way, the truth, the light..

Maybe he came as a child to our southern border
as a test of our belief in his principles
and we were found wanting.

Anyway, who's to say he would come
to the sparsely settled North
rather than to Palestine?
Maybe the poor in Africa or India
are more deserving of his love and care.

And here's the final rub: which one would come —
He who raised Lazarus from the dead, or the man
who overturned the tables in the Temple?

The Poems of Our Climate

. . . one would want more, one would need more,
More than a world of white and snowy scents.
        Wallace Stevens, *The Poems of Our Climate*,
                1938

Between the great wars of your century,
Stevens, old master, you said the image alone
is not enough to make a poem. The cold
bowl of pink and white carnations

cannot suffice even if it makes our *torments*
easier to bear. The one who sees must be there
in the poem, the *vital I*, no matter how imperfect,
among the *flawed words and stubborn sounds.*

You could not have foreseen how that *I* would
blossom once the wars receded to far-away lands,
how soon all its torments would be personal
as poets confessed their imperfections.

But you knew that poetry must change
to meet the new needs of each age,
no other era exactly the same, no matter
how many turns the wheel of fortune takes.

Now here we are, needing truth from poems,
because it is missing in action, gunned down
by illusions more clever than the eye can see:
political spectacles more fantastic than fiction.

If the poems of our climate can't be completely
true, let them at least *try* for close-ups
of a world we recognize as real, even if
only in shards, beneath the powerful lies.

Peter Piper

As we have known since childhood,
he must have been a politic
judicious man who took advantage
of the season, a citizen in a civil
place that celebrated his right
to harvest more peppers than
one man would need to feed himself.

Perhaps his town did not set limits
on the number of pecks he could pick,
but it probably had a policy to keep
his market safe from plundering.

In his time, whenever that was,
there may have been a council that
decided what to do if his neighbors
protested his habit of pickling peppers
before they were picked.

It's complicated.
We cannot just reject
everything political
as scheming, cunning, lowdown nonsense.
Peter's polity must have protected
his pickles from politics,

which makes the world go around,
often faster than we can say
Peter Piper picked a peck . . . .

Belief

Everyone has to believe in something, and I believe in Poetry. It happened in a high school course on the New Testament. *In the beginning was the Word.* Now there's the Truth, raw as a salmon swimming upstream. I often fear the salmon won't get there. Poetry requires so much good will, attending to the voices of strangers.

I continue to believe in Poetry, *the word made flesh*, precisely because it always lies there waiting at the beginning to shape what we see and don't. Because it still leaps out of the water of syllables into fresh air to change our course.

Because without it, I cannot imagine a good life in my country, where many seem to believe only what they are told from the pulpits of television by corporations now enshrined in the hall of individuals, more powerful than you yourself in front of your morning mirror.

Some days, Venus swims
straight to her half-shell,
to rise in naked glory.

The World Was All Before Them

> where to choose
> Their place of rest, and Providence their guide:
> They hand in hand with wandering steps and slow
> Through Eden took their solitary way.
> John Milton, *Paradise Lost*, XII, l. 643-46

Did Milton foresee our world
as he sent Adam and Eve from Eden?
A land of plenty, tables overflowing
chests and shelves filled with toys
and gadgets, two homes, three cars,
boats of all sizes, and don't forget
the plane or hundreds of friends
on Facebook, followers on Twitter.

Not just fullness but abundance,
bounty, surplus, enough rooms
in one house for several families
in far off times or places, copious
wealth, not just a great sufficiency,
but profusion, excess, a glut of riches
while others go hungry.

No, Eden was nothing like this,
and what our ancestors took away
was not material goods but choice
and providence — preparation,
frugality, care.

They left hand in hand.

Fifty Years Ago

On the occasion of a daughter's 50th birthday

We were so sure that women would soon be equal.
The ERA would finally pass, the rule of law
would make men set aside their privileged state
and they would soon find grace in carrying
half the load of work with half the tasks
of raising children well. Instead they only
seemed to welcome us, after we proved
our worth on their turf, and our presence
mostly spurred them to compete more fiercely.

Yes, we made the case for women in art
our role in changing history, doing science
law, diplomacy, politics, Olympics
in any arena you can name, but we failed
to convince the men in power
that women are fully equal.
Susan B. Anthony and those
who secured the vote for us
would writhe in familiar pain.

Now at the end of an era, passing the torch
to the next generation, we need to say we didn't
know this would be harder than the vote,
didn't admit we needed help, proudly certain
of our ground, convinced we could go it alone.
So, we must say we're sorry. We were wrong
to think equality would come from reason
and reason would prevail in the next election.
It's long past time for change to come.

Still, we have a torch to pass. Some events
were won. Our hope now lies in you.

Robert Okaji

Robert Okaji lives and works in Indiana. He holds a BA in history and once owned a bookstore. His publications include the chapbooks *I Have a Bird to Whistle* (2019), *From Every Moment a Second* (2017) and *If Your Matter Could Reform* (2015). He has also had three micro-chapbooks with the Origami Poems Project: "The Circumference of Other," a chapbook-length work included in *Ides: A Collection of Poetry Chapbooks* (2015), "The Language of Bread and Coffee," included in the 2019 *Oxidant\Engine BoxSet Series*, and *Interval's Night*, a mini-digital chapbook (2016). His work has also appeared or is forthcoming in such publications as *Taos Journal of International Poetry & Art, North Dakota Quarterly, The Zen Space, Vox Populi, Indianapolis Review, Panoply, Ristau: A Journal of Being, The High Window, Boston Review* and elsewhere.

His poetry often blends life's mundane details with a strong sense of eternity and the spiritual. A tulip of double IPA, green beetles, dish washing, bacon, and other everyday life details pile up as he then finds beauty, ghosts, edges, precipices, or eternity growing out of his observations of his, and the earth's, life.

> Yes, yes, we've heard. The dishwasher wastes less
> and cleans better. But Kenkō believed in the beauty
> of leisure, and how better to make nothing
> while standing with hands in soapy water, thoughts
> skipping from Miles Davis's languid notes to the spider
> ascending to safe shelter under the sill. . .

he writes in "The Resonance of No."
Toward the end of the poem "Scarecrow Sees," he writes

> as one entity the crows explode into the blue,
> leaving me alone with the shivering stalks,
> questioning my place and purpose. . .

sending the reader into the contemplation that plagues every human being alive. Who are we? What are we doing here?

Sometimes Okaji approaches the ideal of the imagists like H.D. or the early work of Ezra Pound, turning images into objects that carry symbolic meanings that echo into the long march of literary history. At other times he is clever, humorous, and filled with a joy that bursts out of his contemplations about the large questions present in our lives and the universe.

To the Lovely Green Beetles Who Carried My Notes into the Afternoon

Such beauty should not be bound,
thus I tied loose knots,

knowing you would slip free
and shed my words

as they were meant,
across browned lawns,

just over the cedar fence
or at the curb's edge,

never to be assembled,
and better for it.

What Edges Hold

By which I mean those lines framed in certainty: the demarcation of sunlight and shadow. Kami signifies not spirit, but rather that force above man.

Never religion, but life itself: the mountains, trees, the rocks. Lightning.

Or waves, thundering off the coast, lured by the moon.

Stirring the water with a spear, Izanagi dripped an island into being.
Separate the ordinary through limitation, by practice, by ritual and space.

Another night in the twisted trees. The god-shelf.

Recognize that wind respects no borders.

Knowing that to the east questions may respond to answers I have long suspected, I look elsewhere. After the vowel, the consonant.

Though torii differ in style, each retains two posts and a crosspiece.

After the consonant, the winnowed tunnel, extinguished light.

At the gate, bow respectfully, then enter. Ladle water from right to left, then left to right. Pour it into your left hand, then cleanse your mouth.

Invert and regard the precipice.

I have placed one foot in their sphere. The other still searches.

Scarecrow Sees

Da Vinci maintained that sight relies on the eye's
central line, yet the threads holding my
ocular buttons in place weave through four
holes and terminate in a knot. My flying friends
perceive light in a combination of four colors,
unlike the farmer, who blends only three. The
octopus knows black and white but blushes
to escape predators, while I remain fixed,
evading no one. Certainly my sense is more
vision than sight, and not the result of nerve
fibers routing light. Crows choose colors
when asked, but a certain shade of yellow
eludes them. And who would hear, above
the flock's clamor, my claim to see this world
as it is? Grayscale, monochrome, visual
processing and perceptual lightness measures
mean little to one whose space accumulates
in uncertain increments - what is a foot to an
empty shoe? If I painted, which hues would
prefer my attempts, which would distract or
invade my cellulosic cortex, resulting in
fragmentation or blindness? Fear is not
limited to the sighted alone. I look out over

the field and perceive the harmonious
interaction of soil and root, leaf and sun,
the beauty of atmospheric refraction and
the wonder sprouting daily around me. Then
as one entity the crows explode into the blue,
leaving me alone with the shivering stalks,
questioning my place and purpose, awaiting
the next stray thought, a spark, a lonely
word creeping through this day's demise.

My Mother's Ghost Sits Next to Me at the Hotel Bar

Blue-tinted and red-mouthed, you light a cigarette
that glows green between your lips and smells of
menthol and old coffins, burnt fruit and days carved

into lonely minutes. I mumble hello, and because
you never speak, order a tulip of double IPA, which the
bartender sets in front of me. Longing to ask someone

in authority to explain the protocol in such matters,
I slide it over, but of course you don't acknowledge
the act. The bartender shrugs and I munch on spiced

corn nuts. I wish I could speak Japanese, I say, or cook
with chopsticks the way you did. We all keep secrets, but
why didn't you share your ability to juggle balls behind

your back sometime before I was thirty? And I still
can't duplicate that pork chili, though my *yaki soba*
approaches yours. You stub out the cigarette and immediately

light another. Those things killed you, I say, but what the hell.
As always, you look in any direction but mine, your face
an empty corsage. What is the half-life of promise, I ask. Why

do my words swallow themselves? Who is the grandfather
of loneliness? Your outline flickers and fades until only a trace
of smoke remains. I think of tea leaves and a Texas noon,

of rice balls and the vacuum between what is and what
could have been, of compromise and stubbornness and love,
then look up at the muted tv, grab your beer, and drink.

Diverting Silence

Wren canyons down the morning's edge, proclaiming dawn.
Unpapered, unfettered, fearless, he abides.

I say "he," but sexual dimorphism is not apparent in the species.
Accepting signals, we process and choose, freighting gender aside.

Listening requires contextual interpretation, as does belief.
Shrilling to the porch screen, he spears a moth, veers outward.

An acquaintance claims birds are soulless, existing only to serve God.
As temple bells exist solely to announce, and rain, to water lawns.

Faith's immensity looms in the absence of proof.
Spherical and hollow, *suzu* bells contain pellets.

The search for truth without error does not preclude fact.
Even tongueless bells ring.

To the Light Entering the Shack One December Evening

No prayers exit here, nothing
limits you. I never knew
before.

The pear tree's ghost shudders.

Water pools in the depression of its absence.

For years I have wandered from shadow to
source, longing. Now, at rest,
you come to me and fear

evaporates. I would like to count
the smallest distraction.
I would like to disturb.

You are the name
I whisper
to clouds.

Will you leave if I open the door?

A carnival germinates in my body.

You are not death, but its closest friend.

Darkness parts, folds around you.

I close my eyes and observe.

September in April

Already I have become the beginning of a partial ghost, sleeping the summer
sleep in winter, choosing night over breakfast and the ritual of dousing lights.
This much I know: the moon returns each month, and tonight you lie awake
in a bed across the river, in a house with sixteen windows and a cold oven,
where your true name hides under the floorboard behind the pantry door.

*

Differences season our days — from flowers to snow, root to nectar — take
one and the other lessens in its own sight. One day I'll overcome this longing
for things and will be complete in what I own, living my life beyond the page,
past the white space and dead letters. When I mention hearts, I mean that
muscle lodged in my chest. Genetics, not romance. Tissue. Arteries, veins.

*

Dark cars on the street. Cattle grazing in the damp pasture. The liquor store
sign glaring "CLOSED." Separate yet included, we observed these scenes but
assigned them to the periphery, grounded in our own closed frames. In a
different time I would transcend my nature and strive to withstand yours.
Look. That star, the fog silhouetting the tombstones. A bobbing light.

*

Love is a gray morning, a steel-toed shoe or coating of black ice; nothing you do will repeal its treachery. There, on my stone porch, I will inhale the smoke of a thousand burned photographs. The sun will descend but you won't share it, and I'll no longer hum your tune. When I rise no one sees. Or everyone stares. Imagine that great cow of a moon lowing through the night.

Two Cranes on a Snowy Pine (after Hokusai)

Who knows where bird
begins and tree

ends,

which branch shifts
snow, which bears

eternity. This, too, will share

joy,
elusive green

and breath,
with no thought

of flight

and night's
fall.

Thomas Davis

Thomas Davis's historical novel, *In the Unsettled Homeland of Dreams*, winner of the 2019 Edna Ferber Fiction Book Award, is about Washington Island in Wisconsin and slaves who escaped the boot-heel of Missouri using the Underground Railroad. He has published two epic poems, *The Weirding Storm, A Dragon Epic* (2017) and *An American Spirit: An American* Epic (2019). His non-fiction book, *Sustaining the Forest, the People, and the Spirit*, about the sustainable development practices of the Menominee Indian Nation, has sold in countries around the world. He has published three other novels as well as poetry, scholarly essays, plays, and chapters in books published by the Smithsonian and the University of Nebraska Press. He has edited three magazines and helped edit one poetry anthology, *The Zuni Mountain Poets*. His book of poetry, written during the founding of the tribal college and universities and world indigenous nations higher education movements, *Meditations on the Ceremonies of Beginnings*, was published in 2020.

A powerful orator and oral interpreter, he has given speeches and readings at colleges and universities in the United States, New Zealand, Australia, and Canada. Davis is also an educator who has been a significant figure in the United States tribal colleges and universities movement and the indigenous higher education movement. Twelve podcasts about his involvement in the tribal college and university movement can be found at https://tribalcollegejournal.org/our-history-memories-of-the-tribal-college-movement-podcast-1.

In all of his writings, Davis makes impressive use of his remarkable character development skills. His professional experience creating dynamic solutions with people from many cultures provided a key to many lyrical doors, including the human capacity to overcome deep-rooted impediments of the mind, body, and spirit. As in the following passage from *The Weirding, A Dragon Epic*, Davis makes his characters confront the shadows inside themselves, creating and developing strong tensions with enchanting resolutions to the obstacles blocking their souls' paths:

> And then he saw the spirit bear refracted
> Out of his walking body on the snow.
> His arm hair stirred with skin that tinged fear
> Into the coldness of the snow and light.
> He'd lost the battle that he thought he'd won.
> He'd sent the bear into the nothingness,
> But now he was Ruarther *and* the bear.

He was a monster walking on the earth.
He looked again and felt the shadow bear
Inside hm as he walked across the snow.

What should he do, he thought? What could he do?
The witch and bear were locked in mortal combat,
And he was in the center buffeted
By forces greater than mortality
Could hope to face and still survive intact.

The exceptional use of iambic pentameter in Davis' epic poetry creates a dreamy and compelling mood for the reader, much like the baritone waves of his rhythmic speaking voice. Ringing softly alongside the triumphs of the characters is a rare symphony, one composed specifically to transcend the old fears and shortcomings in the human experience. Through a lifetime of achievement in writing, Davis gifts the world with a deep art, one that will sustain its relevance long into the psyche of future generations.

A Lover's Song

We strung along a priceless string of stars
And made the moon a pendant just for show.
I cut the night into a dress, the bars
Of moonlight setting stars and dress aglow.

You laughed with love deep in your doe-brown eyes.
You swirled the universe upon your hem.
As dizzy as a lover filled with love's first lies,
I watched your eyes grow dazzled by your gems.

Then, with a shrug, your dress fell to the ground.
The night became a carpet at your feet.
Stars glistened in a heap, their skies cut down.
The moon gleamed silver-cold without your heat.

We swirled together deep into the night,
Our years illuminated, blazing light.

Of Bees and Flowers

We drove to Mesa Verde as the San Juans rose
in morning sunlight green, majestic, soaring.
I've met this girl, he said. He rubbed his nose
as if he had a pounding headache starting.

But I don't know, he said. I feel like smiling
whenever thoughts about her make my day.
She's with another guy she's basically supporting.
He sighs. Sometimes I think she'll walk my way,
but then she hesitates, he says. I sway
as if I'm in a storm that generates
emotions strong enough to make me flay
myself as who I am deteriorates.

Love isn't what it really ought to be,
he said. The flower should accept the bee.

Break to Manhood

Before we reached the bank two twelve year olds
were on the water in the good canoe.
Both Brand and I looked at our sons, their coup
apparent as they grinned at us, both bold
enough to know that, ten feet out, they controlled
the moment even though the wind still blew
and rain was falling hard, the clouds a stew
of swirling turbulence and whipping cold.
Okay, Brand said. Inside the inlet, calm
prevailed, but as we moved into the lake
the waves were higher than our heads. The qualms
I'd had at seeing youngsters make their break
to manhood with such resolute aplomb
unmanned me — as they left me in their wake.

His Mother's Arms

He died enveloped by his mother's arms.
The two of them alone, she felt so tired
from lack of sleep, she'd thought about the charm
of closing eyes and drifting off, transpired
into a dream where waiting, dread, and love
were not commingled with each ragged breath
he took. But then his breathing changed. She shoved
herself out of her chair and smelled his death.

She put her arms around him as his eyes
flew open, glancing one last time at light,
and then his breathing stopped. The cloudy skies
leaked rain. Eyes stared without the gift of sight.

Her daughter said, she brought him to the earth,
her love the bridge between his death and birth.

The Insight

She was different suddenly.
Not in the way she looked:
young woman, small, black eyes intense,
her mouth used to smiling
even when she did not feel like smiling —
but the tone of her voice had changed.
Always, before, she'd had a touch of whining
in the way she used words,
the way she thought about herself.
You could always tell she had an inner fire.
She was going to make something of herself
in spite of all the burdens she'd faced:
she'd had a child when she was too young,
and an uncle who liked to cut her down
when she was most vulnerable,
the reservation woes that went on and on
with family and addictions and anger
so deep it seared the spirit
with a flame too intense to be seen.

You could tell that she'd end up with a degree
in spite of the whine in her voice,
and in spite of the edges of not-good-enough
in the way she approached everybody at school,
the problems that beat her down
and held her back from who she was.

"I've found out something," she said.
She waited, looking at me.

"I'm glad you came to see me," I answered.
"It's always good to see you."

"I found out that I internalize oppression,"
she continued. "I gather up wrong
everywhere I find it, and then I use it
to beat up on myself and everyone around me.
It's made me needy in a way
that demands everyone help me all the time,
even when I should help myself."

I leaned back in the big black chair
that I'll only occupy for a short while
as a new president for the college
is being sought.
I felt stunned, as if suddenly blackbirds
were surrounding me and singing
in a spring rainstorm and a field of wildflowers.

I had always liked her,
watching her grow toward maturity
while she fought ferociously for a place in life
where she could feel comfortable.
But this new insight into herself seemed unlikely,
a step too far away for her to reach.

"That's pretty insightful," I said.
"You've started to grow."

"I feel awkward seeing that," she said.
"I keep listening to myself,
and I see what happens when I start telling myself
that I'm not good enough

or somebody tells me that I shouldn't be having
the problems I'm having,
and then I don't know how to act or even think.
I want to blame somebody, anybody.
But I don't want to blame myself
while I'm really blaming myself,
and even though I see the oppression
building and building inside me,
I still can't stop it from making me do things
or say things
or even be things that I know aren't good for me."

"Wisdom begins in the discovery of self," I said.
"You've made a huge breakthrough.
I'm proud of you."

"I've had so many people close to me die,"
she said. "Classes have been too hard
this semester, and all I've done is cry.
I've wanted to drop out of school
so many times I don't understand why I'm here."

I smile.

"You're here because here you can make discoveries
about yourself, your life, and everything you need to learn,"
I said. "I don't even want to hear
about you thinking about dropping out.
I have faith in you and who you are."

"My uncle yelled at me the other day
and told me that my problems were my fault,"
she said. "I believed him
until I told him that it didn't matter what he thought.
what mattered was that I am going
to keep on going on until I'm the first one
in my family or his family going back forever
who walks across the stage at graduation
and gets a college diploma in her hot little hand."

Getting up and going out the door,
looking over her shoulder, grinning.
"I guess I'm learning something here after all,"
she said, then quickly walked away.

Mother Earth's Song

I rummaged around in words all day,
changing this one, discarding that one,
snipping, pruning, and adding, a gardener
working in a field of meaning flowers.

Now, at this hour before dawn,
sitting in silence while first light smudges horizons,
I wonder where all the words
written, recorded, spoken, chosen, discarded, go.
Intelligence is not what distinguishes us
from an orangutan with its long, kind face.

Books stamp from printing presses.
Armies march with words
squeezed and polished into diamond thoughts.
Lovers touch each other's faces
and speak of what is in the other's spirit
as they forget they are caught in time
and will spin from where they are into a lifetime's days.
Speakers breathe deep and reach
into throats, minds, and emotions to spew words
as arms wave and bodies lean forward
in an intensity of eyes that demand,

look at me, look at me, and listen.

All over earth words are made and remade and remade.

But what do they mean?
What happens to a blue whale's song sung in ocean depths?
Where does buzzing and wing-fluttering
of worker bees go after they have danced
a map to a field of spring wildflowers?

Do all words and sounds on earth,
monkey clattering, elephant trumpeting, earthworms sliding, whisper of mon-
arch wings in Mexico fluttering tree branches into motion, purple finch song,
haunting wind-moan echoing through a sandstone canyon, falling rock rum-
bling in isolated wilderness,
meld into a symphony pulsating planets, suns, and galaxies?

Is Gaia poet to eternity?
The singer whose songs sing meanings more profound and beautiful
than our words?

Peach Cobbler, the Beautiful Baker's Song

Unable to sleep, she got up at three
and went outside where silver moon horned night
below a star glittering and dancing in a twinkle.
She went over to the back yard's three peach trees
and waved her hand in darkness along branch bark
until she had picked a large, round peach from each tree.
Inside the kitchen the song the universe was singing
was a little off-key, as if her being up in the middle of night
was unkiltering the lining up of stars and moon.

She went to the cupboard, pulled out flour
ground from sunflowers and daisy essence
and peeled huge peaches
whose slices failed to fit into her largest bowl.
Smiling to herself in the moon's dim light,
she lit the old wood stove before rolling out peach cobbler crust,
mixing honey, nectar, and the sound of the flight of bees
into the rich, shining peach slices,
covering the cobbler with petals of red and yellow roses
picked the evening before from beside a dark pool
glimmering starshine and a faint trace of moon.

In the great cast-iron oven fire crackled and danced.
Bats flew from the attic to swoop crazily in the kitchen
as the woman wiped hands on her apron
and hummed a silver song that had no words,
but bubbled and popped into the cobbler's fillings
as cooking peach smells mixed with firewood smells
and woke a symphony of night, stars, sky, moon, and earth.

When the cobbler was done and out of the oven,
the wood fire stoked,
the woman took a deep breath and yawned.

"Maybe I can sleep now," she said.

She left the kitchen, climbed the stairs
to where her husband was snoring oblivion,
and closed her eyes as sun sent yellow fire
over hills and the day's horizon.

I Imagine Hard Bitten, Cold-Eyed Men

riding across the Texas panhandle,
dust rising behind them as they flee demons they created
through alchemy of bank robberies, thuggery, and lies.

I come from legends vague as hints of mist:
outlaws; dirt farmers in Oklahoma and Texas
    standing in awe as black dust gathers and sweeps
    lightning and the end time toward straggling crops;
migrants following seasonal harvests
    by getting out of old cars and pushing them over Colorado mountains;
preachers without Bible training forming congregations
    in small mountain towns where fervor
    warmed winter when snows piled to rooftops,
    and smoky wood stoves frosted crust inside tiny window panes.

Generations fade backward into men and women
who lived, loved, died in waves of meaning and thoughtlessness.

Young, I watched my big-boned Irish/Scottish grandmother
come out of her adobe house and walk into chicken pens
where she grabbed a squawking, flapping, speckled white, black hen
and with a single movement of wrists and big hands
    snapped the hen's head off,
the headless body running around, silent as a tomb.
"Good eating tonight," my grandma said.

On another day my cousin Lee and I watched
my dark, short, round grandmother come out
of her adobe shack not far from the Gunnison River's banks
with a whipped meringue-topped chocolate pie.

"Bet I can eat more than you can," Lee said.

Ten minutes later Aunt Stella came around the house's corner
and saw two small boys with chocolate hands and faces.
"What are you boys doing?" she demanded.
"Don't you know there's starving people in the world?"

When I was young my father told everybody,
"I'm finer than frog's hair sitting on a split wood fence blowing in the wind,"

and I say, even as I imagine hard-faced me
as filled with flight across the panhandle
as a young mother on ancient Colorado plains
fleeing strangers who have cut her off from her people,

let us sing who we are.
Let us sing dawn as it fades to day.
Let us sing sunset as it blazes toward night.
Let us sing night as we settle beneath heavy quilts
and slip into the dream of our lives.

The Song of Taliesin

1

This is the center — where the fireplace rises, stone
On stone, into the sloping ceiling, inner stones
Charred black by countless morning fires; lintel stone,
Clay colored, massive, square above the morning flames,
An anchor, root, foundation for the song of stone
And space that flows into the early morning light
Which spills onto the oak wood floors, the furniture,
The oriental pots and plates and statues strung
Around the room like rare and priceless deep-sea pearls.
The space explodes with inner vistas, angles thrust
Into the slope of angles, point and counterpoint,
Until, at last, above the ancient panel painted blue
And white and gold, above the wooden cabinets,
The stonework, rough and natural, climbs toward a ledge
Beside three western windows where a Shinto god
Looks down upon this room of earth and light and space
And art and stone.

2

Outside the window, down the hill's
Steep slopes, beyond the brush and trees that spill their life
Onto the valley's meadow floor, five geese swim regally
Upon the pond. The profile of the tree-dark hill
That gently rises to the east is cast upon
The waters. Stillness shines reflected light back to the sun.

This is the song, man's song, upon, into the hill;
The other hills about this hill sing other, older songs
That rise in point and counterpoint against, into
The stone that rises out of earth, above the pond —
An inner space that holds, inside, a morning fire.

3

The plate glass windows lay in molten crystal pools
On charred, hot courtyard stone. The man stared, scarred,
At smoking ruins. Isaiah strode about the sky
As lightning danced away into the eastern hills:

> *"Therefore, as a tongue of fire consumes stubble,*
> *And dry grass collapses into the flame,*
> *So their root will become like rot and their blossoms blow away like dust."*[1]

And in the dark — The smoke and ash, destruction, death,
Despair, an anguish hot as any fire, a sense
Of doom, a searing of the spirit, soul:

> *That lurid crowd! During the terrible destruction the crowd stood on the hilltop,*
> *faces lurid, lit by flame. Some few were sympathetic. Others half sympathizing*
> *were convinced of terrible doom. Some were already sneering at the fool who*
> *imagined Taliesin could come back after all that had happened before. Others*
> *stood there stolidly — entertained?*[2]

---

[1] From the Book of Isaiah, the King James version of <u>The Holy Bible</u>.
[2] Frank Lloyd Wright's description of the aftermath of the second major fire at Taliesin. The first fire was set by Mr. Wright's Barbados cook, Julian Carleton, and took the lives of Martha Borthwick "Mamah" Cheney, Wright's mistress, and her children. The second fire destroyed Taliesin for a second time. From Mr. Wright's <u>Autobiography</u>.

4

Behind the house, below the hilltop, near the two
Blue pools, a garden, filled with phlox, impatiens, white
And yellow daisies, spider plants, and other flowers die
Into the fall. The roofs about the courtyard rise,
A symphony of levels, vistas blocked, revealed,
And outlined by the ever-rising texture of the stone.
A huge, black oriental bell hangs from an oak
Tree branch as shadows stretch into the light

That crowns the hill with sun. And from this hilltop, from
The dark green oak leaves, the hillside runs into a vale
Like other hills beyond, the evening shadows long
With night defeating, melding with the ending day.

This house is earth and fire and water, of the hill
Not on the hill, a song that accents earth and rings
Into the song of Taliesin, home and farm and school.

This is the center. From this place the song goes out
Across the hills, onto the prairie, out toward
The mountains and the forests and the deserts, bold
And brash, American.

                    I sit inside the song
And feel it ebbing, surging with its waves and tides
Into the world. The blackness from the fire is gone.
The stones sing point and counterpoint to all the songs
That rise in chorus from the ever-living earth.

Four Windows Press
231 N. Hudson Ave.
Sturgeon Bay, WI 54235

Email: fourwindowspress1@gmail.com
Website: www.fourwindowspress1@gmail.com

copies of this anthology can be obtained from bookstores, online retailers, and the publisher's website.

Books published by Four Windows Press:

An American Spirit by Thomas Davis
The Glowing Pink by Standing Feather
Halfway to the North Pole by the Door County Poets Collective
The Healer by Ethel Mortenson Davis
Here We Breathe In Sky and Out Sky by Ethel Mortenson Davis
How to Improve Study Habits by Christine Reidhead
I Sleep Between The Moons of New Mexico by Ethel Mortenson Davis
Johnny Sha Sha by Dorothy Windmiller
No More Can Fit Into the Evening, edited by Thomas Davis
        and Standing Feather
Salt Bear, a children's novel by Thomas Davis
Seeing-Eye Boy, a young adult novel by Terence Winch
Skipping Stones by Betty Hayes Albright
Under the Tail of the Milky Way Galaxy by Ethel Mortenson Davis
Waiting on the Monsoons of His Desert Soul by RedWulf DancingBare
White Ermine Across Her Shoulders by Ethel Mortenson Davis

CPSIA information can be obtained
at www.ICGtesting.com
Printed in the USA
FSHW020009261120
76178FS